LAST OF THE ROCK ROMANTICS
PETE DOHERTY

LAST OF THE ROCK ROMANTICS
PETE DOHERTY

ALEX HANNAFORD

EBURY
PRESS

1 3 5 7 9 10 8 6 4 2

This edition published in 2007
First published in 2006 by Ebury Press, an imprint of Ebury Publishing

Ebury Publishing is a division of the Random House Group

The Random House Group Limited Reg. No. 954009

Addresses for companies within the Random House Group can be found at
www.randomhouse.co.uk

A CIP catalogue record for this book is available from the British Library

The Random House Group Limited makes every effort to ensure that the
papers used in our books are made from trees that have been legally sourced
from well-managed and credibly certified forests. Our paper procurement
policy can be found on www.randomhouse.co.uk

Printed and bound in 2007 by Cox & Wyman Ltd, Reading, Berkshire

Interior designed by seagulls.net

Photo credits:
Chapter 2: Libertines performing, 2002 © Brian Rasic / Rex Features
Chapter 4: Libertines © Patrick Ford / Redferns
Chapter 6:Libertines at White Chapel tube station © Eva Edsjo / Redferns
Chapter 8: Libertines performing, 2004 © Nicky J. Sims / Redferns
Chapter 10: Pete Doherty, 2004 © Lex Van Rossen / Redferns
Chapter 12: Pete Doherty, Islington, 2005 © Rex Features
Chapter 14: Pete Doherty, Live 8, 2005 © Richard Young / Rex Features
Chapter 16: Pete Doherty, Trafalgar Square, 2005 © Getty Images
Chapter 18: Pete Doherty, Ealing Court, 2006 © Getty Images

ISBN 9780091910792

Acknowledgements

Thanks to Court for all your love, encouragement & putting up with a library's worth of books and CDs piled around the flat. Pat, Pete and Liz – as always. Jake, Claire, Sarah, Rae and all at Ebury for their hard work – it's a pleasure working with such a professional (and lovely) team. Mari for having the patience of a saint. My 'gurus' William Hall and Stevie Chick for their never ending advice and encouragement. Tony Linkin, Banny Poostchi, Chas Hodges, Simon Bourcier, Christian Datsun, Roger Morton, The Paddingtons, Johnny Triad, Hugh Barnes, Jim Dewar (for letting me raid his contact book), Rob Mendik, Clare Drummond, Tom Green, Andrew Asplin, Triona & Spirit of Albion (an amazing resource), and JM for your help, trust, encouragement and Christmas card – it meant a lot.

If I've missed anyone, it's one in the morning, what do you expect?

Alex Hannaford, London, January 2006

To Courtney

CONTENTS

FOREWORD

BY JACKIE DOHERTY

Carpe diem – seize the day! These are the first words that went through my mind when I was asked to write a foreword for this book.

To date, there have already been a few books written about my son, Pete Doherty. What a difference a year can make in a person's life! This time last year I was writing my own book, *My Prodigal Son*, when a young gentleman of the press rang to tell me that he too was writing a book, entitled *Last of the Rock Romantics*. And he had high hopes, no doubt, of securing an interview. Instead, what he heard was a mother crying inconsolably into his earpiece as she struggled to cope with yet another invasive phone call. Alex Hannaford, the said journalist and author, quickly and sincerely set about apologising for the upset that he thought he had caused, not knowing that his untimely phone call was merely the latest in a long line of them that morning.

And so, a year has come and gone and Alex has single-handedly restored my faith in the press, when once it had reached an all-time low. He has shown himself to be trustworthy, and it is with a certain fondness that I recall a Latin phrase that sums up my esteem: *multi famam, conscientiam pauci verentur*, which translates: many fear their reputation, few their conscience. It is for this reason that I now feel honour-bound to write the foreword.

It is my belief that this book has been written with a deep desire to tell the truth. As has happened in the past and, indeed, in the present, the truth isn't always revealed when a third party writes about events or another person. The reasons for this are complex: sometimes the true facts are not available; sometimes the so-called true facts are not 'true' at all and are assumptions or pure conjecture.

This book, I believe, sets out not to knock Peter from any pedestal but to present as near-accurate a story as possible. It's a book for fans, charting Peter's winding and tumultuous journey – a journey that hasn't reached its end yet; a journey that he has embarked on, step by step, in the glare of the media. This book also often offers a lesser-known insight into the more widely known persona of my son. It's written by a journalist who, I feel, writes with passion when expressing the bond between Peter and his fans. It's by a young author who, I believe, is also on his own journey.

Jackie Doherty, October 2006

INTRODUCTION

|BEING|PETE|DOHERTY|

It was 11 September 1999,
and The Libertines – Pete Doherty, Carl Barât, John Hassall and their
stand-in drummer, seventy-year-old Mr Razzcocks – had just exited
the small, cramped stage at the Hope & Anchor pub in Islington.
Maybe a few people that night realised they had just witnessed an
incendiary live set from the most important band to emerge from
London for a long time. One *NME* hack there certainly did, reviewing
the band a few nights later at the Bull & Gate pub in Kentish town. For
almost two years afterwards the three-piece plied their trade at
London's smallest rock 'n' roll venues in the hope that the elusive A&R
scouts would be somewhere among the teenage crowd. But no record
deals were on the horizon …

Now, in the early part of the new millennium,
Pete Doherty has come to epitomise British rock 'n' roll. He's an
enigma: loathed by the establishment but worshipped by his fans, he
lives his life as both pariah and idol. Television documentaries have
attempted to deconstruct him, books have tried to expose his character,
and articles in the music press, broadsheets and tabloids have – on an

almost daily basis – served to perpetuate his legend. But all have made vain attempts to understand him.

Back in the heady days of 1978 when punk rock was at its meanest – prodding, poking and generally infuriating the establishment – two of its biggest icons, Sid Vicious and Nancy Spungeon, checked into the Chelsea Hotel in lower Manhattan after heading for America to start a new life and wean themselves off drugs. But Sid was still injecting heroin or prescription methadone on a daily basis. The self-destruct button had been pushed a long time before and there was nothing anyone could do.

A couple of months after the couple arrived in the city, Nancy died from a single stab wound to the stomach. Sid was implicated in her murder but was out on $50,000 bail courtesy of Richard Branson's Virgin record label. From his holding cell he was checked straight into rehab at Rikers Island, but it was no use. Four months later, Sid was dead too – after overdosing on smack.

Sid Vicious entered into rock legend. According to Jon Savage in his book *England's Dreaming*, punk was 'infected by a Rimbaldian script: live fast, disorder your senses, flame brightly before self-immolation'. In the 1950s it was Kerouac who was championing these rare human beings who 'burn, burn, burn like fabulous yellow roman candles'. And before that the Romantic poets: Blake, Shelley, Keats, Coleridge and their ilk were the punks of their generation: feared by the mainstream, revered by their fans, living fast and – in some cases – dying young.

Fast-forward to February 2005 and Pete Doherty, erstwhile singer with The Libertines, is sitting in the back of a police van on his way to Pentonville Prison after his record company failed to pay his £150,000 bail. In an hour the skinny, pale-faced musician will be sitting in a sweaty white cell that stinks of vomit, facing robbery and blackmail charges. Like Sid Vicious before him, Pete is addicted to heroin and has spent time in rehab. He has also played in one of the most talked-about new rock 'n' roll bands of his generation.

A few hours later and Britain will be reading the latest instalment in the soap opera of the 'drug-addicted rock star boyfriend of supermodel Kate Moss'.

Just a few months before, twenty-six-year-old Pete had picked up the 'Cool Icon of the Year' gong, along with Carl Barât, at the influential *New Musical Express* annual awards.

His life had become one of unpredictability; at once admired and vilified.

This book explores the myth of Pete Doherty – from his childhood, in which, despite travelling around constantly, he enjoyed a status as a kind of Pied Piper, to his aptitude for poetry, The Libertines, right up to the present days of rock 'n' roll excess in Babyshambles. He is the last of the Rock Romantics.

'Everything he touched turned to
gold – he was a jammy bastard ...
such a loveable guy.'

ANDREW ASPLIN, SCHOOLFRIEND

ONE

DAD'S ARMY

There's an image of Pete Doherty conjured up by Libertines biographer Pete Welsh in his book *Kids In The Riot*: the rocker is sitting cross-legged on the floor of his friend's Camden flat, strumming an acoustic guitar while belting out Chas & Dave songs. Welsh even jokes that, rather than realising he was party to the future of rock 'n' roll, he simply 'saw a peculiar kid playing Chas and fucking Dave and got a night bus home'.

It's a poignant image. When Chas & Dave sang 'Ponders End Allotments Club', 'Edmonton Green', and 'London Girls', they were chronicling life growing up in a London Pete could have only dreamed about. In their songs, Chas & Dave evoked the spirit of happy working-class life that seems to have all but disappeared from the city; and despite having had to deal with the rougher elements of north London life, it is a place they look back on with great affection. Theirs was a childhood full of the romance of the street: terraced houses, Mother gossiping over the fence in the back yard, Dad down the pub, violence, football, cups of tea, fishing, fighting, playing with pals in the road, running about filthy dirty – always the last one in the bath.

Pete Doherty's childhood was very different. But he'd romanticise this working-class existence and it would later inform his songwriting;

his was a rose-tinted vision of an England in which he wished he'd lived.

'Your street was your whole world,' Chas Hodges remembers. 'Me and Dave had similar upbringings and down our streets you knew everyone; you knew where the roughs lived; you knew where the nice people lived.

'There was a lot of sadness too,' he says. 'My dad shot himself when I was three years old – we'll never know why – and mum brought the family up on her own. It was a poor upbringing but it was a happy one and music helped to bring me, my brother and sister together. I have a great respect for the London way of life and that's reflected in our songs. When we wrote songs we'd think about growing up in London; we'd put the memories of our mums and dads down on paper. Sometimes it was subconsciously coming out – just a feeling. At the end of the day even a musical passage doesn't have to have a lyric to convey a feeling.'

It's 2003 and Pete Doherty is standing mid-stage at the Kentish Town Forum, bare-chested, sweating profusely, sharing a microphone with his comrade-in-arms and fellow Libertine Carl Barât.

The Libertines play the song 'Up The Bracket' at breakneck speed, referring to Vallance Road in the East End, and the 'Cally' Road in north London. Finally Pete too is conjuring up the London he's come to know – not in childhood, but as a twenty-four-year-old boy in a band.

Tonight, Pete's heroes Chas & Dave are the support act, hawking their jaunty knees-up to a slightly fresher-faced crowd than they're used to. Pete is in his element, squaring up to Carl as if the pair are about to start brawling, flailing his arms around, snarling into the microphone.

Pete's father, also called Peter, was born in Paddington, London, to a gas company inspector from Ireland – his mother, Doris, had moved out of the family home when Peter Sr was still a boy. Peter went on to work as a corporal in the Royal Corps of Signals – the army communications experts (although his wedding certificate would incorrectly say he was with the Parachute Regiment).

Pete's mother, Jacqueline, was the daughter of Liverpudlian taxicab proprietor Percy Michels. She was serving as a lance corporal in the Queen Alexandra's Royal Army Nursing Corps and met Peter in Aldershot while she was working at the Cambridge military hospital near his barracks. They married on 28 October 1976 in Hampshire.

The family name, Doherty, is one of the oldest hereditary surnames in Ireland and translates from the Gaelic as 'obstructive' – ironic considering the image of the 'hellraiser Pete' that the media likes to portray today.

Peter and Jackie's first child, Amy-Jo, was born in February 1978. Peter Sr had by now been promoted to sergeant in the Royal Signals and the family had moved to the Albermarle Barracks near Harlow Hill, Ouston – a small village near Newcastle. Pete junior was born on 29 March 1979 at Hexham General Hospital in Northumberland a few miles away; his sister Emily was born seven years later.

It was the beginning of a fluid existence for the young Pete: picking up sticks every year or so and moving to the next army base where his father was stationed. The Doherty family would stay in Ouston just two years before moving on to Catterick in North Yorkshire, then to Northern Ireland, Cyprus, Germany, Dorset, Birmingham and Holland. They would eventually return to Blandford Forum in Dorset where Peter Sr would be stationed at the local military base, in use by the British Army since 1914.

The Dohertys spent two years in Cyprus. After the country was granted independence in 1960 two army bases were declared British sovereign territory and are maintained to this day. In 1989, Peter, Jackie, Pete, Amy-Jo and Emily packed up their life there and moved to the town of Krefeld near Düsseldorf in Germany. Peter Sr had been seconded to the British Army of the Rhine, just a few years before it was officially disbanded by Prince Charles in 1994.

It must have all been pretty exciting for a young boy. For Peter and Jackie, Düsseldorf offered all the benefits of a cosmopolitan European city: sights and theatres, cute pavement cafés, the elegant Königsallee shopping boulevard known as the Kö. At night the promenade alongside the Rhine was unchallenged in its beauty. British Army families had lived in Germany in dozens of small communities since the end of the Second World War. Certain shops offered little tasters of home such as Cadbury's chocolate, marmalade, Marmite and tea bags. But creature comforts didn't come much better than the waffles Jackie cooked, served up with vanilla ice cream and maple syrup. Like American air force bases in Britain, British servicemen and women also had their own cinemas, bingo halls, hospitals and radio station and it wasn't uncommon for a family to spend years in Germany without learning any more than a few phrases of German.

Peter Sr frequently disappeared from the family home with his job. Iraq had invaded Kuwait in 1990 and by January the following year over half a million Allied troops – a coalition led by the US – were stationed in Saudi Arabia. In 1991 Peter Sr headed out to the Gulf and was eventually awarded the MBE in recognition of his bravery after foiling a plot to blow up an oil tanker during the first Gulf War.

Pete was sent to Dalton Middle School in Ratingen. For the most part, the school taught the children of those serving in the British Army, but in addition there were a handful of Polish and American children, and occasionally a couple of Japanese students would pass through. Pete was always bringing friends home – Japanese kids, American kids. He loved the mix of nationalities. He also excelled academically and loved sport; it wasn't long before he was playing for the school football team, and was just as adept on the athletics field. In short, he was pretty good at everything. Inevitably, his teachers loved him.

The kids in Pete's year had awarded their German teacher the moniker 'Dracula Collars' – on account of the heavily starched, upturned collar of her white shirt. In every school there are one or two teachers who come in for a good ribbing from the students. Dracula Collars was one of those teachers, and some time during the hot summer of 1991 she made the mistake of popping out of the classroom for a few minutes.

Because of the heat, the double doors at the back of the room, which looked onto the huge playing fields, were open. Pete had an idea. Within minutes the entire class of boys and girls were running at full pelt around the perimeter of the field. 'Come on,' he shouted, leading from the front. 'Quick … she'll be back in a minute.'

Ten minutes later Pete and his pals were back in their seats, sweat dripping from their faces, panting loudly: the boys' shirts were soaked and clung to their chests and the girls' long hair stuck to their shiny foreheads. When Dracula Collars came back into the room everyone acted like nothing had happened. At the back of the class a girl with braids looked deep in thought as she stared out of the window; one boy was writing in his exercise book, and at the front, Peter Doherty looked like butter wouldn't melt in his mouth.

It's interesting that later on, with the success of The Libertines and the increasing interest in Pete's background and personal life, he would tell journalists that he'd had a lonely childhood. 'The only life I knew was moving on, changing schools,' he'd say. He described it as a 'rootless existence' and said that for the most part he was alone, 'living in dreams, kicking footballs against walls ... devouring literature'. 'I had no choice really but to disappear into myself,' he said. In their book *Pete Doherty: On the Edge, Daily Mirror* journalists Pete Samson and Nathan Yates claim he became 'a solitary, introverted teenager' and that his childhood had been 'one long period of retreat into his interior'.

The truth was a little less romantic. Yes, his life was constantly disrupted by his father's job, but he was rarely alone. Wherever he went Pete seemed to attract friends and followers. He was incredibly popular: the life and soul of the party and a relentless practical joker. Everyone fell under his spell – even when he was just twelve.

Pete's best friend at Dalton Middle School was Andrew Asplin, whose father was in the Royal Logistics Corps based a short drive away from Krefeld in Duisburg.

'I knew Pete for the two years he was there – 1990 to 1991 – and he was one of the most academically clever people I've ever met,' Asplin remembers. 'He was in the top set for everything he did; one of those lucky bastards who was immensely popular, good at football and got all the best-looking girls. Everything he touched turned to gold – he was a jammy bastard and a bit of a bruiser too; he didn't go round punching people but he could handle himself and everyone knew it. It got that bad, people even wanted to copy his handwriting – I know I did.

'I remember we were all in little gangs at school. Our gang was called the Funky Crew and everyone in it was given two-letter names, which always ended in J for some reason. I was AJ, Pete was PJ and our mate Ben was BJ – if only Ben knew then what he knows now.

'We even had special handshakes and secret meetings; it was great fun. And the girls had their equivalent.'

Evidently an early developer, at school Pete dated a string of pretty girls. Tanya Robinson was two years below him and during their dalliance he was the envy of the male half of the school. Tanya Robinson went on to become a model and one of the first of *FHM* magazine's 'High Street Honeys', winning the 'competition' in 2002.

'There was another girl,' Asplin says. 'She was the school hottie. And one winter morning at about a quarter to nine, just before school started, Pete was standing outside the classroom with her in the freezing cold, and he was leaning with one hand on the wall and the other hand down her pants. It was hilarious.'

Pete was a jack-the-lad. And all his fellow pupils looked up to him. His favourite teacher was Mrs Wadsworth, who taught French and physical education, and she took a particular shine to Pete, the brilliant and lovable rogue.

Pete's love of words hadn't quite made it into song form at this stage but he had taken a liking to freeform poetry. 'He'd make up little rhymes – stupid ones,' Asplin recalls. 'But they were quirky and clever. He made up stories too that would have everyone in stitches – ridiculous stuff about his mates falling off donkeys and stuff like that. He'd take a classic poem or nursery rhyme and make his own words up. And everyone loved it.'

Jackie had always sung to Pete when he was younger and read him stories. He would later say how vital this was for a child's creativity.

At this age there were few clues to his future musical career. 'We liked New Kids on the Block at that time – everyone was into them,' Asplin says. 'SNAP, the Fresh Prince, Kriss Kross. When you're younger you like anything that sounds good. I guess it's only when you mature that your musical tastes follow suit.'

In 1990 New Kids on the Block had shot to number one in the UK with their single 'Hangin' Tough'; two months later it was another of Pete's favourites – Snap, with 'The Power'. In a year when acts such as Bombalurina could stay at number one for three weeks with 'Itsy Bitsy Teeny Weeny Yellow Polka Dot Bikini', it's safe to say the charts were lacking cultural kudos. However, it wasn't all Vanilla Ice, Milli Vanilli and Jive Bunny. Just two years before, Rough Trade had released The Smiths' live album *Rank*, recorded on the band's Queen Is Dead tour. The Stone Roses' debut had come out a year later, and in 1990 – the year Pete was rocking out to New Kids on the Block – The Charlatans' *Some Friendly*, The Happy Mondays' *Pills 'n' Thrills and Bellyaches*, and The La's debut record hit the shelves.

It's fair to say Pete's tastes hadn't fully developed.

'When I found out years later that he'd formed The Libertines, Jesus Christ, that was the last thing I ever thought he'd do,' Asplin says. 'I expected him to have joined the army as an officer or become a lawyer, accountant or merchant banker.'

Pete knew even then that he was cut from different cloth; he wasn't so much anti-war, but he had tired of the transient life of an army kid, so couldn't see himself following the same career path his mum and dad had taken. He was more creative and loved literature. He knew he wanted to write; he just wasn't aware at that point that he'd end up penning lyrics that would be devoured by hundreds of thousands of fans in a few years.

'But without a shadow of a doubt he had that magnetism back then – he was such a lovable guy,' Asplin says. 'He was very funny and had such a great sense of humour.'

In 1991 it was time to move on. Again. Peter Sr had been given a transfer and the Dohertys headed back to England, this time to Dorset in the south-west.

Eleven years later – towards the end of 2002 – Asplin and Pete exchanged a few emails. It was the first time the pair had been in touch since they were children. Pete particularly liked speaking to someone who for him represented his life before the mayhem of The Libertines. He told his old friend he had formed a band and was about to tour Japan. But it didn't register with Asplin – there was no way he meant *The* Libertines who had just released a record on Rough Trade. Asplin thought he must have been talking about a college band. The pair lost touch with each other again and for the next two years Asplin could only watch the madness unfold on TV and read about his old friend in the pages of first the *NME*, then the national press.

Shortly before a Babyshambles gig at the Mill in Preston in the autumn of 2004, Asplin handed security guards at the side of the stage a copy of an old photo of him and Pete from Germany. When Pete finally made it onto the stage he dedicated the first number – 'For Lovers' – to Asplin. After the show the pair hugged but Pete wasn't making any sense; he was incoherent and didn't seem to recognise his old mate. By this time Pete had succumbed to one of the inevitable by-products of rock 'n' roll: hard drugs.

Ten minutes later Asplin was alone in his car. He cried on the way back to his home in Blackpool.

The Dohertys moved into a house in the pretty town of Blandford in east Dorset. Pete was placed in year nine at the Blandford School and it was here that his love of football would blossom; he was ecstatic when he was picked for the football team and, outside of the school gates, the Royal British Legion under-thirteens. He was a champion goal-scorer. Peter Sr encouraged his son's love of football, driving him to matches in his VW camper van. Pete was already hooked on Queens Park Rangers by this time, with a love bordering on obsession.

Pete's close friend was Dean Daniels. Daniels, too, remembers Pete as being a swot but not the extrovert he seems to have been in Germany. Maybe it was finally dawning on Pete that with a father in the forces he was never going to be able to settle down. Every time he got used to a new town or city and made friends, his family was off again. Pete felt settled at Blandford – he loved playing football for the two teams and he could see a future there – at least until the end of his school days. But it wasn't to be; the Dohertys would be moving again after just one year, but in that time Pete again blew his school-mates out of the water, winning the most academic merit marks of the entire year.

Of course, Jackie and Peter didn't want their son to end up like some of the other kids in the area – bored and indulging in petty vandalism, brawling and drugs – but Pete was far too immersed in liter-ature to present a worry to his parents. A couple of his teachers even suggested he could stay on in Blandford and live with them; he was so bright they just didn't want to see him go.

Jackie felt that she and her husband were ruining Pete's life. Every time he seemed settled, excelled at his studies, joined the local football team and formed friendships, they were off again. But they were a mili-tary family and they had to go; Peter and Jackie had little choice. They were about to move to Birmingham, 160 miles away; it wasn't as if Pete could see his old friends at weekends – he'd keep in touch for a short while but inevitably the friendships would fade.

At thirteen Pete was enrolled at Nicholas Chamberlaine school in Bedworth, and the family moved into a house in Nuneaton.

Academically, he would fit right in. It was here that Pete remembers giving his first ever public performance – singing a song called 'Billy The Hamster' in assembly. It wasn't quite punk rock but it was a performance – in front of a crowd – and he instantly knew he'd caught the bug for the stage. But while he excelled in class, he was also beginning to daydream; he'd often romanticise about the lives of people he admired, be they on TV, in books, or, more frequently, on the football pitch.

The same year that Pete moved to Birmingham, he witnessed an event that would be etched in his memory: on New Year's Day, 1992, before 38,000 spectators at Old Trafford and in front of a live TV audience, his beloved QPR thrashed Manchester United 4–1 on their home turf. Pete was ecstatic and decided to write a letter to Dennis Bailey – the man responsible for all those goals.

Bailey wrote back to thank the young Pete and advised him to read Genesis – the first book of the Bible – as that was specifically what had inspired him. While the reply wasn't exactly what Pete had expected, he nevertheless flicked through the pages of a Bible he had once used at Sunday school and tried to imagine how his hero had used the passages to help his career. Contrary to what journalists would later write, Pete was not raised as a Catholic. Jacqueline was raised in the Church of England and although Pete would never turn out to be overtly religious, he did go to the interdenominational garrison camp churches and Sunday school, and was fascinated by just how powerful the Bible could be in shaping lives. He wanted to get inside the heads of these people; find out how they ticked.

As for his own writing, the jokey rhymes he had played around with as a cheeky schoolboy back in Germany had matured into some seriously heartfelt verse. He had a gift for poetry, and Jackie and Peter didn't need to encourage him: he had books piled from floor to ceiling.

He loved Oscar Wilde, Graham Greene and George Orwell – particularly *Down and Out in Paris and London*. He loved the Romantic poets of the late eighteenth and early nineteenth centuries, such as Wordsworth, Coleridge, Byron, Shelley and Keats. They were champions of the imagination – in 'Intimations of Immortality', for example, Wordsworth had claimed a child's intuition was far superior to adult reasoning. Pete, who was beginning to enjoy the company of his own thoughts more than that of his 'temporary' school friends, found a kinship with these poets. But he was also fascinated by their private lives. Byron, with his looks, oppositional politics, fame as a poet and a 'Satanic danger' that made him sexually alluring, had been the Jim Morrison of his day. The poets' lives had been marked by tragedy and scandal, and the public lust for any sort of contact with them had echoes in the growing lust for celebrity played out in the pages of the daily newspapers that his mum and dad would get at home.

Pete was both inspired and moved by poetry. He knew 'Suicide in the Trenches' by Siegfried Sassoon by heart and would linger on the images it conjured up. Sassoon wrote of a 'simple soldier boy' who put a gun to his head after trying to survive the trenches in winter. The snarling epilogue criticises the smug crowds who cheer when soldiers march by, telling them to pray they'll never get to find out first-hand the hell their bravest and best had been put through. Pete knew the reality of war was far from romantic, particularly as his dad had fought in the Gulf.

And there was more to it than the words Sassoon wrote. Pete saw Sassoon's life as the embodiment of the romantic spirit. The poet had been born into a wealthy family and had lived a privileged life, hunting foxes, playing cricket and writing poetry. One day he waved it all goodbye and went off to join the army where he was exposed to the horror and brutality of war; both his friend and brother were killed, and Sassoon returned to England vehemently opposed to conflict, finally finding solace in religion.

For the impressionable sixteen-year-old Pete, Sassoon was the ultimate hero, at once quintessentially English, but also a rebel and a romantic.

Pete had settled into life in Nuneaton and had begun to feel at home there. Deep down he knew that any attachment would only lead to heartache, as it had done so many times in the past, and he almost didn't want to let himself get too close to people. But his addictive personality meant this was easier said than done. Everybody loved Pete.

He ended up passing all eleven of his GCSEs, with nine A grades and two Bs. Jackie and Peter even discussed with his teachers putting him up a class but Pete was modest; he didn't think he was particularly academically gifted.

During his A-levels Pete would put his bicycle on the train and travel from Nuneaton to Birmingham to study in the city's main public library. He'd sit outside for hours talking to tramps on the big stone steps of the library. His mother would later describe him to friends as 'Orwellian' – he had so much respect for the man way down the social ladder. His ability to romanticise the lives of people he admired wasn't confined to the rich, well-heeled or academic. He also romanticised the working classes, the vagabond and the down-and-out. They all epitomised a life free from the constraints of mainstream society – whether reached through great art or by 'opting out' and living in squats or sleeping rough.

Pete was at an age where he wanted some level of independence. Peter Sr heard there was a paper round job going and the seventeen-year-old Pete decided he'd apply. He had a lot to do for his A levels but he'd only have to deliver the local free paper once a week for a couple of hours and Jackie thought it would be a good idea.

After just a couple of weeks, Pete managed to persuade all the neighbourhood kids to post his papers for him. He pocketed £10 a week for his 'trouble' and would entertain the kids as they went round doing all his work for him. When the troops arrived back at the house, Jackie would have a bag of lollipops at the ready. Pete was like the Pied Piper. But just one year into his paper round it was time to move on once more.

A little later in life, Pete would become obsessed by British post-war comedian Tony Hancock. Hancock would become not just a source of inspiration to Pete but also someone he would repeatedly refer to in interviews. Hancock had joined the RAF in 1942 and, like Pete forty-odd years later, found his life had become nomadic. Home for him would be wherever the army sent him, entertaining the troops and boosting morale with the Ralph Reader Gang Show in Weston-super-Mare, Bournemouth, Scotland, North Africa and Italy.

In 2006, Pete Doherty has become the living embodiment of the itinerant musician: addicted to touring, living out of suitcases, sleeping on friends' floors. Even though Pete is undoubtedly a wayward spirit now, when he was growing up he wanted nothing more than a regular childhood, a place he could call home.

TWO

MAYBE IT'S BECAUSE I'M A LONDONER

Pete and his sister Amy-Jo

had been the first generation of the Doherty family to stay on at school and do A levels; Pete toyed with the idea of going to university, but there was really only one thing on his mind: getting to London. Amy-Jo was already there; she was two years into a drama degree at Brunel University in Middlesex. Pete was still stuck in the West Midlands on the army base with Jackie and Peter.

She'd been telling him about a guy from her drama course she was hanging around with, called Carl. He had long dark hair, pale skin, a strong jaw and model looks. And he played guitar. In turn, Amy-Jo told Carl about her little brother – this aspiring young poet who was hooked on The Smiths and Chas & Dave.

Carl Barât was a little older than Pete, born in Basingstoke to hippy parents – a contrast to Pete's relatively strict upbringing. But Carl was fascinated to hear about Doherty family life, moving from one army base to another. He was reticent, however, about the fact Pete liked The Smiths; he thought they were crap.

Brunel's campus was at Uxbridge, and although most of the students liked this quieter, more relaxed corner of west London, Pete wanted to be in the heart of the city. He had gone to visit Amy-Jo for a few days and it gave him a glimpse of what life could be like if he moved away from the West Midlands.

That morning she'd left him in her room, staring out of the window at the Thames, and had told her mate Carl to introduce himself while she went to her lecture. The pair clicked immediately, even though Pete had a habit of provoking people. Carl remembers this lanky lad – over six feet – sitting there calmly trying to wind him up. 'He'd watch people go into a whirlwind, and of course I fell for it,' he says. They bonded over an acoustic guitar, which Carl could play perfectly. Pete was still learning.

A year later Pete moved to London. At the very least it would allow him to spend some time in the Smoke and hang out with Carl.

In 1978 The Jam hardly glamorised the city; in 'Down In The Tube Station At Midnight' Paul Weller painted a vivid picture of its underlying violence – an image of businessmen heading home on the train to the safety of their suburban houses, wives and 2.4 children, while back in the city, its youth had to face the crime that the businessmen had read about in that day's paper. In '"A" Bomb in Wardour Street' the picture was no less gloomy in its depiction of random violence. Even The Clash's London saw its streets teeming with police and thieves and in *London Calling*, one of their best known songs, its lyrics dealt with police brutality. It wasn't pretty. But while its streets may not have been paved with gold, they were certainly alluring. And for Pete Doherty, even in the 1990s, London's dark alleyways, polluted thoroughfares, grimy subway walls and run-down tenement blocks had a poetic beauty.

His father had been born on a council estate in Paddington and couldn't get out of the city fast enough; for Peter senior the inner city had spelled poverty and deprivation, not opportunity. Jackie too preferred life in the countryside. Pete admits he 'was romanticising what they were trying to escape from', but for a seventeen-year-old London was alive with possibility and adventure; the prospect of living there awakened something in Pete's soul.

London has always been a city of immigrants; in his biography of London, Peter Ackroyd writes of the eighteenth-century city: 'Here was a centre of worldwide experiences, with outcasts, refugees, travellers and merchants finding a place of refuge.' He says that in other cities many years must roll by before a foreigner can ever feel accepted. But in London it takes just a few months. The secret to assimilation is to 'consider yourself a Londoner'.

Pete got the opportunity to move in with his grandmother in her Dollis Hill council flat near Kilburn – hijacking her sofa wasn't the height of comfort, but it was a home of sorts and a starting point.

Kilburn had been redeveloped after it had suffered extensive bomb damage during the Second World War. Labour was provided by Irish immigrants, many of whom eventually settled in the town. It sits in the London borough of Brent, which has always been very culturally diverse, and by the 1960s the Irish community was sharing its home-town with the Indian community; today, 50 per cent of its residents are from ethnic minorities.

Sandwiched between the expensive celeb-heavy hangout of St John's Wood and the run-down ghettoes of Willesden Green and Neasden, Kilburn was an unlikely mix of inner-city mayhem and subdued subur-ban sprawl. For Pete it was perfect. And it was only ten stops on the tube from Camden – the heart of London's live music scene.

In another parallel with his hero, Pete had followed in the footsteps of comedian Tony Hancock. After the war Hancock moved to London. Servicemen could be 'demobilised' anywhere they wished and he had chosen London. His first stop had been a room in the Union Jack Club opposite Waterloo Station; after that it was a bed-sit in Baron's Court and a 'chocolate-brown basement in Holland Park'.

To some extent Hancock also romanticised this down-at-heel existence. In her biography of Hancock, his wife Freddie writes of his 'general feeling that if there were hard times around he was not going to be deprived of his fair share of them'. Among the contradictions in Hancock's character were that he hated squalor but frequently lived in it.

Pete Doherty, who probably felt as if he'd been demobilised from the army as well, had also headed to London. At the age of seventeen he did exactly what Ackroyd had spelled out in his book: he assimilated; he became a Londoner. And within a short period of time he had contacted his friend Carl Barât.

Pete found a job filling graves in Willesden Green cemetery – his first proper wage since leaving school. Mechanical diggers dug the graves, and after funerals Pete and his co-worker – 'Old Joe' as he was known – worked shifts filling them in. The job was just that – a job – but for the sensitive Pete Doherty, it wasn't one from which he could emotionally detach himself all the time. Inevitably he'd become affected by the sometimes tragic circumstances behind the funerals. Years later he would post a slightly cryptic message on an Internet discussion board devoted to his band Babyshambles in which he'd mention the murder of a teenager, a 'family home burnt to the ground' and 'a toddler shot dead'.

'The community rallied round that afternoon,' Pete wrote. 'Families who were sworn to loathe one another over ancient pettiness and babies and rival dealers were arm in arm on New Road. Crowding the churchyard and sweating out their grief beneath heavy suits on a muggy summer's rainy day.

'It was a day all on its own, in gloomy isolation from the rest of the calendar, from the rest of ever all time. Clouds spelt out E A R L E and crowds swirled ghostly and whispers shrieked through streets like speeding cars suddenly slowing down and silent as they disappear forever.'

This was an unpublished snapshot into Pete's world, only for the eyes of those closest to him: his fans. Pete might have become slightly desensitised to the work – the tips were good after all – but on this particular day he felt numb and later said he wanted 'to be a million miles away'.

Although the money he was making at the Willesden Green Cemetery wasn't bad, Pete still hadn't decided what to do with his life. He'd called Carl – or Carlos as he was sometimes known – and the pair talked about hooking up and writing songs together. Both were frustrated with the state of the British music scene. It was 1997. The Spice Girls seemed to be on a roll with three number ones; Aqua's Barbie Girl had sold over a million copies, and when Elton John re-wrote 'Candle In The Wind' for Princess Diana, who was killed in a car crash in August, the song became the biggest-selling British single of all time.

That same year *Vanity Fair* carried a photo of the Oasis singer Liam Gallagher and his then-wife Patsy Kensit on its front cover, sprawled out under a Union Jack bed cover. Tony Blair was at the forefront of the move to push Britain's credibility abroad, boasting a new generation of pop groups, style magazines, celebrity chefs, actors and designers. The press was happy to act as the mouthpiece for 'Cool Britannia', loudly proclaiming that London was swinging again. For Pete Doherty, holed up in his nan's council flat, it was a different story. 'England was starved of the kind of songs I somehow knew the pair of us could craft,' he said. 'It's about time British kids had something in music to say was truly theirs.'

It was ten years since Morrissey and Marr's 'severed alliance' had split up one of the only bands that mattered to Pete – The Smiths. They were exactly what he was talking about (although Carl didn't agree). For Pete, Morrissey's lyrics engaged with England's many eccentricities. These songs weren't depressing; they were subtle and wry and often hilarious, chronicling an England that songwriters simply couldn't see – possibly out of sheer stubbornness.

In the song 'London', Morrissey described the smoke lingering round his fingers as the train moved on to Euston. In 'Panic' he managed to voice what Pete had been trying to say for the past year: that the music all around him said nothing about his own life. And in 'Alsatian Cousin' his vision of England was one Pete too could identify with – his vision of British man with his tweed coat and leather elbow patches was one that could only be recalled in black and white films from the 1950s or 1960s; an England in which Pete had never lived but one in which he was increasingly able to see himself.

Jackie had long described her son as 'Orwellian'. Now in London, this trait would shine even brighter. George Orwell had been born Eric Arthur Blair into a relatively wealthy family which worked for the Indian Civil Service. Working in India as a policeman, he had experienced the lives of the poor and downtrodden first hand. A few years later, Blair lived among the poor in Paris, then returned to London where he lived as a tramp in the East End before finding work as a school teacher. It was then that he wrote his first novel: *Down and Out in Paris and London*, under the pseudonym George Orwell. The working-class poor were people Pete could identify with too, even if, unlike Orwell, he had never experienced real poverty himself. Another of Orwell's works, *The Road to Wigan Pier*, which examined the lives of poor miners in a Lancashire town, must have also struck a chord. Again, there was an element of Pete romanticising this life, as the reality was undoubtedly harsher than he could ever have imagined.

'I do have utopian fantasies,' Pete later told the *Socialist Review*. 'But they relate more to the imagination and the individual. For me socialism is a way of trying to put far-fetched ideas into everyday use, trying to find a way to bridge the gap between that fantasy and reality, and reaching out across that gap to the people who can actually do something to make the change.'

By the summer of 1998, Pete had moved out of his nan's place and into a flat in Whitechapel in the heart of London's East End. Forming an eastern gateway to the city, Whitechapel was home to the Blind Beggar pub, in which the notorious local gangster Ronnie Kray had executed George Cornell in the 1960s; the Royal London Hospital, which has stood on this spot since 1752; and a melting pot of cultures. Although it wasn't home to Pete for long (he would end up moving to north London before coming back east again), it would always be fertile ground for a dreamer like him. Its shabby streets steeped in history were perfect for Pete's poetic leanings – and later his songs.

Jackie and Peter were so proud the day their son called to say he'd been offered a place at the University of London to study English literature; their belief that he had a natural gift for poetry was finally vindicated. As for Pete, it meant he could stay in London longer and it was a chance to get some money together in the form of a student loan. It would also enable him to realise a dream he had been having for quite a while: to start a band.

The fact that at this stage Carl and Pete needed each other cannot be understated. Pete wanted to settle somewhere – for once in his life.

He loved London, and had found a soul mate in Carl Barât. But a year into his English degree he'd already had enough. Carl still had a year to go on his drama course but he too wanted to jack it in. The pair decided to leave university early and move into a flat together in a run-down block called Delaney Mansions on the Camden Road.

Their neighbour was Steven Bedlow – better known as Scarborough Steve – and as luck would have it, he was looking to start a band as well. Pete would have been content rehearsing in his flat, strumming his guitar while sitting on his unmade bed, but Steve had been in rock 'n' roll bands before and wanted to do it properly. It was decided Steve would be the singer – after all, his model looks, rock 'n' roll haircut, pouting lips and rib-thin waist gave him the air of a younger, prettier Mick Jagger. Pete and Carl would play guitar.

Pete had often thought that music could accompany his poetry. He wasn't a brilliant guitar player by any means but he could play some basic chords; enough to write some simple songs. Carl on the other hand was proficient; Pete was impressed with his ability to take these half-formed ideas and basic snapshots and turn them into proper songs. He would play barre chords and could pick as well; Pete thought they sounded brilliant. His simple ideas had been transformed into full-blown tunes – singles even.

In the early days they called the band The Strand but the name didn't stick. For Pete, The Libertines were born one afternoon on the side of the canal near Camden. He, Carl and Steve sat on the edge, trying to hit a glass bottle floating in the middle by pelting it with stones. Whoever hit it first could decide the name of the band. Arguments over who eventually won the game were a preview of bigger, fiercer arguments to come. In truth, nobody could remember. One thing was certain: The Libertines had been born; the name came from a book called *The Lust of The*

Libertines by the Marquis de Sade, and the threesome later swore a blood oath on the back steps of Delaney Mansions on the Camden Road.

For the next few months a succession of drummers and bass players came and went. Eventually Steve suggested a local lad he knew called John Hassall. This guy apparently lived with his mum in Kentish Town and owned a lot of expensive music equipment: amps, guitars, all sorts. He sounded too good to be true.

John Hassall had played bass for as long as he could remember. He was born in north London – the only Libertine able to make that claim – and had done his A levels at the unlikely venue of Camden School for Girls, which had a mixed sixth form. Up until the final two years the school was – as its name suggests – for girls, and these tended to be hardcore north London lasses who would rip your earrings out if you double-crossed them; there was a lot of attitude. The sixth form was vastly different and although it was a comprehensive school there was a high intake from private junior schools due to an impressive reputation for a top art department: Emma Thompson was a student, and Britain's elite from the performing arts world sent their children there.

John was a quiet lad but settled in comfortably with the in-crowd at school, particularly a group of girls known as Jess, Jess and Bella, who are now close friends with Ms Dynamite. Although he seemed reserved, he was a bit of a rebel; he'd miss classes and would party hard at weekends. During term-time he'd bring a set of bongos to school and play them sitting on the kerb. He could also play guitar and was a self-confessed Beatles nut. He'd been in bands since he was fifteen. And when he met Pete, the pair inevitably clicked.

Minus a drummer, The Libertines were almost complete, and from this moment on the lives of three of the four members at least were to change forever.

'If it's nostalgia, it's nostalgia
for a time that didn't exist.'

PETE DOHERTY

THREE
ENGLAND'S DREAMING

The Libertines would ultimately become so closely connected with England's capital that they would be seen as being as much of a London mainstay as, say, The Jam, The Clash or The Sex Pistols. And even though John Hassall was the only member to have been born there, very few other London bands seemed to play up the association as extensively as The Libertines.

But while London was important to all of them, for Pete particularly it was England that had a far greater hold on his imagination.

Morrissey once discussed his affection for the soap *EastEnders* with the writer Will Self. Self said The Smiths singer 'let slip a yearning for a very populated, very unmiserable arcadia'. Morrissey said: 'I think people wish that life really was like that, that we couldn't avoid seeing forty people every day that we spoke to, that knew everything about us, and that we couldn't avoid being caught up in these relationships all the time, and that there was somebody standing on the doorstep throughout the day. Within *EastEnders* … there are no age barriers. Senior citizens, young children, they all blend, and they all like one another and they all have a great deal to say, which isn't how life is.'

Pete, too, knew that wasn't how life really was. But he wanted to live in a fictitious world in which that was the reality. He called that imaginary world 'Arcadia' – a poetic vision of England in which no one was tied to society's rules, and where, like the London in which Chas Hodges had grown up, your street was your whole world.

And just as George Orwell had aroused nostalgia by praising English institutions such as horseradish sauce, Stilton, Yorkshire puddings, red pillar boxes and comic seaside postcards, so Pete would seek his fictitious vision of England by immersing himself in the British TV shows, films and literature of the 1950s and 1960s. Popular culture has been described as 'the battleground for identity' and Pete's quest to discover the meaning of 'Englishness' saw him poring over endless episodes of *Rising Damp, Dad's Army* and *Hancock's Half Hour.*

There was one small problem: the council estate that Pete's dad had come from, and the streets that Chas & Dave had known as young boys in north London, weren't all about cups of tea on the front steps, cockney banter and street football. Life was tough; there was violence, alcoholism and depression. To a large extent the England Pete was looking for doesn't exist now and didn't exist back then. His vision of London was opaque, looking at it as he was, through rose-tinted glasses.

But it wasn't just Pete who pined for this lost and possibly fictitious era. In 1997 social historian Jeffrey Richards suggested that, as the millennium loomed, Britain was undergoing a crisis of national identity. Pete was against the Americanisation of society, of which Orwell had also warned; he certainly didn't want to see a world lacking in religion and culture, where ambition and drive – the survival of the fittest – replaced imagination, tradition and ideology.

Early on in their musical career, shortly after they signed their first record deal, Carl and Pete would be asked by the BBC who or what had inspired them. 'Sid James and Sid Vicious,' Carl would say. Pete would expand: 'Whatever it is that gives you that feeling inside to get out of bed, get out of London and do something. Whatever inspires you to do that – to be alive and to dream.'

Sid James appeared in countless British films, including the comedy *The Lavender Hill Mob* alongside Alec Guinness. In the early 1950s he began working with Tony Hancock on the BBC's *Hancock's Half Hour* radio programme, which was later televised. Sid James parted company with Hancock shortly before the final series and plunged head first into the *Carry On* films for which he would be best remembered. Despite being born in South Africa, he was the archetypal cheeky cockney with his infectious, cheeky cackle.

Pete loved Tony Hancock. Hancock's ability to bring his characters vividly to life was nothing short of incredible and clearly based on observation. Pete's passion for Englishness was inextricably bound up with Hancock's world of saveloys and brown ale. 'As far as I'm concerned, anyone who flogs meat pies is British,' Hancock said in one episode. 'I don't care where he was born.' Pete also loved the absurdity of Hancock's humour. The comedian loved to head to a café in Chalk Farm with his friends Spike Milligan and Larry Stevens and order 'three boiled rice and three raspberry jams' just because it sounded funny.

The England portrayed in the so-called Ealing comedies, such as *Hue and Cry* – the story of a gang of criminals foiled by an army of school kids – or 1949's *Passport to Pimlico*, in which the inhabitants of a London street discover buried treasure and documents proving they are really citizens of Burgundy and declare their independence, was as far removed from reality as you could get. But Pete loved the escapism. These films weren't only amusing, they were uniquely British in character and featured ordinary people plunged into extraordinary situations.

Pete would watch these films of the 1950s endlessly. Compared to the sexually liberated and politically radical films of the 1960s, they were slightly backward-looking. The Ealing comedies now tend to be dismissed for their narrow-mindedness, sexual repression and 'sentimental nationalism' – but it was exactly this sentimental nationalism that Pete loved. Escapist comedies were his bag. Yes, 1950s cinema may have remained unquestioning about Britain and its class system, reinforcing a cosy view of England, but Pete wasn't interested in the sociology of it. He loved the world the films evoked, even if it was entirely different from the world in which he lived. That was the point – he could escape there in dreams if he wanted.

By the 1960s, British television was reflecting the English national image far clearer than the films on the big screen that were pouring out of Hollywood. *Dad's Army* – one of Pete's favourite shows – was a comedy about the Home Guard during the Second World War. Jeffrey Richards says its image was one of 'muddling through, whimsical ingenuity and dogged individualism' and that English comic writing was 'the richest and wisest kind of humour, sweetening and mellowing life for us'.

The novelist J.B. Priestley describes the England during the war that saw the evacuation of Dunkirk not by warships but by seaside pleasure steamers as one, which 'seemed to belong to the same ridiculous holiday world as sandcastles, ham-and-egg teas, palmists and crowded sweating promenades'. Richards says there was a 'humanity … in the determination of … the misfits and the outcasts to do their bit, part of the long-standing British affection for underdogs and losers'.

Pete was hooked on this England. *Dad's Army, Hancock's Half Hour* and the Ealing comedies all seemed to exaggerate these peculiarly British traits of class and snobbery, a love of amateurism, and a gentlemanly 'code of conduct'. They also exaggerated the notion of 'the good old days' where children were taught good manners, to read and write properly, respect their elders, and that crime didn't pay. Of course, as Richards says, this wasn't a historical reality. The picture he paints in his book *Films and British National Identity* is of a 'golden age', a 'restructuring of the past into an amalgam of myth, reality and ideal'. But what is important is that 'this world conjured up in the imagination affects the way you look – at the present'. Nostalgia preserves the best of the past.

Pete began to adopt an image that conjured up this vision of England, fusing the English gentleman (jacket, tie, pork-pie hat) with the crudeness of 1970s punk, the freedom, imagination and disregard for authority of the Romantic poets and occasionally the violence of English soccer hooligans. Together with Carl they likened themselves to the characters in the film *Withnail & I* – two artists who had hit rock bottom, living on the fringes of society in a wet, dreary Camden Town, struggling to keep warm, losing themselves in a heady haze of narcotics and alcohol, trying to 'create' while looking at the world through an irreverent black humour.

And with this British resolve, the pair of them headed off into the unknown, determined to become successful on their own terms. 'Albion' was the poetic Roman name for Britain. For Pete and Carl it represented their vessel – 'the good ship *Albion*' – in which they would set sail on an adventure to find Arcadia, or their vision of an imaginary England, drawing on the best bits of the past. The dictionary defines Arcadia as 'a representation of life in the countryside believed to be perfect'; it was also a pastoral, mountainous region of Greece – the birthplace of the shepherd god Pan, whose mother was a nymph – and features in Romantic poetry. Oscar Wilde wrote: 'O goat-foot God of Arcady! / This modern world is grey and old'. For Carl and Pete it didn't have to be in the countryside. Their Arcadia could be found in the grimiest parts of the city; they saw beauty in the crowded, cold streets of London. But it was still a paradise or utopia, and Pete summed it up on his Internet message board thus: '*Albion* is our vessel, Arcadia is our destination, and our starting point. One needn't have a classical education or a British passport; only an imagination. Let it be what your heart desires, but let not your actions or desires infringe upon the liberty of others.'

Their mission was to 'sail the good ship *Albion* to Arcadia'. 'The band could have been called The Albion, but it's a shit name for a group,' Pete would later tell the *NME*. 'It's like photo booths and squeaky beds. What else do you need to know? It's just a word.'

Arcadia was not in ancient Greece, he insisted, but in the mind, a vision of a better place.

Carl added: 'It's just about the realm of the infinite, and is capable of anything as radical or as beautiful or as sick as you can conjure up.'

A few years later a fan would post the following message on The Libertines Internet message board: 'I think that Arcadia is beyond simple definition. It's more a feeling, a freedom in your heart and mind.'

The roots of this English imagination could be traced further back than the likes of Oscar Wilde: to Shakespeare and Chaucer. Author Peter Ackroyd says with the Bard it lay 'in his mingling of high and low, king and fool, prince and grave digger, commander and soldier, scholar and buffoon'. In Chaucer's *Canterbury Tales*, 'it's the same slightly embarrassed and furtive and jokey attitude toward sexuality'. Chaucer was, Ackroyd says, 'the quintessential English writer' who refused to take himself seriously. In Pete Doherty's world, for Chaucer's jokey attitude towards sexuality, read the *Carry On* films of Kenneth Williams and Sid James.

Ackroyd even wrote a book called *Albion*. The *Independent* newspaper called his vision 'an old-fashioned place ripe for rambles and daydreams'. This summed up Pete and Carl's vision too – and it was about as far away from the England of today as you could get. Ackroyd's England lay in the distant past, and it's precisely this England that had fired Pete and Carl's imagination; they longed for this place.

Will Self said Morrissey possessed a 'peculiarly English brand of Ortonesque camp'. Pete was similar, but preferred Kenneth Williams's campery to Joe Orton's. Morrissey and Pete shared a passion for Englishness, but whereas Morrissey's vision was 'wedded to an exquisite taste for the most subtle kitsch of the recent English past and slathered in Yank worship', immortalising dour seaside towns and evoking 'bedsit angst' (according to Self, Morrissey's perceived 'miserablism' came from that 'archetypally grim, ravaged provincial city', Manchester), Pete's England was slightly more appealing, albeit less realistic.

But Pete and Carl weren't content simply to borrow from the comical world of *Dad's Army*, *Hancock's Half Hour*, *It Ain't Half Hot Mum* or *Carry On*. There had to be an element of rebellion in there too, an attitude that was personified in British punk bands of the 1970s. Carl probably liked punk music more than Pete – he loved its balls, its aggression, and how basic chords could marry with cynical, politically astute lyrics. In punk there were no self-congratulatory guitar solos. Pete loved the rebelliousness. Compared to the bland music in the charts or on the radio, the punk rock of twenty years ago had so much attitude – something Pete felt was sorely lacking from the British music scene.

Both Pete and Carl loved the audience participation in punk: was there another genre of music in which audiences were actively encouraged to pick up a cheap second-hand guitar themselves and told that anyone could play three chords and start a rock 'n' roll band? Audience participation was paramount. As the rock journalist Caroline Coon pointed out: 'When for months you've been feeling that it would take ten years to play as well as Hendrix … there's nothing more gratifying than the thought, "Jesus, I could get a band together and blow this lot off the stage". In addition, there was also very little difference between the way these punk acts dressed on stage and the way their audiences dressed; in fact, occasionally the audience made these bands look positively straight.

Despite being seduced by punk's DIY ethic and the smaller divide between artist and audience, in the beginning the music of The Libertines was a long way off punk rock. It was almost the opposite – they were a skiffle band, with a drummer and a cellist called Vicky. It was enough to give Johnny Rotten a heart attack.

'Skiffle' had been coined in the 1920s to describe the British bands who had replaced expensive jazz instruments like the trumpet and sax with home-made or improvised instruments like the washboard, kazoo and tea-chest bass, but who still drew on black American roots music for their inspiration. Lonnie Donegan was one of its most famous proponents and his influence on the young John Lennon has been well documented – Lennon's first band was a skiffle act called The Quarrymen. Interestingly, like punk, skiffle boasted the 'anyone can play' mentality and so, regardless of real musical talent, young would-be musicians formed bands, wrote music and took to the stage.

The Libertines' first gig was in Carl and Pete's tiny flat in the Camden Road. At the time they couldn't have known just how much this evening would come to define their gigs in the future. The Libertines would pioneer the 'guerrilla gig': impromptu performances in their living room, with the nominal fee going straight to the band, cutting out management commission, booking agents' fees and doing away with the need for financial 'tour support' from the record label (which is ultimately recouped from record sales anyway). But that was all in the future. In early 1999 they were just beginning to ply their trade on the streets of London: the Seen bar in Soho, the Empress of Russia – a real-ale pub a stone's throw from the Sadler's Wells theatre – in Angel, and Filthy McNasty's.

By the summer Carl and Pete decided that if they were going to get anywhere in the business they would need a demo. And so, along with their new bassist John, they disappeared into Odessa studios on the Upper Clapton Road for a few days to put down some tracks. Still devoid of a drummer, the studio sound engineer suggested an old guy known as Mr Razzcocks, who did session work for £50. There was one person missing from the new line-up: 'Scarborough' Steve Bedlow. Carl and Pete had begun to write songs on which they could share vocal duty; Steve wasn't needed for these demos.

By September 1999 The Libertines – albeit a hotch-potch of characters at this point – were ready for their first important live show: a gig at Islington's Hope & Anchor pub at the top end of Upper Street. The underground venue was tiny – the stage was barely big enough for the band – but it was legendary. U2, Joy Division, Elvis Costello and Madness had all played there. It was, and still is, a key pub on the London circuit for aspiring rock 'n' roll bands.

On 11 September The Libertines joined the list of bands that read like a roll-call of definitive British and Irish talent. It also marked the beginning of playing venues often populated by the music press and the occasional A&R scout. It was around this time that the *NME* began sniffing around.

FOUR

|LIBERTINE|

If you head west from Angel underground station along the Pentonville Road and take a left into Amwell Street, a short way down the hill you'll come to a pub. In the past, Filthy McNasty's whiskey bar has seen Shane MacGowan and the Pogues grace its tiny backroom stage and Nick Cave prop up its bar.

Its red interior is set off by black and white pictures on the walls, and a letter written in memory of the late, great Joe Strummer. Its tattered sofas reek of cigarette smoke, and during the day you'll find the old, local boys nursing pints of Guinness, keeping out of the cold.

In 1999 an Irishman known as the Rabbi was booking the bands there; everyone knew the jovial man with the beard down to his knees. He also seemed to be able to drink gallons of Guinness in an evening and not suffer.

Tuesday night was 'open mic night' run by an American musician called Geoff McIntire, who was dating one of the girls behind the bar. The standard of musicianship on those nights was high: the majority of the crowd were in bands or played instruments. Ex-members of festival favourites Dodgy would get up and entertain the audience; there were members of the now defunct Britpop band Menswear. The Libertines liked to play there too.

Performing in front of just thirty people, Pete, Carl and John loved it at Filthy's. Mr Razzcocks would sit behind his drum kit, crammed in with his back up against the fireplace, and there was little if any space separating Carl and Pete from the front of the crowd. It was also hot. Very hot. But it was an intimate atmosphere and The Libertines' songs went down well.

Apart from Razzcocks and Vicky the cellist (who later was to leave the band of her own accord), the lads wore black vintage suits with tapered trousers, white shirts and black ties. Like latter-day Beatles they were instantly recognisable. And on stage Pete and Carl's mic-sharing antics and verbal word play were beginning to set them apart from other bands.

But these open mic nights weren't always about music. There was the female poetry reader with an afro who'd talk about contraception; there were old guys who looked as if they'd been propping up the bar all day, who'd sling acoustic guitars over their necks and play blues songs like they'd just stepped off a plane from Louisiana. Anyone could play at Filthy's, and everyone was encouraged to play. Occasionally even the Rabbi would step up to the mic and belt out a couple of old Irish traditionals. Pete was in his element – this was exactly the sort of creative environment he had imagined in his vision of urban bohemia in London.

The 'look' among the mostly twenty-something crowd at Filthy's was tight vintage Levi's jeans, flared at the bottom; rock 'n' roll 'mullet' haircuts; Converse trainers; vintage silk scarves and studded belts.

Clare Drummond, another cellist, who occasionally accompanied Geoff McIntire on stage, says this early incarnation of The Libertines was unforgettable. 'They were brilliant,' she says. When Vicky later left the band, Carl asked Clare to step in but she was living in Brighton at the time and the commute meant it was impossible.

McIntire had some contacts at Universal Records and Pete and Carl bristled with excitement when he told them an important producer who had worked with the French band Air was popping down. The producer never materialised; or if she did, she was never interested in The Libertines. But despite still living in a hovel in Camden, playing Irish pubs and somewhat lacking in the financial department, the band were determined to lead the high life.

'There was a really good cook at Filthy's called Maria,' Clare remembers. 'The Libertines used to order oysters and champagne when they were doing these open mic nights – and this was before they got a deal. They already had airs and graces about them.

'At the time, Carl was in a serious relationship with a blonde girl and they'd cosy up to each other after the show. She was lovely. John's long-time girlfriend used to come along too. Pete was dating this crazy, elfin Italian girl and they'd be constantly fighting. She had this mad dress sense and would wear long black gloves up her arms; she was very pretty and very stylish. They were passionate and volatile to say the least and always seemed to be in a bad mood with each other. She loved drinking champagne too. It was like they were all living this rock 'n' roll lifestyle before they'd even signed to Rough Trade.'

Offstage the band would flounce around Camden in 1970s cast-offs from the market – suede or sheepskin jackets were the order of the day. Looking back, Clare says Carl had the most style. 'He had the long haircut – almost a bob – like Paul McCartney in the seventies. Pete was scruffier – on stage he always had stuff written on his hands and his hair looked like it hadn't been washed in a week. Most of the girls fancied Carl; there was something romantic about him and he was quiet. Pete was a bit of a show-off. He was nice but a little more self-assured than the others; more of an extrovert. I think that's the attraction though –

he had charisma and character; definitely the wild card of the pack, and possibly less approachable than the others. There was something indefinable that set him apart.'

In 1999 Roger Morton – now manager of Razorlight – was working as a reporter on the *NME*, but he'd begun to get itchy feet. He'd sit in north London pubs with his mate Andy Fraser, who worked as a press officer, trying to work out why they were still sitting in the pub while the bands they were helping to promote were becoming rich and famous. 'The next good band we find, we'll manage, and see what happens,' they decided.

And as fate would have it, at the end of summer The Libertines had lined up a gig at the Hope & Anchor in Islington. Morton had a musician friend called Su Goodacre – a protégé of trip-hop pioneer Tricky, signed to Virgin Records – and she had encouraged him to come along to see the show.

'I used to see Su at a lot of gigs and she mentioned that this band called The Libertines were playing at the Hope & Anchor,' Morton recalls. 'They were appearing on stage in the basement and I remember the first thing I thought was, despite the fact they were a bit shambolic, they had a huge amount of charm and there weren't any other bands like that in London at the time.

'They were a great band despite the fact their music wasn't really together at that point. But they definitely had ideas about how to write classic songs even though they hadn't written too many yet. That was obviously their ambition, though, and they had a really defined aesthetic. Live, they were shambolic, and with the cello player they were frankly bizarre – it was like The Kinks with a cello player.

'The Libertines were coming from somewhere completely different and were very endearing. I immediately thought: you should be on the cover of the *NME*.'

Morton's hopes of a cover feature weren't to be realised for another few years but, along with Fraser, he did go on to manage the band.

'Pete had once worked at the Prince Charles cinema so he managed to blag a gig there,' Morton says. 'So Andy and I went down to see them live again – along with thirty other people – and we were sitting in these cinema seats while The Libertines played through the cinema's PA system. It was all very strange. Afterwards we had a meeting with them in a grave-yard off of Wardour Street and tried to convince them to let us manage them. And so The Libertines became the first band I ever took on.'

Jackie and Peter had been understandably upset when Pete had left university after a matter of months. He'd been going on about Albion and Arcadia and this band he was setting up with his friend Carl, but in truth his parents thought he was wasting his talent. Certainly nothing seemed to be happening. But this, they felt, was a good sign: Morton was an *NME* hack and had contacts. Maybe Pete had something with this band of his, The Libertines.

The Libertines' first *NME* live review appeared on 18 September 1999, after Morton saw them at the Bull & Gate pub in Kentish Town, north London. The band were, he said, 'fresh, wry, flow-ery and savage ... as much precious neophytes as twisted ol' souls'. But the music The Libertines were playing circa 1999 was quite different to what they would play two years later. Morton described their sound as 'all light and skiffley' with their blend of both acoustic and electric guitars, Vicky on cello and Razzcock's jazz drumming.

But one thing Morton did note in 1999 could just have easily been written five years later: that 'puppy-eyes frontman Pete [was] casting his poetry pearls among the appreciative onlookers'. In addition, Pete's songwriting was already embracing his passion for England's past: Morton noted that one song referenced comedian Tony Hancock. He also said the band made funky numbers seem 'like the most alluring thing since opium lollipops'.

They obviously impressed an *NME* hack who had been there through the early days of indie music in the late 1980s, and charted the rise of dance music in the early 1990s and later Britpop. Morton had seen a lot of good bands come, go, and even stay, but The Libertines really floated his boat. '"Brick Road Lover" and "You're My Waterloo" evoke The Kinks or early Beatles,' he said, 'while "Music When The Lights Go Out" is more anthemic.' They were, he concluded, 'Proper London Oxfam aesthetes with dirty minds, dusty books, nice tunes and a future.'

Only 'Music When The Lights Go Out' would make it onto a Libertines album. The song became a classic, standout track on the band's second album for Rough Trade, released in 2004. It was arguably more poignant five years after Morton first heard it that September night at the Bull & Gate. By the time it actually made it onto the reel-to-reel in the studio, drugs and fame would have damaged Pete and Carl's relationship, possibly irreparably. The song's lyrics said it all, recalling the excesses they had shared together that would stay with them until their dying day, but emphasising their fractured friendship.

'Brick Road Lover' was an error on Morton's part. There was a song called 'Breck Rd' – a reference to the A road in Anfield that slices past Liverpool Football Club – that would be dropped from The Libertines first album. On the album's handwritten track listing the song is scribbled out, replaced by 'Boys In The Band'.

In the same issue as that first *NME* review, DJ Richard Fearless's dance project Death in Vegas had made the front cover. Inside the magazine, next to The Libertines piece, was a large review of a gig by the Norwegian industrial metal musician Mortiis – or 'some pointless goth band' as Morton says, leafing through the old issue. Unfortunately the *NME* scribe who'd written the Mortiis review didn't agree. 'We desperately need more freaks like this,' he said.

'Even Bernard Butler had a review,' Morton sighs. 'The hangover from years ago' – who went on to record The Libertines' first singles. 'There's Sparklehorse, Public Enemy who have been away for years, a full-page live review of a Blur gig. This was 1999. People still hadn't recovered from Britpop, and for the kids who were sixteen, seventeen and eighteen, this wasn't their music, it was their uncles' music. The Libertines were perfect for that generation but the record industry hadn't noticed.'

The record industry wouldn't take any real notice for at least another year and a half. But for the next eight months, Morton and Fraser would help point The Libertines in the right direction, securing them gigs, persuading music publishing companies to give them studio time and putting the word around that this band was the brightest thing to come out of London for ages.

Aside from the music, Morton was also taken with Carl, Pete and John's personalities. 'They were all very amusing,' he says. 'Back then John Hassall was exactly as he is now – kind of quiet and didn't give much away but a really lovely guy. Carlos was a bumbling, theatrical, funny bloke. Pete was a bit more calculated and keen to be an enigma. One could say that.'

Morton was also impressed by their almost encyclopedic knowledge of the music of the 1960s and 1970s. 'I thought they were very unusual. I didn't have any experience of any kids in their early twenties who were that heavily into this music,' he says. 'They came round my flat and there was a piano there and they could play covers of classic 1960s songs – Bowie, The Beatles, Kinks and Stones. I didn't think their generation gave a shit about that, particularly as 1999 was still in the aftermath of house music and the bands scene was so crappy. It was an eye-opener to me.'

Image-wise, The Libertines were wearing – in Morton's words – anything they could get their hands on from the second-hand shop that looked vaguely 1960s. But even if Morton and his business partner Fraser were sold on the band, persuading the record labels to sign them was going to prove difficult, if not impossible. 'No one was really interested at all,' Morton remembers. 'Mike Smith from EMI Publishing [who later actually signed them to the publishing house after Morton had left The Libertines] gave them some free studio time. We then sent that demo off to a number of labels but nothing came of it.'

One of those labels was Instant Karma. Rob Dickins, former chairman of Warner Music UK and the British Phonographic Institute, had started the boutique label earlier the same year. Instant Karma had thought The Libertines were interesting but ultimately turned them down. Morton recalls taking the band down to the label's head office. 'Everyone was really excited but it was a meaningless chat that never turned into anything,' he says.

Understandably Pete, Carl and John were disappointed. 'He took us to meet some poncey record company executives who definitely did not like us,' Carl would later recall.

Music was all they wanted to do, and signing a record deal would mean the music they were making could finally be heard by more people. Reality bites hard for bands struggling to get signed. Even having a manager on board like Morton, with all his contacts, was no guarantee of immediate success. It looked like this was going to take time. Evidently 1999 wasn't the right time for The Libertines.

Morton still has the tattered guest list from a gig in the winter of that year. It's interesting to see which labels were showing a glimmer of interest then, even if none of them actually made the leap to sign the band. 'All these labels that came down to see them play,' Morton says. 'Sony Publishing, East West Records, Warner Chappell Music. The guy from Parlophone isn't ticked off on the gig list so he obviously didn't turn up.' He laughs.

There was never any game plan. Morton says The Libertines were simply this romantic gang that was vaguely delinquent. Pete was working in a pub called the King's Head to pay the rent, selling speed and marijuana to top up his income.

'We'd sit in meetings and everyone would look at each other and say, "Well, what are we going to do?"' Morton says, 'and of course they'd look at me and I'd go, "Er, well, I've got a mate who runs a club night and I'll talk to somebody about something," but they certainly didn't have a coherent, conscious idea about how to manipulate their innate qualities.'

Gigs were booked at the Water Rats in King's Cross; at the Blow Up venue – which in 1999 primarily hosted club nights, but which would, after its move to Oxford Street two years later, become instrumental in breaking new bands; and the Kashmir Klub – an acoustic night run out of the basement of a pizza restaurant in Baker Street by singer-songwriter Tony Moore, ex-keyboard player from 1980s outfit Cutting

Crew. All three venues were important on the London circuit: the Kashmir Klub had hosted Damien Rice before he signed to East West Records, and Gemma Hayes before she signed to Source. But unfortunately for The Libertines, their shot at fame fell short.

As a band they seemed to gravitate to north and east London, playing self-booked gigs at dives in Hackney or Islington Green. These venues may not have been where the record industry gravitated, but it gave them a chance to hone their skills as musicians, experience playing in front of a crowd, and develop a feel for the stage.

'The music was refreshing,' Morton says. 'What was so good about it was that it was linked to their environment. They weren't aping American bands. It all belonged in London. They did have that comical thing with Chas & Dave but it was all fitting and they were writing songs that romanticised the environment in which they were living. That element was missing from all the other bands that were around at that time.'

Even back then Pete would talk at length about his notions of *Albion* and Arcadia. 'He clearly had that idea in mind,' Morton remembers. 'They were inventing their experience as young people in London and romanticising it in a way no one else was. They were clearly a gang that did lots of mad things together – had parties, some of them took drugs – and there was clearly a scene within London at that time of which they were a part. And while that was going on, the *NME* was writing about Leftfield. That's no good if you're sixteen years old and want to sneak out and go to see a band.'

Pete had begun putting on what he called 'Arcadian Cabaret Nights' at Finnegan's Wake and the Foundry on Great Eastern Street, an old bank transformed into a 'space' for music, poetry and art by former KLF musician Bill Drummond.

The following year Mairead Nash began to help The Libertines out. Mairead, who would later become immortalised on the Von Bondies second album *Pawn Shoppe Heart* and start the DJ act Queens of Noize with her friend Tabitha Denholm (one-time girlfriend of Pete's), was working as a booker at the 333 Club in Old Street. It was while booking the DJs and bands that Mairead became friends with Pete, Carl and John, and she'd give them regular slots on the stage in the club's basement. It was a small space, dingy brick walls and no natural light, but the 333 Club was to become the mainstay of the 'Shoreditch scene'. Mairead, a pretty, jet-black-haired wild child from Coventry, envisaged the 333 becoming the focal point for a new scene in British music. 'The London equivalent of CBGBs,' she would later say. And in 2000, it was still young, fresh and exciting.

Another name that cropped up around this time was that of the young Johnny Borrell. He had known John Hassall from school and Morton had seen him that first night he'd been to watch The Libertines play at Islington's Hope & Anchor. Borrell was also a musician and, like Pete and Carl, desperately wanted to make it.

'I first saw him in the bar upstairs, above the venue,' Morton recalls. 'I'd never seen him do anything musically but I clocked him and thought: you look like a rock star. I was introduced to him and then saw him again when The Libertines played a gig at a bar on the edge of Islington Green.'

That night, Johnny appeared wearing a cowboy hat and carrying a William Faulkner novel under his arm. Johnny and The Libertines were inhabiting the same dream; they had the same fantasy. Both Pete and Johnny wanted to be bohemians. 'I thought, not only did he look like a rock star, he also had the affectations of a rock star as well,' Morton says. 'And he was indicative of the crowd that were hanging around with them at this point. They wanted to live this bohemian existence in a movie that was never made about England in the 1960s. And maybe they still do.

'Poetry was important too. Johnny always carried round books of lyrics and Pete was always scribbling things down. They saw themselves as poetic troubadours. It was really engaging and great to see that. For me as a journalist, there was actually something to write about these guys. They weren't just aping American bands. There was no romance to a lot of [what the American bands were doing], but these people were specifically inventing their own fantasy.'

Morton says that together, this band of troubadours – Pete, Carl, John, Scarborough Steve, Mairead – were like a gang. 'Who dated who and for how long, and how many people were in the bed was extremely confusing.' Morton laughs. 'In fact, I don't think even they can remember.'

Morton shakily videoed an early performance by The Libertines at the venue near Islington Green. That 30-minute VHS tape would be enough, he thought, to generate interest if he was ever able to get to play it to an A&R executive from one of the major labels.

It was a few months later that the meeting with Mike Smith from EMI Publishing took place. The pair sat down in the middle of the EMI offices in front of the TV and video player. 'I was asking Mike to get the band a demo session and the only thing I had to convince him to do it was this video,' Morton says. 'And the only place they had to watch it was on this machine in the centre of their office.'

While the tape rolled and the band strutted their stuff on screen, Morton and Smith were interrupted by a visibly excited, chubby-faced

man with wild red hair. Morton had known James Endeacott for a while
– as the A&R guy for Rough Trade records, Endeacott was a familiar face
on the British music scene. This particular day he came bounding up to
Morton and Smith and sat down on the seat next to them. His excitement was because Terris – a band he had been involved with – had just
made the front cover of the *NME*.

'Here's a good band, James,' Morton said, pointing to the screen.
'You should check them out.' But Endeacott seemed uninterested. He
continued raving about Terris and upped and left after a few minutes,
while Pete, John, Carl and Razzcocks continued to plough their way
through their set, pouring with sweat in their black suits under the
stifling stage lights on screen.

Just under two years later James Endeacott would sign The
Libertines to Rough Trade and, in a whirlwind of publicity, watch as the
band's rise became nothing short of meteoric.

The *NME* would, in no small part, help catapult the band to this
level of fame; between 2002 and 2004 rarely a week would go by without some mention of The Libertines – whether it was a cover, news
story, feature, tour diary, live review, album review or single review. But
a couple of years earlier the *NME* had failed to latch on to the scene
The Libertines had begun to spearhead. Yes, at the behest of Morton
they had commissioned a live review, but that was it. In terms of page
space, Mortiis – the death metaller from Norway – was deemed far
more worthy.

Roger Morton had started to feel that The
Libertines needed to begin playing electric guitars on stage if they
wanted to get signed. It was crucial, he thought, if they were to be taken

seriously as a rock 'n' roll band. They had some powerful songs but it wasn't quite working as an acoustic skiffle act. It was too low-key. They needed to make an impact and they had the songs to do just that.

Two years later he would watch as The Libertines became marketed as London's answer to New York rockers The Strokes. 'Raw energetic nu-punk came to Southampton this week,' came a BBC review of a 2002 Libertines gig at the tiny Joiners Arms pub in the city's St Mary's district. 'They could be the saviours of punk,' said a review of their debut single 'What A Waster'.

'Someone at the label had obviously given them a strong push in that direction,' Morton says now. 'I was always extremely confused when those first reviews started talking about them in the context of some sort of punk band, which they absolutely were not. Yes, they were slightly anarchic and would fall over and get drunk a lot, but that's not a punk band. Musically there was nothing punky about them; they were too lightweight. The Libertines were songwriters.'

But for now nothing much was happening. Morton and Fraser couldn't continue in their position as managers and parted company with The Libertines. Morton went on to manage Johnny Borrell, who would front Razorlight and sell 100,000 copies of his debut album.

The Libertines, meanwhile, met a woman called Banny Poostchi.

Poostchi – who the band would later describe as 'a Persian she-devil whose family escaped the revolution' – had originally cut her teeth at Simons Muirhead and Burton in Soho, assisting a lawyer acting for Oasis. Two years later, at the start of 2000, she left to take a job with Warner Chappell Music Publishing. It was a few months later that she first met Pete and Carl. Her boyfriend Alex Clarke, a writer, filmmaker and poet, had begun raving about a band he'd seen several times at Filthy McNasty's. 'They have this old drummer and a cellist,' he'd said. 'And they look and sound incredible.'

The band had no manager and Pete, intrigued by Clarke's bohemian spirit, tried to persuade him to manage The Libertines. The fact that Clarke was then working for Malcolm McLaren on his campaign to become Mayor of London was no doubt also a big attraction, but Clarke declined the offer. He was more interested in making films and went on to later direct the video for The Libertines' single 'Don't Look Back Into the Sun'. He recommended his girlfriend; after all she had just spent over a year working solidly for Britain's biggest band and was now based at a major music publishing company. He arranged a meeting between Pete, Carl and Poostchi and when she first saw The Libertines she immediately thought they had something. It was chaotic, but through the chaos Poostchi thought she could spot a talent for songwriting. There just didn't seem to be another band like them.

Clarke had also been going on about this unlikely gang of misfits to a producer friend called Simon Bourcier. 'The first time I heard about them was at a party,' Bourcier recalls. 'Alex was there talking about this band he'd found. He mentioned Pete and said he was this poet and that they were all really talented. I still have their first demo that Alex handed me which features the band on the cover with their original drummer, this old geezer who's about sixty, Mr Razzcocks.'

Poostchi and Clarke organised several gigs for the band throughout the summer and autumn of 2000 as well as a photo session. But for Poostchi, something was missing. She wasn't convinced by their line-up and felt their acoustic strumming lacked bite and energy. Quite simply she thought it failed to make the most of their talent as songwriters. However, back then she was reluctant to interfere with either the line-up or the musical direction that the band had already settled upon before she came along. Instead, by the winter she suggested it would be in their best interests to find someone willing to work with what they already had in place. They parted amicably and were not to see each other again for several months, except occasionally at Filthy McNasty's.

Pete threw himself back into the poetry that he'd been absorbed in since he was a child. A group of Russian poets had headed over to London for a cultural exchange hosted by Bill Drummond's Foundry venue on Great Eastern Street and funded by the British Council in Moscow. Pete had given readings at the Foundry and was interested in heading to Russia on the exchange trip. A four-day visit to Moscow was scheduled for September that year and Pete found out he was going. It was to prove to be a memorable trip. Pete had what he referred to as an 'awakening' in Moscow. Once again he was able to romanticise the experience. 'Making love in these huge Stalin tenements with the bed falling through the floor,' he'd say.

Accompanying him was fellow poet and actor Tam Dean Burn, who has since appeared in the Scottish soap opera *River City* and Irvine Welsh's movie *Acid House*. Burn would compère at the Foundry when Pete was starting out as a poet. Of the Moscow trip, Burn told the *Guardian*: 'I turned up without a clue where I was going and the guy at the airport met me with a bottle of vodka. It all got a bit blurred after that … the trip has gone down in legend. Who says you can't mix poetry and the rock 'n' roll lifestyle?'

Jackie and Peter believed their son was a gifted writer but there was always a nagging awareness of their own bias. Now, with a visit to Russia to read his poetry, they felt vindicated.

In the period that followed, things were changing within the band which would lead to The Libertines' original line-up changing for good.

The friction was caused largely by Pete's desire to play gig after gig at Filthy McNasty's and what seemed like a disinterest in graduating to more important venues on the circuit, like the Camden Monarch. This frustrated John Hassall enough to leave the band, and he was swiftly followed by Mr Razzcocks. Pete readily admits that wasn't the only reason. 'It was also to do with the brown as well,' he says. 'Brown' is the street name for powdered heroin in its most common form. Pete was apparently beginning to develop quite a penchant for it. How true this was or whether it was part of Pete's self-mythologising is anybody's guess but this was news to those working with the band who became aware of his use of the drug much later on.

Somewhere along the line Scarborough Steve had rejoined the band as their occasional singer and had moved into a Peabody Trust housing association place in Tottenham with Pete. But Carl didn't think The Libertines needed Steve at all.

Without a permanent drummer or bass player, and with the friction between Carl and Steve, plus the friction caused by Pete's drug-taking, The Libertines broke up. Pete and Steve would rehearse in their house in Tottenham in a haze of narcotics and Carl became a stranger.

It would be another nine months before Pete would feel re-energised and keener than ever to kick-start The Libertines again.

Meanwhile, in America, something was stirring.

'He is very much a poet with a romanticised view of life and I can understand how he could get a lot out of being a fantasist.'

SIMON BOURCIER, PRODUCER

FIVE

YOU'RE SO OLD STREET

In late 1990s Detroit, behind the walls of the city's handful of tiny rock clubs, something very special had begun to happen.

In addition to Motown, Iggy Pop, the Stooges and Wayne Kramer's MC5, the city wore a legacy of race riots from the 1960s heavily round its neck. While city workers ventured from their offices to secure car parks via overhead walkways – an attempt to keep them away from the crime-ridden streets below – and while addicts, their faces buried in paper bags of glue, walked like zombies along the desolate streets past burned-down, empty and decaying buildings, a new music scene was still in its infancy. Rock 'n' roll was about to come back with a vengeance. Garage rock was on the verge of erupting from Detroit's mean streets: a new soundtrack for a disaffected generation. It was to be spearheaded by a duo known as the White Stripes, but would also give birth to bands like the Dirtbombs, Paybacks, Detroit Cobras, the Hentchmen, Bantam Rooster and the Von Bondies.

Six hundred miles away something similar was happening in New York. Julian Casablancas, son of founder of the Elite Model Agency John Casablancas, had teamed up with childhood friend Nikolai Fraiture to form a rock 'n' roll band. Fraiture played bass and Casablancas could sing. Together with guitarists Nick Valensi and Albert Hammond Jr and drummer Fabrizio Moretti they had formed The Strokes in 1999, quickly becoming a key fixture on the city's Lower East Side.

Casablancas's laid-back, effortless vocals combined with Hammond Jr's punchy, punky guitar riffs and the band's perceptive lyrics, catchy tunes and a fashion sense straight out of the style mags meant it wasn't long before a rock 'n' roll starved audience over the pond beckoned.

The first we got to hear of this 'new rock revolution' – as the *NME* would brand it – was as 2001 dawned. The Strokes' *The Modern Age* EP sparked a bidding war not seen for years among record labels. Their music was like a breath of fresh air to anyone who had tired of Craig David, Ronan Keating, Eminem, Spiller and Sonique. Inevitably The Strokes became the subject of unprecedented hype – something of which everyone would also begin to tire as 2001 came to a close.

But in the beginning it was fantastic. The Strokes were the 'saviours of rock 'n' roll', according to a hungry music press. These five rockers from New York with their leather jackets, pencil-thin ties, snotty-nosed cool and East-side punk chic were exactly what we needed. The buzz was unprecedented for a band yet to release an album.

One reviewer said they looked 'like extras from Mean Streets'. An Irish journalist summed up the hype in the Belfast Newsletter: 'A year ago The Strokes were playing to fifty people, now A&R men are rumoured to be offering them seven-figure cheques ... when we tell you The Strokes are going to be huge, believe us, we mean massive.'

The band's first London headline show was at the Camden Monarch. A journalist from the *Independent* newspaper was there. 'Only their first London headline show, New York quintet The Strokes have sold out this murky room in advance,' he wrote, 'so eager are the punters to soak up their unashamed tribute to the great past bands of their home city, captured on their superb *The Modern Age* EP … for the moment nothing can stop them.'

Their gig shortly afterwards at the Heaven nightclub under the arches near Embankment station ensured their legacy would remain. On stage they didn't really need to do much at all – Casablancas stood stock-still at the mic for the majority of the performance – but live the songs translated and it was a breath of fresh air after rock 'n' roll had spent so long in the wilderness.

Then, a couple of months later it was the turn of The White Stripes. The late DJ John Peel had been championing this young Detroit duo – billed as brother and sister but later 'outed' as a divorcee couple – for months. Then a young *NME* hack named Stevie Chick reviewed their gig at South by Southwest – a music festival in Austin, Texas and one of the most important on the industry calendar. Their legend too was assured. 'Stripped back to its barest elements,' Chick wrote, 'dipped in dirt and sex and explosive passion … [they have come] to save rock 'n' roll.'

From Sweden there was all-girl rock outfit Sahara Hotnights, Division of Laura Lee, Soundtrack of Our Lives and The Hives. The Hives was the new signing by Alan McGee, the man who had discovered Oasis. With their sharp black and white suits, good looks, Ramones-meets-The-Stooges garage rock and unlikely but brilliantly inventive names like Howlin' Pelle Almqvist and Matt Destruction, they were incredibly refreshing. From Australia came The Vines, and from New Zealand, The Datsuns and D4.

You knew the *NME*, although overstating it somewhat, had a point. This was a revolution of sorts. Rock 'n' roll was back with a vengeance and it wasn't long before the style and fashion press caught on: The Strokes became fashion icons for the new millennium. The only trouble was it was all coming from across the pond.

Something had changed in the British music scene too. Whereas once the music magazines had been first to latch onto a new scene, the first to discover new bands – sometimes even before the record companies had got there – by 2001 the mainstream press in the UK had caught up. The *Independent, Telegraph, Evening Standard* and others were sending reporters to cover 'unsigned' events like South by Southwest and Manchester's In The City. They were there in the smoky Camden Monarch, picking their way across the chewing-gum-strewn floor. They were there at the Boston Arms in Tufnell Park, soaking up this new wave of talent from across the pond, chronicling the new rock explosion. But what they and the music press hadn't spotted in early 2001 was the talent on their own doorstep.

In Detroit, the scene had been allowed to flourish away from the prying eyes of the music press or tabloids. There, bands had a chance to grow, to develop and hone their skills for years sometimes before the press got wind of them. In London things were very different at the dawn of the new millennium – there was nowhere to hide. If record companies had seen The Libertines in their infancy – which some had, under Roger Morton's tutelage – they can't have been impressed. But The Libertines were beginning to gather quite a fan base around them. Their own scene was starting to form, quite apart from this new rock explosion from America and elsewhere. In London, The Libertines were thrashing out their brand of very English rock 'n' roll.

A year before The Libertines' debut album would astound a music industry hungry for a British band to replicate the wave of raucous, energetic rock 'n' roll sailing into these shores from the States, there was a small fan base already listening to songs that spoke to them, songs about the England they knew and loved.

At first the 'rock revival' seemed to centre on a few tiny, grungy clubs at various locations across London: Cherry Jam in north London, Metro on Oxford Street, Death Disco at the Notting Hill Arts Club, the Boston Arms in Tufnell Park, and – particularly for The Libertines – the 333 Club in Old Street.

While The Libertines didn't feel part of the new wave of rock 'n' roll bands, they would inevitably be grouped in with them. As Roger Morton recalls: 'The crucial thing is that The Strokes happened and suddenly every label in the UK had a different idea about what was viable. They could suddenly see something in a band like The Libertines.'

Banny Poostchi had seen The Strokes live and knew instinctively that a British band along a similar vein was sorely missing in the UK. She got back in touch with Pete and Carl in the summer of 2001. The pair were without a band and Poostchi proposed that they should work together again to develop their songwriting, replacing the light skiffle acoustic tracks of before with new songs using electric guitars, and adding a bassist and drummer. In short she told them to get their act together. 'We can fucking do this,' she told Carl. This time Poostchi would have a bigger role in the new line-up and the direction of the band. She told them that if they did everything she said, she would get them signed within six months. Carl and Pete agreed.

A month later she left her job at Warner Chappell and moved to East West Records, a subsidiary of Warner Records, where she worked as a business affairs manager.

'Banny saw The Strokes and heard a cash tone ring in her head,' Pete would later tell *Rolling Stone*.

The buzz surrounding The Strokes was incredible and Poostchi decided she would contact the New York producer Gordon Raphael, who had worked with them on their EP and was about to produce their debut album.

Producer Simon Bourcier recalls: 'Gordon was interested in producing The Libertines and Banny said I would engineer the record. That was the vibe at that time. There was also some talk of Jarvis Cocker having heard one of their demos and the record industry was starting to sniff around at this point. But for one reason or another Gordon didn't do it.' Although Poostchi was in regular contact with Raphael she was ultimately more interested in getting feedback on the music.

Poostchi arranged to meet Bourcier at the Dome café just outside her office. There was still no record deal on the table and she asked him whether he'd be prepared to foot some of the bill for putting The Libertines into the recording studio again. Poostchi had a tentative plan: if Bourcier came on board now and could show he was serious, when they eventually signed a deal – which she felt wasn't far away now – he could possibly produce their debut album, however nothing was ever actually agreed.

They considered the idea that The Libertines needed to head to a studio in the country with Bourcier and lock themselves away so they could rehearse and get a really tight set together. It was late summer 2001 and Poostchi felt sure their time was now but they needed to rehearse and demo as much as possible. Her priority was making sure Pete and Carl wrote some decent new material and found a stable line-up, nevertheless she didn't see any harm in them spending time with Bourcier who she felt was a talented producer.

'I got a call from Banny one night,' Bourcier recalls. 'Pete and Scarborough Steve [who had reappeared for the evening] were doing a gig at Riverside Studios in Hammersmith at some poetry reading evening. Banny wanted me to work with Pete and Carl and told me to come along to the show.

'When I arrived at Riverside, I was introduced to Pete and this 60-odd-year-old trumpet player he'd picked up that same afternoon; he'd discovered him busking somewhere and had asked him to play with The Libertines live that night. Carl was in Bristol and Gary still hadn't come on the scene at this point. Pete was a really nice guy. I remember thinking how tall he was; he was incredibly lanky, really thin, and looked great: he wore a black suit and pork-pie hat and I could sense a sort of arrogance.

'When the poetry readings began, Pete, Steve and Banny were taking the piss out of all of these awful poets. The atmosphere was fucking tense and everyone was getting incredibly pissed off; it was a very tiny space. Towards the end of the evening Pete climbed on stage with this trumpet player, sort of ad-libbing. Then Steve began making his way from the back of the auditorium, crawling on his chest, army-style, as if he was in the trenches. Pete began playing Chas & Dave style bar-room music on the guitar and I thought we were going to get chucked out at any minute. Eventually Steve made it to the mic – it took him about half an hour – and then did absolutely nothing. He just stood there, at which point Pete actually broke out into a couple of Chas & Dave numbers. It was hilarious.'

Carl turned up late after travelling back from Bristol. After the impromptu art-house performance had ended, the entourage followed Bourcier back to his studio in Conlan Street near Notting Hill. He planned to record some rough demos to see what he had to work with. It was going to be a long night.

When they arrived, Pete began serenading a group of girls who had accompanied them to the studio. As the clock ticked away and Bourcier recorded Pete and Carl's 'greatest hits' to digital audio tape, the drugs were in full flow. 'It turned into a drug-fuelled session,' Bourcier says. 'One of the girls that was there disappeared to the toilet, and when I went downstairs I found her on her hands and knees, having tipped out the entire contents of her handbag looking for drugs. It had got to that stage in the proceedings. And this went on 'til seven in the morning.'

Despite the excess that was already starting to help define The Libertines as a band, the session proved productive. Pete and Carl managed, relatively coherently, to run through twenty songs they'd written. 'There was good stuff in there,' Bourcier says. 'Intelligent lyrics and arrangements. I wasn't really doing anything. I thought they were good guys who hopefully would achieve something. I wasn't really there as a producer or engineer at first; I felt my job was simply to make them feel comfortable enough to elicit the best performance I could. I wanted to create a vibe in the studio whereby they could be fucked up if they wanted to be, or not. Whatever – it didn't matter. I would just pour them a beer now and again or suggest a chord here and there.

'There were a couple of girls at that recording session and they were sitting on the sofa while I was behind the mixing desk. One girl in particular would open her legs so I could see under her skirt every time she spoke to me. She was wearing this pair of panties with a star on them and I was really trying to be polite but I couldn't help but have a sneak preview every five minutes. Every time I'd look over, her legs would go akimbo; she was definitely doing it on purpose.'

Clarke and Poostchi envisaged Simon Bourcier as a 'George Martin' type character: in Bourcier's words, 'a posh guy who does music, having an influence on the band'. According to Bourcier, Pete was 'obsessed with public school and the aristocracy' and this appealed to him.

It's interesting to note this perceived 'obsession' with class. Growing up, Pete had romanticised the notion of a working-class existence: of a London inhabited by Chas & Dave, rag & bone men and cockney wide boys, with a community spirit he'd never himself experienced. When he first arrived in London he described himself as a 'foppish schoolboy' – imagining himself as a dandy, a word usually attached to the upper classes.

'I think maybe he looked at all the different structures in society and imagined himself in all of them; how he might fit in, and what that world might be like,' Bourcier says.

In the late 1960s, the Rolling Stones had begun hanging out with a number of prominent movers and shakers in the London literary and art world – most of whom came from upper middle-class backgrounds. As such the young Mick Jagger's eyes were opened to art and literature that he would possibly otherwise have missed. One book he was particularly fascinated with was *The Master and Margarita* by Russian author Mikhail Bulgakov – considered one of the best novels to emerge from the Soviet era. The focus of the story is a visit to earth by the devil, known as Professor Woland, and the tricks he plays on those who cross his path.

'When the Stones were recording *Beggars Banquet*, Jagger was heavily influenced by this book,' Bourcier says. '*The Master and Margarita* influenced "Sympathy for the Devil". And I think that, like Jagger, Pete is intrigued by class and differences. Maybe he looked at the different scenarios in both; at how he would have operated as a performer, writer and poet living either a working-class existence or a middle-class existence. He is very much a poet with a romanticised view of life and I can understand how he could get a lot out of being a fantasist, especially exploring genres, film and literature like he does.

'I think he views Chas & Dave as heroes of a particular sector of society and perhaps compares them to old-school heroes of a different genre – a modern-day Byron and Shelley. It's nothing to do with being pretentious; I think it's about not having any boundaries in your thinking – whereby you can actually transcend any situation. Some people will see that as pretentious because they might not have the imagination to go on that journey to that place Pete's talking about. Who knows where his mind is going, but that's what makes Pete Pete.'

Poostchi felt that talk of recording and producers was still premature; that they were running before they could walk. Pete and Carl needed new material and that was not all that was worrying her. The trouble was that bassist John Hassall had gone and they still needed a permanent drummer.

Gary Powell was the boyfriend of Poostchi's PA when she worked at Warner. Born in New Jersey, he had spent a lot of time in England as a child and his family ended up emigrating to the UK in the 1980s. Gary had always been into percussion and in the US he had played in a marching band. When he got to England he quenched his thirst to play by drumming in a variety of rock bands, but he didn't think he could make a living out of it. Gary moved to Birmingham and became a marketing consultant, but the bug never left him and he was soon moonlighting as a session drummer. When he got the chance to play on some tracks with Guyana-born reggae musician Eddy Grant, he was sold on the idea. He moved to London permanently and began to play music for a living. At the request of Banny Poostchi in October 2001, Gary Powell joined The Libertines.

'Gary was really straight. A little too straight for my liking,' says

Bourcier. 'But we recorded so many songs. They played through all the tracks that you've now long since heard The Libertines play.'

At Poostchi's insistence Pete and Carl had written a new batch of songs that were proving to be a departure from their earlier sound – songs like 'Time For Heroes', 'What A Waster', 'May Day', 'Boys in the Band', 'Up the Bracket', 'Horror Show' and 'I Get Along'. With new material and a drummer now in place, things were finally coming together. During the autumn and early winter of 2001 Poostchi booked a timetable of regular rehearsals at local studios so the band could focus on tightening the new sound. She attended each rehearsal and only when they had perfected their set was she prepared to even let a record company get a look at them. And she already had in mind the label she would sign them to.

Scarborough Steve would rehearse only once with Gary. He had signed a modelling contract with Select Models and headed off to New York. That night in the rehearsal room was the last time he'd play with The Libertines.

For the rest of the gang, a deal with Rough Trade Records was just round the corner.

Johnny Borrell was still writing songs, reading poetry and hanging out with The Libertines. Long before Razorlight, and seeing as John Hassall had parted company with Pete and Carl, he asked whether he could play bass for them. It was a short-lived arrangement. Pete and Carl later spoke of how they felt let down by Borrell after he failed to show up for possibly the most important gig of their career – a showcase at which Rough Trade Records would be making an appearance.

Although Poostchi was intent on signing the band to Rough Trade, a London-based indie label called High Society, run by a man called James Mullord, was also sniffing around.

Mullord really wanted to release a demo Pete had put together. It contained just three songs but Poostchi didn't feel it was ready to send to Rough Trade. Pete was keen on signing a deal and because of Mullord's persistence and genuine passion for the band (plus an offer of £1,000), Pete was sold on the idea of signing to him.

However Poostchi had different ideas. By mid winter 2001 she finally felt that Pete, Carl and Gary were ready for her to implement the final step in her plan – contacting the label she hoped would sign them.

By November 2001 Rough Trade's inimitable A&R man James Endeacott had finally heard of The Libertines. It was impossible for him not to: Poostchi badgered him almost daily for a month. With some rehearsal space booked just off Old Street and The Libertines in place, Poostchi turned up in a smart minicab outside the Rough Trade offices in Golborne Road, just off Ladbroke Grove. Plying Endeacott with beers, Cokes and crisps, they headed east into the night. 'They're going to be the new Lennon and McCartney,' she told him. Endeacott had heard it all before but he admired her persistence. And he knew only too well that all the labels in the UK would soon be hunting down British rock 'n' roll bands after they had tired of the American invasion. Endeacott was ahead of the game. But comparisons with the Beatles or Stones didn't wash with him.

Carl, Pete and Gary played just four songs that night. Twice over. And Endeacott was impressed. 'It was amazing,' he later said.

The only demo Poostchi had to give him was the one Mullord had raved about but which she wasn't too keen on. Poostchi's hunch was right: Endeacott felt slightly disappointed – he didn't think it did justice to what he'd just seen in the shabby rehearsal space near the City. Still, he'd keep The Libertines in mind. When they had another gig on, he wanted Poostchi to give him a ring and he'd be there. Meanwhile, she was determined the band wouldn't be signing to High Society. Rough Trade was the right label for The Libertines.

The next gig happened a month later at the Rhythm Factory in Whitechapel. And it didn't go quite according to plan. Gary didn't have a drum kit and was forced to borrow a horrible gold kit. All the toms were assembled with bits of string and he recalled, a metal clamp with cymbals hanging from ropes. 'It was the worst kit ever,' he said.

Pete and Carl began breaking strings and ended up asking the audience if they had any replacements. In short, it was a shambles, but Endeacott remembered the songs as the band played through them. 'I was just so, so excited,' he later said. 'It was mind-blowing.'

The band's former manager Roger Morton recalls: 'They had definitely been encouraged in a rock 'n' roll direction by the people around them, and when they saw it was working they thought they'd do a bit more of it. But a band like The Libertines suddenly became viable, and James Endeacott – all credit to him – saw that first.'

Still, the irony was thick as this was the same band Endeacott had seen almost two years before on the flickery video at the EMI offices – admittedly with a new line-up and an arsenal of new material. After the Rhythm Factory gig, Endeacott was more than convinced and persuaded his boss, Rough Trade Records founder Geoff Travis, to add The Libertines to a roster that included The Strokes, The Moldy Peaches and The Detroit Cobras.

John Hassall got back in touch with Pete and Carl and asked whether they needed a bass player. He'd heard they were getting signed to Rough Trade. Pete and Carl did desperately need a bassist. John, they decided, was back in the band.

Here was a four-piece playing back-to-basics rock 'n' roll. They had an image – just as important and marketable as The Strokes. And Rough Trade – the label that had boasted The Smiths and Joy Division back in the 1980s – snapped them up.

After Christmas 2001, talk turned to the first Libertines single. Poostchi was keen for the band to explore working with a few producers before making a final decision and so in early spring 2001 asked Bourcier if he would have a jam session with the band.

Bourcier's regular, bill-paying nine-to-five job involved running a studio. Poostchi called him to see whether he'd be willing to go into the studio with The Libertines again and he said he could possibly work evenings. Just before the next session he received a phone call from Poostchi. 'Pete, Carl and John are on their way over,' she said. 'Don't let Pete have any drugs at all. Don't encourage him or anything.' Drugs were not starting to become a problem for Pete yet but Poostchi wanted the band to stay straight and focused when there was work to be done.

'When they turned up, inevitably Pete wanted drugs,' Bourcier says. 'It was hilarious; Banny had told me not to get him anything an hour earlier and there was Pete sitting cross-legged on the sofa just looking at her with puppy-dog eyes. He said he'd been on detox for the past week and just wanted a blow-out. He'd obviously spun Banny this massive fucking yarn about not doing any drugs whatsoever.

'Pete was definitely doing fair quantities of drugs at this point. I think I paid for it that night actually – he still owes me for a couple of Gs. But he wasn't doing anything too bad as far as I was aware – it was

Charlie, ecstasy and spliff. And so this guy came up with a couple of grams and we got stuck into the recording session.

'It went really well. John Hassall was playing drums; I had this set of electronic pads called V-drums and he was playing those – they had a nice feel.'

One track they recorded that night was called 'New Love Grows On Trees' – later to appear on the Internet in a simple acoustic form with just Pete singing, taken from the now-legendary 'Babyshambles sessions' in Paris. That night the song was a full-on rocker with electric guitars and a Happy Mondays-esque vibe. 'It was wicked,' Bourcier recalls. 'Everyone was excited about the potential of this as a track and Pete, Carl, John and Banny really liked it.'

It starts with a Stone Roses-style solo as intro before Pete's vocals come in. The guitar solo is played by Bourcier's friend. 'They were too fucked to do it themselves,' he says. 'I think it's got a bit of a Stones vibe to it; at the end they all stand round the mic singing backing vocals. There's a bit towards the end where you can hear the coke really kicking in – the track starts to speed up; we did try a click track but it didn't work. But that was a demo; there was no time to mic the drums up properly or anything like that, I had to literally get it while I could – while Pete was still on the case. But done properly I think it would be an awesome track.

'At one point I remember Carl coming up to me with a CD case with lines of coke on it. He physically put the bank note in my nose for me so I was hoovering up while I was setting up the mic. It was nutty. It would be getting to five o clock in the morning and I'd say, "Listen, guys, I've got to be here again at 9am to do another session," and Pete would pull an E out of his pocket, hand it to me and say, "Come on, take this and you'll get a second wind."

'Let me put it this way. In that situation I think it's OK to do drugs because you're not trying to get a finished product together. You're jamming ideas, you're throwing things out there that might sound shit the next day but you might have a couple of ideas that work. Pete might be writing things at home on the acoustic guitar straight but when he takes those ideas into the studio and takes some drugs he may come up with some trippy ideas, and later, when a producer is involved, that could be developed into a really nice part. I respected Pete because he was somebody who would listen.'

Poostchi thought Bourcier would be a good choice to produce the band's first single 'What A Waster', and B-sides 'Mayday' and 'I Get Along', primarily because she felt he would record the band "live" and capture their energy. Rough Trade, however, wanted ex-Suede guitarist Bernard Butler to take over the controls.

'I met Bernard down at the studio and he was really aggressive,' Bourcier recalls. 'Really territorial and stuff. A lot of politics began to kick in as soon as the Rough Trade thing happened. Banny took my side and said, "Look, I want Simon to do these tracks." So in the end we both did them – myself and Butler, separately – the same three tracks.'

Bourcier and Butler would get The Libertines for three days each. The tracks that sounded the best would be the tracks that were eventually released. 'We had no time to mix down even,' Bourcier says. 'In the end I remember Bernard Butler went to RAK Studios in St John's Wood and he was given extra sessions and weeks to do it, and he was able to mix down in the Strong Room.

'I took The Libertines to Livingston Studios in north London and had three days. Livingston Studios has three live rooms but you can see each other through the glass. It was a perfect set-up and I wanted to record the band doing live takes, seeing as we only had three days to do three tracks. Then we'd go back and record guitar tracks again if we needed to, then the vocal tracks on the third day.

'They all turned up bang on time to the studio; there was no lateness. We'd be drinking a couple of bottles of whiskey at the end of the day, loads of beers and hoovering up a few fuckers. At the time Pete had this dealer whose nickname was Dollarman. Conveniently, behind the mixing desk there was a table that had all the outboard gear, compressors and pre-amps and stuff underneath. But the surface was glass. As soon as we saw the glass surface we were like, "Oh great, let's call Dollarman".'

Bourcier had been working with an American band that had told him a story about a producer in the States who had laid down the law about drugs in the studio before their session. He had given the band 'pep talks' about staying off the drugs until their parts had been recorded. After a hard day's work, they were free to party. So Bourcier thought he'd try this tactic on Pete.

'On the third day I took him aside. I thought I'd have a little pep talk with Pete. I just said, "Look, we're doing vocals today and I'd really appreciate it if you didn't do any drugs beforehand." He did say, "Oh come on!" but I told him that the voice doesn't work too well on coke. I couldn't tell him what to do, nor was I trying to. But my job was to bring out the best in them. I'm just a vibe person – interjecting when necessary in a diplomatic way. So I suggested that he refrain from drugs then get fucking blasted afterwards. He said, "What about a spliff?" and I said, "It's up to you." And Pete Doherty did no drugs. He actually listened to me and gave some great vocal performances. He was on the case, focused, did his thing, then went off and got trashed, like we all did.

'That's why we had that pep talk. Why not be responsible in the studio when you need to be responsible?'

On the flip side, Bourcier says Powell was really straight. 'I found him a bit too much. His drum kit had far too many toms on it – not very rock 'n' roll. I asked him if he could remove a few toms but he wouldn't. He had a squareness that wasn't really needed. He'd call me "Cap" – short for Captain. "Hey, Cap, all right, Cap, can I get a bit more of that left tom, Cap." I always thought Gary was a bit annoying actually.

'But one thing I've got to say is that Pete Doherty is a very loyal guy. I once asked whether he'd thought about getting another drummer, and he just said, "No way, Gary's our man." He was the same with Carl as well. At this point The Libertines weren't the band they would become. We'd arrived at the studio and I asked Pete whether we should just crack on without Carl. He was 100 per cent unequivocal: "No way." He said Carl was his brother and that nothing happened without him.

'Conversely, Carl was always whingeing from day fucking one. "Pete this", "Pete that", "Why does Pete have to be the frontman?" While we were at Livingston Studios I remember Carl coming up to me a couple of times and whingeing. I'm sure he wouldn't like to hear this but it's true. "Why does Pete have to always be the one on lead vocals?" But Pete wouldn't hear a bad word against any of his bandmates. Carl and Pete obviously have the vibe they have together, and it works. But in a way Pete was just doing his thing and maybe Carl had a bit more of an agenda, possibly.'

After the session, Poostchi telephoned Bourcier saying she loved the tracks he'd produced. Ultimately though, possibly because they sounded better, possibly because he was a 'name' (although this counted against him as far as Poostchi was concerned) it was Butler's tracks that were used.

The Libertines began rehearsing at a studio in Old Street, ready for the barrage of gigs that would have to accompany their debut single –

scheduled for release in June. Carl and Pete moved in together to a flat in Bethnal Green. 112a Teesdale Street would go down in rock 'n' roll history after later being branded 'the Albion Rooms'.

Their first gig as the line-up that everyone would know as The Libertines was at the Cherry Jam club on Porchester Road in Royal Oak. On 21 February 2002 the music press would be there to see Rough Trade's new signing: a band being billed as the saviours of British rock 'n' roll; England's answer to The Strokes.

Already the hype was going to be hard to live up to. But Pete, Carl, John and Gary were determined to give it a shot.

That gig also garnered their first reviews as a signed band. The music website rockfeedback.com said although the critics 'were bound to pick up on the fact that their razor-sharp riffs and tight display of unobvious yet warm melodies are reminiscent of The Strokes', they were also supremely talented. 'Hear us now,' it said. 'The Libertines rock and roll with the best of them. And it's about time a London band is poised for such recognition.'

That recognition would materialise far more swiftly than perhaps anyone, most of all The Libertines, could have anticipated.

A second gig at Cherry Jam was reviewed by James Oldham for the *NME*; the magazine's role in championing The Libertines cannot be underestimated, but it was something that left Morton pleased for the band he had discovered back in 1999, and at the same time slightly frustrated. He had tried to get the *NME* to sit up and listen back then but they weren't interested. 'It was ironic that James Oldham took up the cause at the *NME* – the magazine began insanely hyping the band – because it was the same band I was in the pub with a year and a half before,' he says.

'Thank God for The Libertines,' Oldham wrote. Despite describing them as a 'four-piece from *London*' – something journalists would frequently assume – he said they had 'the lyrical dexterity of The Smiths, the taut energy of The Jam and the raw melodies of The Strokes'. It was some eulogy.

On stage the band had chain-smoked their way through their seven-song set in under half an hour, but none of the scenesters in the audience felt short-changed in any way.

The Libertines' relationship with drugs would be documented from the off (although at that stage there were little signs of the hard drugs that would help define Pete Doherty later on). 'You can see they're so wired their eyeballs are almost touching the back wall of the club,' Oldham wrote. There was clearly an unprecedented level of excitement about this band ('Think the Beatles in Hamburg at 4am in the morning,' he said, 'it's impossible to take your eyes off them'); there were also the perhaps inevitable Strokes comparisons. Pete, Oldham said, was the spitting image of Julian Casablancas, and Carl, Paul McCartney.

By March 2002 Poostchi had negotiated a publishing deal with Mike Smith of EMI, signing Pete and Carl to the company for their song-writing. By May she would leave her job at East West Records to manage the band full-time.

Emerging as they had so soon after the American wave, combined with the fact they were signed to the same label as The Strokes, the comparisons with the American band were inevitable, but it wasn't long before it became glaringly obvious that The Libertines were saying something uniquely English. 'The Libertines scrap the gritty New York cool and add something as English as *Carry On*, chips and *Coronation Street*,' one reviewer wrote. There was an element of the danger and aggression of British punk as opposed to the more laidback, slightly safer image The Strokes conveyed.

In The Libertines, for the first time since The Smiths, there was a band singing directly to an audience that could understand and appreciate what they were singing about: they were chronicling a city that deserved to be name-checked in song, a country that had somehow eluded reference in popular music for far too long. For years it had been cool for American bands to sing about their homeland. When Bob Dylan sang 'Highway 61' that stretch of road sounded incredibly cool; the A11 just didn't have the same ring. Whether it was Neil Young's 'Ohio' or 'Alabama', Bruce Springsteen's 'Atlantic City', Green Day's 'East 12th St', or even REM's 'All the Way To Reno', the vast, empty American continent was ideal inspiration. In the 1960s it was OK to name-check England too: The Beatles' 'Penny Lane' was quintessentially English with its blue skies and portraits of the Queen in the pouring rain, and the meter maid in 'Lovely Rita' could only have been an English belle as she was wooed with a cup of tea; The Kinks chronicled an England everyone could identify in 'Waterloo Sunset' and 'Dedicated Follower of Fashion'. A little later The Clash and The Jam were unashamedly English. And a decade after that The Smiths pulled it off as well, unafraid to sing about their England in 'Take Me Back To Dear Old Blighty' or 'Panic'. But since the 1980s there had been a reluctance – an embarrassment, perhaps – to reference England in song. Blur did it cryptically on their *Parklife* album, but just listen to the lyrics of 'London Loves' or the album's title track: it was Britain but not one that was recognisable and therefore hardly spoke to the kids. Blur's was a far too cynical view of London; too ironic.

America has been a constant, uninterrupted source of lyrical fodder for musicians since the Blues. Its musicians have never been embarrassed to sing about their homeland. But in 2001, when The Strokes decried the antics of the 'New York City Cops', The White Stripes described the run-down, decaying Detroit building 'Hotel Yorba', Brooklyn's Radio 4 were shouting about 'Our Town' and The Dirtbombs were once again extolling the virtues of the 'Motor City Baby', it may have come as some surprise back in Blighty that The Libertines were single-handedly ensuring London (and England) not only rocked again, but would be immortalised in song once more.

The Britain in which The Libertines lived had changed from the bright, confident Britain Tony Blair was promoting as 'Cool Britannia' when he came to power in 1997. Back then Liam Gallagher and Patsy Kensit adorned the cover of UK *Vanity Fair* and Oasis cosied up to Blair at Number 10. But four years on, the world had witnessed the devastation caused by Operation Enduring Freedom in retaliation for September 11. American cluster bombs had rained down on civilians, protesters called it unjustified aggression, there were peace rallies in New York and London, and by the summer of 2002 talk had turned to the possible invasion of Iraq as well.

Disillusionment has often been a force for change in music, sparking vibrant movements, but The Libertines didn't seem overtly political. It was as if their music was a form of escapism. The songs Pete and Carl were writing were bound up in an idea of Englishness a million miles from the England Blair had created. Pete wanted his audiences to escape with him to this Arcadian vision of England. While half the world's population were seriously questioning both Britain's role as international policeman and its motives, accusing it, as they did the Americans, of screwing the globe for its own gain, Pete wanted to celebrate England. He wanted to be patriotic; to reclaim the flag from the Blair government; sing about his local community, sing about life in London.

He was proud of England – but quite possibly this England only existed in his imagination.

Just two days after their last gig at Cherry Jam, The Libertines got the chance to join The Strokes on tour, supporting them at the Birmingham Academy and Leeds University. It was a coup, but as they were on the same label and shared an A&R man in James Endeacott, it was hardly surprising. Still, Carl, Pete, John and Gary were ecstatic.

'Playing with The Strokes was almost the ideal,' Pete said. But he was disillusioned when the audience didn't seem to be getting into The Libertines' music. 'I want movement in the crowd,' he said, 'but people didn't seem like they wanted to dance to songs they didn't know.'

After that they headed out on a UK tour with The Vines. As if in an attempt to underline their unpredictability, Pete and Carl played a 20-minute improvised jazz number at the first stop on the tour. It may have understandably confused a large number of the onlookers who were eagerly anticipating Britain's best new band, but at their own shows, people were starting to 'get' The Libertines. By the time of their gig at the 93 Feet East venue in London's trendy Brick Lane – an area that houses a melting pot of Bangladeshi restaurants, organic cafés and gentrified loft conversions – their fan base had already expanded. A lot of the kids in the audience were already sporting the same look as the band.

It was an *NME*-sponsored gig and Pete and Carl pounded through their set, from 'Horror Show' to 'Boys In The Band'.

NME's reviewer Pat Long described the 'heavy-lidded Peter steadying himself with the mic stand' as Carl 'sucks his cheeks and hops about looking like a blue-blooded decadent from *Brideshead Revisited*.' 'Mayday' was punk rock, he said, in the same way Blur once did punk: 'garbled lyrics and Top Man yobbery'.

It was another short set but the *NME* at least needed no more convincing. This was the best band to come out of Britain in ages. Their tour continued with gigs in Harlow, Bedford, Northampton, Southend, Southampton, Birmingham and Nottingam. 'I got head-butted in Wolverhampton,' Pete would recall later. 'Carl got snogged in Northampton, and I won't even tell you what happened in Southampton. Basically Carlos gets the love and I get all the head-butts, it seems to be the way of things.'

Will Jenkins, reviewing the show for *Crud* magazine, warned that nationalism was never a kind thing and that patriotism would 'always lead you astray' before joining the ranks of the faithful and declaring his love for The Libertines. 'The ego confrontation between Peter and Carl of desperately trying to steal the attention of the crowd here tonight exhilarates the whole gig,' he said. He was also particu-larly taken by Pete's attire – a Kevin Keegan football T-shirt from Spain, 1982.

All this publicity flooded Britain before The Libertines had even released their first single. But the best (or worst, depending on which way you look at it) was yet to come. The *NME* was about to put the boys on their front cover to coincide with their debut single. It was unheard of, and there were whispers in the record industry's dusty corridors of power that this could be suicidal for a young band. Pete, Carl, John and Gary's mischievous pouts glared out in front of a Union Jack flag on the cover of the magazine: 'The best new band in Britain'. 'They're on this week's cover for a reason,' James Oldham wrote, 'and the reason is simple: they're the best British band of the year. No question.'

When 'What A Waster' finally came out in June, the *Daily Mirror* – admittedly not quite the benchmark of taste that music fans looked towards – claimed it was 'over-produced' and 'lacked originality'. But what did the *Daily Mirror* know.

This possibly marked the beginning of Pete Doherty's fractured relationship with the mainstream press. *Daily Mail* readers were never going to like The Libertines but The Libertines would never need – or want – to rely on *Daily Mail* readers for a living. The single – released on 3 June – was immediately banned from daytime radio due to the amount of swear words it contained, but an edited version made Mark and Lard's 'Single Of The Week' on Radio 1.

Pete didn't expect their debut single to do so well. 'I'm as happy as a parrot really,' he told the *NME*. He also proudly played the song to his father, who he claimed 'started eating my cigarettes and telling me to fuck off. He started dancing around the room and saying it reminded him of the Goldhawk Road in 1969.'

The single came out the same day as the Queen's Golden Jubilee. A couple of weeks later Oldham bemoaned the fact that the 'nation's young hipsters' remained unmoved at the Jubilee, whereas twenty-five years before, at her Silver Jubilee, The Sex Pistols had threatened to undermine the moral fabric of the nation. The only voices of dissent, he claimed, were Liam Gallagher, 'who announced with typical flair that he was taking "a rather large shit that day"', and The Libertines, who 'dismissed the Queen as "a skanky old hag"'.

Dotmusic.com said the single was 'redolent, in spirit as well as sound, of the urban collision of the likes of The Jam, Buzzcocks and The Clash'. Reviewer Ben Gilbert said it was a 'spitting cauldron of punk urgency'.

Their inaugural tour as a signed band took The Libertines across the length and breadth of the UK. At the Cockpit venue in Leeds on 6 June, Dave Simpson of the *Guardian* remarked, 'As they plug in their guitars, the transformation is extraordinary ... They are young, moderately, if scruffily, good-looking and hilarious ... Their deranged guitar solos sound like 33 rpm punk albums speeded up to 45.'

In Glasgow, however, the *Sunday Mail* said they failed to live up to the hype. 'Despite their sulky charm, their music let them down badly,' David Pollock wrote. 'There was plenty of energy but aside from new single "What A Waster" and the glammed-up "Boys In The Band", there was scarcely a proper tune all night ... Three chords might make a decent punk song, but two decent songs don't make a good gig.'

Everyone was entitled to their opinion, but Pollock was clearly wrong. Plus, he perhaps didn't bank on the *NME*'s persistence.

Back in London, The Libertines played the first of what would become a regular fixture: the secret gig. It happened at the Metro on 27 June and a handful of writers were notified by phone just a couple of hours before. The club night was called 'Death Disco' – hosted by Creation Records founder Alan McGee – and The Libertines clambered on stage at half past midnight.

During the shambles that ensued, in which microphones were knocked over, Carl and Pete clashed heads and the audience pogoed relentlessly, pouring with sweat and punching the air to the catchy songs. Here was a band that was more electrifying and relevant than anything they had seen in years. More importantly, this was happening now and they were standing on a stage just inches from their audience.

Of course, singing about a mythical vision of England is all very well for English people, but what did they make of it abroad? Were The Libertines going to translate as The Beatles had – after all, the Fab Four did sing about 4,000 holes in Blackburn Lancashire, something that surely didn't translate in Milwaukee. But our ability to sell rock 'n' roll back to the Americans in the 1960s – the so-called 'British invasion' –

worked back then; the Yanks fell for The Beatles' quick-wittedness, their tunes, their haircuts, their clothes, their Britishness. Could it work at the dawn of the new millennium? The Americans had reinvented rock 'n' roll once more, we had lapped it up over here and become inspired again. Could we now spit it back at them and, more importantly, would they buy it? That was the burning question. If anyone had a fighting chance, it was The Libertines.

SIX

|ROUGH|TRADE|

2002 was the year in which Britpop finally bit the bullet. Far from standing on the shoulders of giants, Oasis were standing in the shadow of the behemoth they once were. Blur had all but split up. It was also the year that, in addition to the show-stopping antics of The White Stripes, Strokes, Datsuns and Vines, British rap – in the form of Ms Dynamite, Roots Manuva and Mike Skinner's The Streets – finally provided an alternative to the frankly irrelevant world portrayed by rappers from across the pond. It was also to be The Libertines' year.

But by the time Carl, Pete, John and Gary had signed their deal, in one respect their Arcadian dream was already on the road to ruin. They had the money to buy more drugs and their music was finally out there for their increasing fan base to hear. But although they'd 'made it' in one respect, in another, living in the squalor of London's bed-sits, waking up bleary-eyed after spending their only cash on drink and drugs and writing songs in desperation had been part of who they were, part of their allure and their appeal. Now that they had money in the bank there seemed less to motivate them.

Pete had never come closer to achieving his Arcadian dream – fuelled by drugs, casual sex and music – than before The Libertines got signed. He may have been skint, but poverty seemed bound up in his idea of the street poet.

Pete knew that signing a record deal – particularly with a label that had been around since the heady days of punk and which had signed The Fall, Stiff Little Fingers and The Smiths – was a move that would allow him and Carl to realise their potential and get their music heard. The very idea of just recording a song had been – in Pete's words – a pure fantasy just a couple of years before. But he would later confess that signing that contract amounted to the best and worst day of his life in equal measures. Carl summed it up: 'It takes all the wind out of your sails … and it was the key to a world of better drugs and a constant supply of them.'

Carl would also recall one night returning to the Albion Rooms in Bethnal Green and discovering their record contract – which had been in pride of place in a glass case – out on the table. He imagined Pete had sat there, reminiscing about the times they'd had in London before Morton, before Banny, before Rough Trade, before there were demands; before they felt they had to prove something.

The Albion Rooms had become the place for parties. Author and singer Pete Welsh claimed in his book *Kids In The Riot* that 'watching the sun come up in a room full of wasted young women lent an air of *Performance* to the proceedings', referring to the decadence of the guest-house Mick Jagger frequents in Donald Cammell and Nicolas Roeg's 1970s gangster flick. 'On the down side, the place stank to high heaven.'

With their fridge stuffed with both beers and £50 notes from their record company advance, they were set. Impromptu gigs at the Albion Rooms – plugging in their guitars to amps in their front room – would, in the fullness of time, spearhead a movement known as 'guer-rilla gigging'.

Considering they had only signed their record deal at Christmas, their rise to some level of stardom was nothing short of remarkable. As well as supporting The Strokes and The Vines and embarking on their first UK tour as a band, they also played the Reading and Leeds festivals. Poostchi and Rough Trade had hired PR company The Coalition Group to look after The Libertines' press. Coalition was a funky firm based in a Chiswick side street close to Independiente Records, and they already had an impressive roster that included The Strokes, Tom Waits, Richard Ashcroft, Marianne Faithfull and Johnny Marr.

NME snapper Roger Sargent had been asking the band's new PR Tony Linkin if he could take their first official photographs and his chance came one afternoon at the Albion Rooms. Sargent recalls: 'They turned up three hours late to their own house for their own photo shoot … there was money everywhere and drug paraphernalia, wraps and powder smears all over the tables.'

That first photo shoot would produce the now iconic shots of the band decked out in red military jackets – the same shot used for the cover of Pete Welsh's Libertines book *Kids in the Riot* and which would be used in their first press campaign. Pete confessed to stealing the jackets from a market stall in Brick Lane.

When The Libertines made the *NME* cover just before their first single dropped, Linkin warned them: 'It's all gonna change after this.' It was true. The lives of the four twenty-something young men that made up The Libertines would change irreversibly.

At a gig at the tiny Joiners pub in Southampton, a BBC journalist asked whether their sudden thrust into stardom had been daunting.

Pete said: 'We've been given an opportunity if we want stardom – I don't think we've exactly got stardom at the moment, but the machinery's all there.'

Carl and Pete's relationship would teeter between bitter rivalry and camaraderie. They would always love each other – they had been through so much together after all – but it was always going to be a fractured relationship; unfortunately, that was something that would end up defining them.

On 8 June the *NME* ran an interview with the band that underscored Carl and Pete's tempestuousness. Pete had begun to wind Carl up about that fact he seemed to get quoted in print more than him. 'Most people fancy Carl more than they do me. For years I've been in his shadow, but now the worm has turned and I'm getting all the *NME* quotes,' he said.

'Yeah, why the fuck do you always quote Pete?' Carl asks journalist James Oldham. 'And another thing, why did you call him the singer? He's a scumbag.'

Oldham recounts how Pete begins singing 'Chim Chim Cher-ee' from the Mary Poppins film close to Carl's ear in a further effort to taunt him and elicit a response. 'Look, this time, can you just make sure you don't say all that kooky shit that makes us sound like some skanky cult?' Carl says.

'I'll say what I like,' Pete shrugs.

Finally Pete claims Carl is a 'psychopath' who had pulled a knife on him 'so many times I've had to call the police about it'.

The interview marked the start of a predilection for spinning journalists a lofty yarn. To this day it's difficult to separate the fact from fiction in some of the interviews they gave. In this first revealing *NME* interview Pete claimed he spent his childhood moving from place to place (fact), 'depending on whether he was staying with his mum, dad or the social services' (fiction).

Carl's ex-girlfriend, he claimed, attempted to stab him in the stomach with a pair of scissors. The same girl, Carl added, emptied a tin of cat food onto his head and later tried to 'gas herself in an electric oven'.

Carl and Pete also claimed they had joined a male escort agency called Aristocats and ended up 'shagging old men in hotel rooms' to earn some extra cash before they were signed to Rough Trade. 'Spanking off old queens', as Pete eloquently put it, 'only lasted for about five minutes. I got all dolled up, but I couldn't deal with it. I used to push the drinks trolley over and make a run for it.'

This habit of teasing the media was an in-joke that the media were just never going to get. The period spent as 'rent boys' would be something that *Daily Mirror* hacks Nathan Yates and Pete Samson would linger on in their book on Doherty, *On the Edge*. Whether the episode is fact or fiction, it added to the myth that as early as 2002 was already surrounding The Libertines. Carl later said they joined the agency but that neither he nor Pete had ever taken part in anything 'physical'.

In fact, in interviews the band was almost always larking about. Asked to describe their songs, Pete said, 'Innocent, emotional and simple,' to which Carl retorted, 'Simple is definitely what I'd describe your music as.'

Their first tour had yielded 'acts of random violence and acts of random goodwill', Pete told the BBC. 'It all adds up to a complete tablet of chaos that you have to swallow – but they never told me it was going to be a suppository!'

While it was a little far-fetched of both Endeacott and the writers at the *NME* to compare The Libertines to The Beatles in Hamburg, there had rarely been a band as quick-witted or charming as The Libertines since John, Paul, George and Ringo.

The band's debut album was scheduled for release in October. Although Bernard Butler was at the helm for their single, Pete was adamant he shouldn't produce the album. He felt he was too controlling; too structured. Even Carl said that it was 'like the master and the pupils'. Butler liked to work nine to five in the studio and Pete didn't think this was conducive to creativity: surely the band and producer couldn't gel together with that ethic. Although the single was a belter and everyone was happy with it (the *NME* said it was 'brilliantly produced' and described it as 'three minutes of smart, frenzied genius'), The Libertines needed someone less adherent to rules for their first long player; someone who was a bit more of a free-thinker. Butler, it turned out, wasn't available anyway, and that's when Mick Jones came into the frame.

The Clash were the archetypal English band; they had helped define the late 1970s and spearheaded the 'new wave' after punk. Jones clicked with Pete immediately and was able to harness that wild creativity in just three whirlwind days. With Mick Jones at the controls the band managed to lay down twenty-three tracks in less than a hundred hours. 'He had this really cool manner about him,' Gary said. 'He'd turn up to the studio late every day. We'd start playing and he'd have a can of beer in one hand and a spliff in the other and would just dance around saying, "That was great. Do it again."'

The studio time was extended and it was to become a period of intense drug-taking, boozing, late nights and, of course, recording. But out of it came the twelve tracks that would comprise their debut album.

Carl had been taking heroin and crack. Pete was also taking heroin, and their experiences were about to be documented in the song 'Skag And Bone Man' on their debut album, although none of this drug taking was explicit to those working closely with the band. Along with 'brown', 'skag' was slang for heroin; a 'bone' was a joint. Carl recounts the story of going to get 'bugle' – or cocaine – in Bethnal Green at four in the morning from 'some bird in a car'. Then smoking it, not sleeping, and turning up to the studio 'ruined' the next day. Their street argot was seeping into their language and Carl and Pete would talk endlessly, slipping into this slang as a form of communicating with each other – and confounding outsiders.

Morrissey before them was fascinated by Polari – British gay slang of the 1960s, famously championed by Kenneth Williams. It featured heavily in sketches on the BBC radio programme *Round the Horne*, and words like 'bona' are still heard (Morrissey wrote both 'Piccadilly Polare' and named his album *Bona Drag* in tribute)

Back in the studio, Mick Jones had seen a photo of some Argentinian riot police in a copy of the *Guardian* and thought it would make a perfect cover for the band's debut album. At first glance it could have been a rock 'n' roll band silhouetted against the red stage lights, but a closer look reveals a car in the background, riot shields and helmets. It was very 'Clash' but it worked – and has become an iconic album cover. The Libertines decided to name their first LP *Up The Bracket* in tribute to the phrase Sid James and Kenneth Williams made popular in the *Carry On* films.

During the studio sessions Pete had also started using the Internet upstairs at Rak studios. He'd Google 'The Libertines' and discover kids were poring over the finer points of the band in discussion groups. It must have been a wonderful feeling to discover that after the release of just one single they had a fan base motivated enough to talk about their favourite band for hours in these forums.

It marked the beginning of Pete's love affair with the Internet. From this moment on he would use it to communicate his innermost thoughts, his poetry, news on the band, impromptu gigs, and his feelings about this strange new world he'd been thrust into.

When it came to mixing down, Jones took no prisoners though. He battled through until the album was complete and everyone was ecstatic – not least Rough Trade, who were desperately hoping their new signing's debut record would live up to expectation.

After picking the twelve songs that would comprise *Up The Bracket*, the album was mooted for an October release.

Meanwhile, the band had gigs to attend to, one of which was the opportunity to support a band as legendary as The Clash. On 25 July 2002 The Libertines would take to the stage in support of The Sex Pistols at Crystal Palace.

'I got the feeling we were booked as a comedy warm-up, like a compère in the old days,' Pete says. 'We went on in army jackets and the crowd were saying, "Fuckin' hell, it's the Beatles."'

Backstage, Johnny Rotten would look on in contempt as Pete and Carl larked about, smashing beer glasses and getting drunk. The king of punk rock had become tired and grey – and, most worryingly of all, conformist – while his protégés had stolen his mantle at his own gig. The Libertines were arguably more complex thinkers than the Pistols, and in 2002 they also possessed far more vigour and ability to motivate the new generation than Johnny Rotten did. Twenty-odd years after the Pistols first came on the scene, Rotten was sadly benign.

It was a punishing schedule but nobody was complaining. That summer they played festivals in Sweden, Germany and Japan. Back in the UK the reviews were mostly glowing. 'All threadbare T-shirts and tiny leather jackets, singer-guitarist Carl Barât and his sidekicks slouch onto stage in the guise of a Grange Hill bully and his accomplices,' the *Coventry Evening Telegraph* reviewer wrote, describing the atmosphere as explosive and Carl and Pete's dynamic as 'tempestuous'.

It was very perceptive: shortly before their show in Scarborough on

3 August, Carl and Pete came to blows in an incident that was played out for all to see, and would be the first of many.

The band had been in the studio mixing down the single with Mick Jones into the early hours of the morning. Pete and Carl were engaging in horseplay when things became heated. It resulted in a punch in the throat for Carl and a knee in the head for Pete, after which Pete disappeared. Carl headed up to Scarborough with just John and Gary, learning the songs in the van on the way up. On stage he admitted having a fight with Pete before launching into 'What A Waster'. Pete reappeared two days later; no one knew where he'd been.

The gigs were becoming increasingly hit and miss. The Libertines could either be brilliant – their sheer energy and enthusiasm matching exquisitely crafted songs in a chemistry on stage not seen for years – or they could be, frankly, pretty awful. There was no rhyme or reason for this, save perhaps for the increasing quantity of drugs they were forcing into their systems, and occasionally their faulty equipment. Their PR Tony Linkin recalls that their show at the Reading Festival was a disaster. 'Everything went wrong,' he says. 'I saw them the night before, warming up in Chelmsford and they'd been brilliant, but at Reading the equipment just fucked up … everyone walked away thinking they were rubbish.'

Carl's parents had come up to Reading to see the show and he was understandably keen for everything to go well. When his amp packed up he was livid, and Pete didn't help matters by giving him a jokey kick up the backside on stage. For Carl, though, it was the last straw, and the pair disappeared off stage after the final number throwing punches at each other.

Other times it was sheer magic. One reviewer described a Libertines show as 'the sound of The Strokes being given a kicking at closing time in East London'.

When *Up The Bracket* came out in October, it predictably met with rave reviews. It was an incredible debut. This was no clinical recording where the note-perfect instruments could have been produced by a computer and the drums kept in time with a click-track. You could feel the energy pouring from the studio. This was The Libertines, warts and all. Occasionally off-key vocals, mic-sharing, missed notes; it was the real deal. 'Horror Show' somewhat cryptically recounted episodes of drug-taking. Pete admits it was about wanting to lie down after being 'down on the brown'; while 'Boys In The Band', which had become a live favourite, was faithfully reproduced without losing any of its power. Still, Pete felt strange singing about getting them out for the boys in the band while watching girls in the audience singing along. It wasn't, he insisted, about 'getting your bangers out for the boys'.

The tour that followed the album's release, however, was not a happy one. 'We were battling so much with each other and with the world,' Pete recalls.

Reviewing The Libertines support slot for British rockers Supergrass at the Shepherds Bush Empire, *Evening Standard* contributor David Smyth was less than impressed. 'Championed by the music press as the most exciting new rock band in Britain today, it's clear that the excitement stems less from their derivative music than their mouthy interviews and general air of unhinged abandon,' he wrote. 'They seem to be in a tremendous hurry, perhaps hoping that by rapid sleight of hand, we won't notice that they aren't as good as we say they are … if The Libertines are supposed to be Britain's fight back against the three-pronged rock attack from America, Australia and Scandinavia, we've lost already.'

It's fair to say not everybody was enamoured with The Libertines. Simon Price, writing in the *Independent*, said they were 'roughly the thirteenth inheritors this year of the *NME*'s ludicrous weekly Your New Favourite Band mantle' and that every song sounded like either The Jam's 'Down In The Tube Station At Midnight' or The Smiths' 'This Charming Man'. But he was man enough to admit that the last time he'd seen Mudhoney live, the third band on the bill were Nirvana 'and they were awful'. 'If I'd had to place all my worldly possessions on which of the two was most likely to change the course of history, I'd be a hobo by now.'

The *NME* summed it up best in an introduction to an interview with The Libertines: 'What do we look for in our stars?' it asked. 'The best ones come from disadvantaged or damaged backgrounds, are a bit weird and have done something brilliant that makes them stand out from the crowd.'

Prior to the interview Pete had managed to consume a litre of vodka, down two pints of Guinness and 'hoover up a lot of cocaine'. 'Being a pop star isn't about the music,' the *NME* said. 'It would be a very dull state of affairs if it was. It's the other stuff that makes The Libertines worth our attention – their attitude and image and reference points; the talk that goes with the walk.'

Drugs, violence and The Libertines had started to go hand-in-hand, particularly in reviews of the band and in interviews – something that was starting to annoy Pete. In one interview he snapped: 'I don't like all of this stuff about us fighting all the time. I mean, do they want to see a fucking bunch of people having a scrap? If you want to see a scrap go and watch ultimate fighting.' While in another he claimed: 'People are saying we've lost it to smack or money or groupies, but smack, groupies and money had far worse effects on us before than they do now. Now we're more united.'

Unfortunately the rest of the band were starting to disagree with

Pete. Ironically, in the same interview Pete would offer something that turned out to be scarily prophetic. Signing to Rough Trade, he insisted, was the same thing as embarking on a suicide pact. When The Sex Pistols split up there was just bitterness, he said.

'That's not the same as us,' Carl argued.

But Pete was adamant it was exactly the same. 'That's how it's going to be with me and you,' he whispered, turning to his friend, ignoring the interviewer. 'It's going to turn sour.'

Press reports about drug-fuelled, anarchic tours had started to ensure The Libertines notoriety. By mid-October, after twenty-two days on the road, they had sacked their tour manager for being 'too strict'. One reporter called it 'one of the most debauched tours in recent rock history'. Their soundman quit in disgust while their tour manager, who boasted twenty years' experience, was fired. The Libertines were becoming infamous for their in-fighting, alcohol consumption, drug use and groupies. Carl and Pete had reportedly blown £10,000 of their publishing advance on a 'massive bender'.

During all this mayhem – in fact, since the very beginning – Pete had been scribbling down all his innermost thoughts, ideas and philosophical meanderings and by year's end he had enough to fill a few notebooks. The Books of Albion, as they were known, chronicled life with The Libertines from the first days at Filthy McNasty's. Carl called them 'tour memoirs'. To Pete they were far more.

By the dawn of 2003, blanket policies would be introduced in some of the bigger record companies in the UK, enforcing a (little adhered to) freeze on signing any more bands from America. Universal said it should be left to the US divisions, and that their UK subsidiaries should be focusing on UK bands.

As Detroit's Von Bondies signed their first major label record deal with Warner in the US, our passion for the new wave of American rock 'n' roll was already starting to wane. Mercury Records was already (wrongly) predicting the next scene would be an indie-dance crossover in the same vein as the 'Baggy' scene that had heralded the Happy Mondays back in the 1990s.

James Oldham, the *NME*'s deputy editor, who had been championing The Libertines for the past year, was headhunted by Universal to front a new label – Loog – which was also given the brief of signing British acts after its initial flirtation with American bands. The Libertines had finally come of age. But although the world – or at least Britain – was now ready for The Libertines, it was as if The Libertines were already nearing the end of their trip.

'Gigs and riots are the only things left that bring about that sense of spirit and community where you can let yourself go'

PETE DOHERTY

SEVEN

SEVERED ALLIANCE

The Libertines were becoming tour junkies. As 2003

dawned they were at it again, but despite being forced to play ever bigger gigs, Pete didn't want to stop playing the tiny pub gigs that had won over their fans in the early days. 2003 would be remembered as the year of the guerrilla gig – impromptu performances announced a few days or sometimes even just hours before, on the Internet. They'd still play the occasional smaller show at the Duke of Clarence or Filthy McNasty's, but Pete would increasingly prefer to open up the front room of his own flat in Bethnal Green. In doing so, the divide between the band and their fans was all but disappearing. It at once made their supporters feel a kinship; that they were no different from the pale, wanton figures on the stage in front of them.

Morrissey used to encourage an excessive and extremely physical devotion from his fans. According to the writer Will Self, it was a case of 'you can touch, but only in this contrived, aberrant way'. In an interview with the former Smiths frontman, Self suggests that stage invasions 'puncture the surface of stardom', to which Morrissey replies: 'Let it be punctured, let it be punctured, that's my motto.' A story is then recounted of a gig in which Morrissey 'goes so far towards puncturing that he almost bodily hauls a would-be stage invader through the arms of the bouncers, past the ranks of monitors and into his arms.'

Pete and Carl had, for a long time, encouraged members of their audience to join them on stage. Pete would often shout 'stage invasion' towards the end of each Libertines set, and a throng of young boys and girls would evidently be only too happy to oblige.

According to Self, Morrissey, however, sought adulation from those 'most indisposed to give it' – the 'Dagenham Daves and Rusholme Ruffians who people his landscapes' and eschewed the advances of those who regarded his talent as poetic.

Pete, however, has always embraced all-comers. For him it was a simple case of breaking down barriers. He was no different from his fans, and the process of getting them up on stage; performing for them in his front room, letting them flip through his record collection, communicating with them on the Internet were all ways of putting it into practice.

Libertines performances were becoming more and more unpredictable too. Journalists didn't have to worry about not filing enough copy: The Libertines gave them reams to write about. At a gig at the Valencia Roxy Discoteca in Spain in January, Carl and Pete 'snogged' each other on stage 'not once but three times' according to one reviewer. The *NME* said the gig was out of this world and that the Spanish fans 'crumbled in their presence'.

A month later they were back in London again, headlining the Astoria. They seemed to have climbed the ladder of success so fast they'd missed several rungs on the way up. The *Guardian* called them the 'bastard sons of Britpop: young, shirtless and out to steal the indie throne'.

Reviewers were beginning to grasp Pete and Carl's concepts of Albion and Arcadia as well. Journalist Betty Clarke said, 'The Smiths and Blur can both stake a sizeable chunk of Albion as their own – but rarely has such literacy looked so cool.'

On stage, as Pete flung himself at his mic stand, dived into the crowd or bashed heads with Carl as they jockeyed for centre stage, any tension between them was hidden. But that wasn't to say it didn't exist.

In February the band headed to the annual *NME* awards where Mick Jones was due to accept a 'Godlike Genius Award' on behalf of his old band The Clash. Pete went along with his mate Pete Welsh, writer of the first Libertines book, *Kids In The Riot*. Little did Pete know but his band would also be picking up an award that night – for Best New Band. But as Welsh recalls, when the award was announced, 'Pete had snuck off to the loo for a pipe' – referring to the glass 'base' pipes used for smoking crack.

Subsequently Welsh said he could trace the demise of The Libertines to this very night at the *NME* awards. Pete's behaviour was becoming more and more unpredictable. He and Carl had almost come to blows in Camden earlier in the day and there was a lot of tension between them. When they finally collected their gong, Pete threw fire-crackers with little or no regard for anyone standing nearby. Carl was furious. Rough Trade head honcho Geoff Travis hated that night. For him, the *NME* awards represented the first time he truly saw the effect drugs were having on his new signing.

Pete Welsh said a gap was opening up between Carl and Pete. It was more like a chasm.

In addition to Pete's drug problem, there were other difficulties that were contributing to Pete's alienation from the rest of the band. James Endeacott recalls Carl was becoming increasingly pally with Supergrass drummer Danny Goffey, while Pete was hanging around more and more with his friend Pete Wolfe.

Like Pete, Wolfe was a poet and songwriter. And like Pete, the biography he likes to tout as his own is slightly questionable. Apparently he was born in Maidstone in 1968, spent two months training to be a professional footballer with Gillingham FC but got mixed up with alcohol, music and the 'wrong crowd', which he terms his 'heavy experiences'. He married a woman of Polish nobility, became friends with Shane MacGowan and lived in New York and Paris before his marriage dissolved, after which his drinking got worse and he attempted suicide.

Wolfe then went back to stay with his father, picking himself up out of the mire and forming a band called the Side Effects, who played their first gig at the 2003 Sundance Film Festival. Back in London, Wolfe met Pete Doherty and the two bonded over poetry, songs and booze.

The pair would later collaborate on the song 'For Lovers', which became a top ten hit, and Pete would pen the song 'Wolfman' as a tribute to the friend who stuck by him through his painful addiction.

But in 2003, when Pete's predilection for class A drugs was beginning to worry those around him, Internet discussion boards were starting to point the finger at the Wolfman as someone who wasn't helping. Wolfe would later tell the *Guardian* that although he took the odd line of cocaine, he wasn't into heroin or crack. 'He won't leave me alone,' he said, referring to Pete. 'It's like having a really needy little brother.' In his next breath, though, the article's author says, 'Wolfe professes deep-seated affection for Doherty.'

Carl was also spending less and less time at the Albion Rooms because of what he saw as a growing circle of Pete's 'friends' connected with the drugs world hanging around. Geoff Travis says he'd never experienced dealing with bands on 'this level of drugs before'. Banny too was starting to have a hard time controlling Pete. She was relatively new to management but Pete was slowly starting to become unmanageable.

At their gig at the Sheffield Leadmill in February, Scarborough Steve's new band The IVs provided support, thrashing their way through a short but incendiary set. It seemed drugs weren't just inspiring and informing The Libertines' songs, as The IVs played their new song 'Green-Eyed Monster' – a paean to amphetamine overindulgence.

Despite the ever-increasing problems within the band, their audiences were growing and reviews were positive, even if at times the onstage antics could best be described as ramshackle. 'The Libertines are well on their way to becoming a national institution,' critic Thomas Lee wrote for the website noripcord.com.

In truth, touring was probably not the healthiest thing for The Libertines to be doing but for a band just starting out in their careers and who had not spent much time playing together before they were signed, it was essential. Pete recalls the routine of travelling on the bus, waking up, stumbling out, doing interviews, playing gigs, getting obliterated, finding girls, sleeping, waking up and doing it all again. There were drugs. There were sleazy clubs. Pete remembers 'fucking this girl in the toilets, on the floor, proper sort of sliding about the tiles,' adding jokingly, 'so there were those intimate, tender, romantic moments.'

One *Telegraph* writer said he 'feared for the health and sanity of The Libertines' and was worried they wouldn't survive life on the road. Their tour bus had become a caricature of itself: leather sofa covered in stains; a floor full of empty beer cans and open bottles of whiskey; the obligatory PlayStation 2 and TV/video hook-up. And that was just downstairs. Upstairs the bunks were strewn with unwashed clothes, bras, boxer shorts and guitar cases. Groupies had been banned but Pete managed to craftily smuggle the lassies back on several occasions. 'And imagine my surprise,' he innocently proclaimed when the tour manager caught him. The same *Telegraph* journalist described it as a 'life positively encrusted in unhealthy rituals built around bad meals, worse drugs, casual liaisons, sleep deprivation and lack of hygiene'.

In typically jokey fashion, Pete simply said, 'At least we've got hot and cold running water here. We haven't got that at home. I have to flush my toilet with Evian. Only the best for the Albion Rooms.'

When the tour reached Glasgow, King Tut's Wah Wah Hut was jammed to capacity. Gary was convinced it was too dangerous for stage invasions but his concerns fell on deaf ears. Pete simply smiled.

Later that night he was sinking in bodies. David Pollock, the journalist reviewing the gig who the previous year had said there was 'scarcely a proper tune all night', admitted his opinion had changed. 'A great show,' he said, after watching Pete invite half the crowd onto the stage with him during 'I Get Along' with the immortal words: 'Pitch invasion.'

On the UK leg of the tour things seemed to be going well. But when the *Telegraph* article eventually appeared in print, there was a note tacked on the end: 'The Libertines were due to play in Hamburg,' it said. 'On arrival, however, singer Pete Doherty was diagnosed with bronchial pneumonia, and the band were forced to cancel the rest of the tour.'

The truth was a little different.

After the Glasgow show, and before the scheduled European leg of the tour, there was still a show to play at Nottingham's Rescue Rooms, with support from Detroit's The Sights and Pete Welsh's band Kill City. Kill City was fronted by Lisa Moorish, with whom Pete had begun a casual relationship. Tickets for the gig had sold out a long time before, and outside the venue, touts were asking four times the face value. At the end, as the intro to 'The Boy Looked At Johnny' kicked in, and in keeping with their mandate to break down the barrier between band and audience, Pete once again asked the audience to rush the stage.

Tony Linkin said it was one of the best Libertines gigs he'd ever been to. They were, he said 'becoming the best band in the country' and Pete was looking more like a rock star. But on his way back from the Rescue Rooms, Pete seemed troubled. The European leg of the tour was just around the corner but something inside was apparently telling Pete not to go.

The band was due to reconvene in King's Cross before heading over to Germany on the tour bus. After a petty row with Banny where she expressed the tour crew's concerns at the escalating danger posed to the band and them from stage invasions, Pete ran off the bus, trying in vain to persuade Carl to join him. As a result the bus left for Germany minus Pete.

Understandably the atmosphere on the bus was fraught. Carl began teaching the guitar technician Pete's guitar parts. He knew Pete needed help and hoped his friend would do something about it back in London. Poostchi stayed behind and over successive days tried to persuade Pete to rejoin The Libertines in Hamburg but it was never going to happen.

As it turned out Carl ended up with flu and was too sick to play, and with Pete missing in action, The Libertines were forced to cancel the entire European tour. At the time it seemed like a setback. On reflection, it was a disaster.

By spring 2003 the broadsheets were still fawning over the 'new guitar bands', now not just from America, Scandinavia, Australia and New Zealand, but Britain as well. But the movement – if you could call it that – was hardly new. The Strokes had arrived on the British music scene at the beginning of 2002. It often takes the mainstream a little while to catch on: as late as March 2003 the *Independent* was 'visiting the barricades of the New Rock Revolution'.

The Libertines were uncomfortable being grouped in with the 'revolution' that the *NME* had heralded the year before. 'There've always been boys playing guitars,' John Hassall said. 'But we will never be like anything else. The chemistry between the four people and the year we're living in all add up to something completely different. We're just trying to express ideas and feelings … art and romance.'

The Libertines also still wanted to play smaller venues, and for this there seemed to be a consensus. Gigs were booked at the Buffalo Bar and the Camden Monarch, even though in audience size terms they could have graduated to venues like the Astoria or even – as would take place later that summer – the Kentish Town Forum. It was just another example of how The Libertines wanted to stay close to their fans. That was Pete and Carl's mandate from day one, after all, and that mandate wasn't about to be compromised.

To underscore this, they had started playing impromptu 'guerrilla' gigs at the Albion Rooms. Pete would post a message on his website's discussion board a couple of days before. Tickets would be sold by a friend standing outside the Blind Beggar pub on the Whitechapel Road, or someone in the photo booth at Whitechapel underground station, or a 'man in a hat' sitting on a brick wall near their block of flats. They'd cost a tenner and people would squash themselves into the lounge of the Albion Rooms or other equally un-venue-like venues, such as rooftops, or the Red Rose Labour Club on the Seven Sisters Road, which was more used to putting on comedy nights and political functions.

Money didn't seem to be the motivation, or at least that was the feeling. The reality may have been slightly different – when a hundred people are paying £10 each that's not a bad payday considering there are no overheads, no management commission, no equipment hire and no booking agent taking a percentage. And considering there was the ever-present *NME* to faithfully record the mayhem that ensued each time, publishing almost weekly accounts, there was publicity too. Either way it was a very clever idea.

But Pete says there wasn't much enthusiasm for the gigs from Carl, John or Gary. Carl, however, claims he loved the gigs but felt bad charging for them. He says he could see from the Internet discussion forums that some fans were desperate to go but were complaining they were having trouble finding the money.

The low-key gigs at the Buffalo Bar (an acoustic set) and the Camden Monarch took place on 27 and 28 March. One young libertine pushed his way through the crowd sporting a red Coldstream Guards military jacket: he had apparently spent £50 to emulate his heroes. At the Buffalo Bar the band looked like they were having fun, that their differences had been pushed aside, at least for the night. They covered everything from Chas & Dave's 'Harry Was A Champion' to 'Dream A Little Dream Of Me', even managing a re-working of Michael Jackson's 'Billie Jean' and The Coral's 'Dreaming Of You'.

The *NME* was unequivocal: 'The Libertines *are* their fans. No artifice, no delusions of grandeur. As the audience leaves, John walks home alone along Chalk Farm Road, carrying his bass guitar into the night.'

But changes were setting in. Tony Linkin recalls there was a different atmosphere in the band by spring 2003. Pete's penchant for hard drugs was becoming even more of a problem, and the people he had begun inviting round to the Albion Rooms were a little unsavoury to say the least. Carl desperately wanted his own space. He'd turn up at the Albion Rooms and find Pete's cronies 'piping' on his bed. Things were going missing too. It was time to leave.

There are three big markets that record labels are usually keen for bands to break: North America, Europe and Japan. Europe was already sold on The Libertines. The band had been to Japan the previous summer – to play the Summer Sonic festival – but it was time to head back for their own ten-day headline tour, including two extra dates added in Tokyo due to overwhelming demand. After that it was time to take their very English brand of rock 'n' roll to America.

On 13 April the band played the Liquid Room in Shinjuku, Tokyo. The response to the gig provided a snapshot of how well the band would go down on the entire tour.

As The Libertines walked casually on to the stage and the opening notes of 'Boys In The Band' rang out, the largely Japanese audience (peppered with a number of ex-pats) seemed to know all the words. Carl, Pete, Gary and John shot through most of *Up The Bracket* and a few B-sides. Jockeying for the mic, Carl and Pete bounced around the tiny stage, slamming into one another and showering the front row with sweat.

During 'The Boy Looked At Johnny' one Japanese teenager pushed his way to the front, clambered onto the stage, grabbed the microphone from Pete and screamed down it before launching himself into the audience. While Carl took over vocals for 'Skag And Bone Man' during the encore, Pete hurled his mic stand over his head and onto the ground to roars from the crowd.

Japan had been a success. The American tour, however, was going to prove difficult. They had planned to record in the States but Pete was increasingly difficult to manage, largely thanks to his drug-taking and what seemed like a regular disappearing act. As if that wasn't enough, the first night of the tour – a gig in San Francisco – had to be cancelled after Pete's grandmother died.

Photographer Roger Sargent flew out to New York to meet up with the band at the legendary CBGBs club where they were scheduled to play, but he was about to find out how difficult it would be to get the band all in one place at one time. Pete had been told that to score crack in New York you should approach homeless people on the street. And that's exactly what he did that night in New York. Eventually, after going up to random hobos, he found someone who could 'help him out'. That person would eventually join The Libertines on stage that night after convincing Pete of his musical leanings, much to Carl's dismay.

Pete would later claim the CBGBs gig was the out-of-tune and uncomfortable. But from a typical New York audience with a reputation for a cooler-than-thou indifference, a handful still managed to bring themselves to join The Libertines on stage for the encore.

'There were a lot of drugs going down on that tour,' remembers Endeacott in *Kids In The Riot*. 'Pete smashed up his room at the Chelsea Hotel and tried to smash up our offices out there. He was just out of his mind.' In the tour bus Pete was endearing himself to his bandmates by blowing fumes from his crack pipe into the back of Gary's head. 'You could have cut the atmosphere with a knife,' Pete says.

Despite the bad gig at CBGBs, Pete's wayward behaviour and the constant worry over his whereabouts, the tour would actually prove to be a success. He'd be there on the tour bus and managed to turn up on stage on time, but in between times – usually while interviews were taking place or soundcheck demanded his presence – he'd be off. And where he went, nobody knew.

Inevitably The Libertines were billed as the British Strokes. But it was their Britishness that would appeal most to the Americans. One critic said their search for Arcadia 'was proving a surprise hit among more esoterically inclined American music fans'.

A smoking ban in force throughout New York meant the atmosphere was a little different from the venues the band were used to playing back at home, but at Brooklyn's Club Luxx The Libertines had no trouble infusing the place with their rock 'n' roll energy. The Libertines exploded onto the stage as if, as one online reviewer noted, 'they were gonna bust the walls down of this tiny club … I have seen rock's present and it is The Libertines.' This may have been a little over the top, but it would make American readers sit up and listen. In between songs the band played slightly bizarre audiotapes of what sounded like an old man crying, and the sound of a crowd applauding.

At the end of the tour they were booked to play *The Late Show* with David Letterman – an hour-long weeknight chat show broadcast from the Ed Sullivan Theater in New York City. Letterman had been a mainstay of American television since the 1980s and his show was one of the most important – and widely watched – chat shows on TV. For The Libertines to bag a slot on the show was a big deal. They were on the right road to breaking America – something so many bands had tried to do and failed. But the band were trying to break America while simultaneously dealing with a frontman increasingly dependent on crack and smack.

They had all turned up on time for soundcheck before the Letterman show and afterwards there were a few hours to kill before their performance. This was the time Pete usually did his disappearing act and James Endeacott was concerned he wouldn't show for their slot.

Pete had to be there for their first national broadcast on American TV.

Pete walked casually out of the stage door telling Endeacott he was off to buy some jeans and a T-shirt. Endeacott said he was bored and would go along for the ride – a ruse with the simple intention of making sure Pete was back in time. Pete sat in the back of the cab that afternoon the happiest Endeacott had seen him for ages. He was elated to be in America; elated to be playing Letterman. At six o'clock the pair of them were finishing up cocktails in a nearby bar and Pete told Endeacott to hurry up otherwise he'd be late for his appearance.

They caught a cab back to the studio. Endeacott was overjoyed. Pete was on the ball and the performance that night on the hallowed stage at the Ed Sullivan Theater was incredible – the best he'd seen them in a long time.

But all was not well in The Libertines camp. Overall, the tour may well have been a success, but Carl and Pete's relationship was suffering – largely due to what Carl had decided was Pete's growing dependence on drugs. He didn't think Pete was the same person he had known and loved back when they'd first decided to form a band, when they'd set out to find their Arcadia and launched the good ship *Albion*.

Pete, meanwhile, felt alone in America; he knew he was overdoing it with the drugs but he didn't like the distance Carl was putting between them.

His mind wandered back to that afternoon on the side of the canal in north London a few years before, where he, Carl and Steve had decided on the name of the band. Afterwards they'd sworn a blood oath on the back steps of Delaney Mansions on the Camden Road. Libertines. Forever.

EIGHT

|INTO|THE |MYSTERIOUSLY |TOMORROW|

After Carl moved out of the Albion Rooms they seemed to have officially closed for business and so Pete moved out too. His friend the Wolfman had a spare and rather comfortable sofa in his flat on Gunter Grove at the Fulham end of the King's Road, and Pete was only too happy to claim it.

Towards the end of May, Pete posted a message to fans on the Internet advertising a gig in Wolfman's flat on Gunter Grove and promising 'a kiss, fine music and accommodation for the night'. It would be a good way, he thought, to repair any bad feeling from the American tour and rekindle his relationship with Carl. Little did he know, the gig would not only go down in legend but would also help widen the already gaping chasm between him and Carl.

Pete and Wolfman had spent the best part of the day getting the flat ready for an army of fans who had promised to descend on Gunter Grove from all corners of the country. John was never able to make the gig and had made his excuses. When Gary arrived later that afternoon, he took one look at the 'druggy crowd' that had started to assemble and fled. But it was Carl's non-appearance that irked Pete most. He felt betrayed.

Pete had become friends with a rock 'n' roll band from Hull called The Paddingtons who, together with The Rakes, The Others, Razorlight, Thee Unstrung and The IVs, were setting basement nightclubs alight across Britain and kick-starting the most exciting British music scene since punk – all spearheaded, of course, by The Libertines.

The Paddingtons were a five-piece and in the early summer of 2003 were yet to release their debut single. They had met Scarborough Steve at a gig in North Yorkshire and through him had become friends with Pete. The Paddingtons were already staunch supporters of The Libertines and had seen them playing live on *Later with Jools Holland* back in October 2002 and the televised gig with The Sex Pistols in the summer of the same year.

'Pete asked us to support The Libertines,' recalls Josh, The Paddingtons' guitarist, 'but first of all he wanted us to play Gunter Grove in Chelsea. We drove all the way down from Hull with our guitars and drum kit for the gig. When we arrived there was this woman on the door collecting money. I said, "I ain't paying a tenner." It turned out to be quite a memorable night. We got on really well with Pete and ever since then he's been like a big brother to us, always look-ing out for us, sorting us out with gigs, mentioning us in interviews. I got a phone call a couple of months ago saying, "Pete Doherty's just mentioned you on TV." He had apparently said The Clash were the past, The Libertines were the present and The Paddingtons were the future. It helps you out when he says that to God knows how many thousands of people.

'You had to get in through the window for the gig at Gunter Grove. Outside there were about two hundred kids trying to squeeze into

Wolfman's tiny flat; his neighbours were milling around in the road outside looking angry – and worried.'

As early as six o'clock Pete had set up his guitars and was strumming through a few numbers. By 7.30pm sixty people had been allowed in via the window and Pete chatted casually to fans as they graffitied the walls of the flat. The 'gig' moved into the garden and then back into the living room. By nine o'clock a hundred-odd people had managed to cram into the flat at Gunter Grove to see Pete Doherty, tired of waiting for Carl to turn up, play the most intimate gig of his career. But not before he and Wolf had entertained the crowd with some freeform poetry.

'The police came, as you can imagine,' Josh says. 'The first time, they just asked us to keep it quiet and this kid told them he just had a few mates round to watch the football– but there were a hundred kids inside. At this point Pete played a rousing version of "What A Waster". The second time they threatened to take the gear, and the third time they started physically taking all the amps and stuff.'

By 10pm Pete had swapped his electric guitar for an acoustic, much to the satisfaction of the police, who disappeared into the night. An hour and a half later, though, the fuzz were back, forcing an end to the proceedings. But it didn't matter. The gig was over and the crowd – and Pete – were satisfied.

Carl later told Pete he would have shown up if he'd known the *NME* was going to cover the event. A few days later the pair met up in Regent's Park. Pete told Carl he was planning another guerrilla gig on a rooftop in Whitechapel in the near future. Carl said he would be there. But once again, he never showed. It was one of the lowest points in Pete and Carl's relationship.

A second Libertines European tour had been scheduled for June. As they had cancelled the first one earlier in the year it was vital they turned up to these gigs or there would be a continent full of irate Libertines fans – not to mention compensation to pay to angry promoters.

Pete decided not to go.

Tony Linkin says Pete's decision not to head to Germany – the first stop on the tour – was because Carl hadn't showed up at the Gunter Grove gig. Carl was worried about Pete's continuing drug use, which he felt was turning into drug abuse. There was talk of Pete joining the band in Spain but it was never going to happen. Still, Pete felt the option was open to him at least, and for that he was happy. He'd stay in London, but if he decided – at a later date – to join Carl, John and Gary, he would.

Then Paris happened.

On 19 June, just before midnight, Pete logged on to the Network 54 discussion forum on the Internet – the same board on which he'd previously announced the guerrilla gigs; the same board on which he'd published his poetry; the same board with which he communicated his innermost feelings to his fans. What he posted was headed, simply, 'Untitled'.

'So just tell me straight, I said, do you want me to come or not?'

'No, Peter.'

'Aah, Carl, surely not this, not now, I need to play.'

Pete described his knee-jerk reaction to being told categorically by Carl that he wasn't welcome on the tour. 'Lose mind,' he said. 'Fly-kick a bus; smash at Abbey National window.'

Pete was determined to go to Paris regardless, but said his passport was taken from him by 'minders' as he slept, referring to two of his friends who had been in touch with Banny to see if they could help him sort himself out. 'Paris becomes more and more distant,' he wrote, but wondered aloud whether The Libertines would have him back for the English dates.

Carl had been on the ferry to France when he called Pete and broke the news. 'I don't think you should come to Paris and do the show tonight,' he had said. It broke Pete's heart. He told Poostchi he was coming whether she liked it or not. 'Carl doesn't want you,' she replied.

It was a difficult decision for the band to reach and Poostchi did not enjoy having to be the one that told Pete where the band stood. But he had failed to turn up to too many shows and needed to realise things were getting out of control.

Pete, it seemed, was out of The Libertines.

Carl told Pete he wanted him to be happy. Pete knew the lads in the band cared for him, and he cared as much for them, but he just couldn't understand. He resolved to go 'off into the mysteriously tomorrow'; to start a new band and 'play the toilet circuit again', the dives that new bands are forced to play on their way up the ladder to success. 'Bon voyage, piggles,' he wrote – bastardising the nickname 'Biggles' he sometimes used for Carl.

Pete had decided to start a new band. He didn't see why it shouldn't be called The Libertines as well – after all, he had just as much right to the name. Tony Linkin was quick to reassure music journalists hungry for a story – an official statement claimed The Libertines were not splitting up and that Pete was still very much part of the band.

Shortly afterwards, Libertines' fans' worst fears were realised when Pete played a *Big Issue* magazine benefit gig at the Tap 'n' Tin pub in

Chatham, Kent, under the name 'The Libertines' but this time led by former band member Scarborough Steve. Interestingly, the Tap 'n' Tin venue would end up featuring prominently in The Libertines' story a couple of months later – even going down in rock 'n' roll history.

'Over the years it's always been the same,' Pete told the *NME*. 'We'll have a little fall-out. Sometimes it'll last six months. I'm not going to sit at home like a wife like I used to back in the day. I've got a new band together and we're still called The Libertines.'

To emphasise his point – that The Libertines could never truly be broken – he showed off a tattoo crafted on his arm. 'That's etched forever,' he said. 'We'll always be The Libertines.'

Pete also posted another message on the website; this time an open letter to another of his casual girlfriends, Katie Lewis (nicknamed Katie Bapples because of her large chest), whom he also referred to as 'Madame Bilo'. 'The morning trembled to mourn a lost boy grateful dead the obvious always unsaid. I'd hold you so dear to cherish and un-suspect, this love is unreal, to see you dance or so, to hold and roll you over and lips to meet.'

It was a frank and poetic declaration of love, but also what seemed to be an acceptance of his deteriorating condition. 'Dear oh dearest girl I adore you so it scares me this unbalance,' he said.

It was also a poem that in some way lamented the man he was becoming. He described his actions as 'selfish manoeuvres' and went as far as to suggest 'something in me wants so badly for you to kill me, as I sleep shoot or stab me for my weird actions that so hurtful result to be'. There were references to 'piping' (smoking crack); there were hidden song titles: 'The man who would be king is your slave', and there was a nod to the Beat poets of the 1960s in his romanticising of 'glorious dawns'.

He cheekily ended the paean with 'Oi, soft girl, giz a kiss', before quoting a variation on Arthur Rimbaud's 1872 poem 'Song From The Highest Tower'. The opening stanza is telling: 'Youth so full of Leisure / Slave to each new taste / In fine choice of pleasure / My life went to waste.' But by no means pessimistic: 'Ah, may the time come / When hearts are as one!'

But Pete's open letter to a loved one belied the sense of outrage he was feeling at Carl's 'betrayal'. He was sleeping on friends' floors, moving from one house to the next and chronicling his thoughts each day on the discussion board. In truth – despite wandering off into poetry about his lovers – he was livid. He said when he first met Carl, Carl was the one into drugs and he wasn't. Pete couldn't believe Carl had – in his opinion – refused to stand by him; he never thought he'd be physically prevented from appearing on stage with his own band.

But while Pete was readily accepting his 'selfish manoeuvres' and 'weird actions' in writing, elsewhere he was denying he had a problem. 'I think Carl's deluded about the extent of my overall deterioration,' he told one journalist. 'I think he hasn't been able to write for a while.'

ON 21 JUNE The Libertines were back in the UK and gearing up to play the Midsummer Night's Scream event in New Brighton, Liverpool. Although Pete considered it home turf, he was still effectively out of The Libertines and wouldn't be appearing at this or any other gig on the band's mini-tour of the UK.

'Rumour has it,' one journalist wrote, 'that Pete is extremely ill and has had to pull out of their forthcoming tour.' Pete's replacement was The Libertines' guitar technician Nick, and the verdict was that Carl seemed to be doing a good job despite the absence of his fellow frontman – and despite the fact the crowd continually chanted 'We want Pete!' between songs.

A few days later they played with Billy Childish's band The Buff Medways at the Kentish Town Forum. All eyes were on The Libertines as their troubles were now common knowledge, played out in the pages of not just the music press but the broadsheets as well. Carl said he felt like it was a public execution. 'It was a shock to the system,' he said of playing at the Forum without Pete. 'It was horrible.'

The general consensus was that Pete's erratic behaviour, fuelled by his drug use, had angered the rest of the band and that they had decided he needed professional help. His fans too had begun to worry that he could he be heading down the same well-trodden path that Gram Parsons, Brian Jones, Hendrix, Jim Morrison and Hank Williams had been down before him.

The verdict was, once again, that Carl had managed to pull off the unthinkable – playing live to die-hard Libertines fans without Pete. They gave a 'palpitating version' of 'Horror Show' according to one critic. Another said 'Don't Look Back Into The Sun' was undoubtedly the best thing the band had ever done.

It wasn't always like that. At the Glasgow Barrowland on 22 June, Carl tried to ignore the cries of 'We want Pete' that threatened to disrupt the gig.

Pete's pronouncements on the whole sorry situation were difficult to decipher. One minute he seemed angry, but at other times almost resigned. He said Carl had called him but then hung up, later texting him to apologise. Pete said he'd then received a letter from Carl with some quotes from Chet Baker in it, and remarked that he was proud of his fellow Libertine.

Playing Glastonbury without Pete was heartbreaking. For some bands the festival is the pinnacle of their career. Run by farmer Michael Eavis since 1970, it's widely seen as the best of all the UK summer festivals – not so much for the profile it offers bands, but for the entire experience.

Carl didn't want to be playing at all without Pete. He just knew it was necessary. Pete's health was deteriorating and to him it seemed the only logical thing to do. Pete, on the other hand, couldn't really see that anything was drastically wrong with his health. All he saw was his band playing the most important live music event in Britain, touring the world and playing *Top Of The Pops*, without him. At the Leeds Carling Festival he was even turned away by security guards who had once worked for him.

In *Kids In The Riot* Pete Welsh says there was no getting through to Pete. 'In classic junkie denial everyone could see this but the kid himself,' he says. Pete had been staying at a hotel in Paddington. His on/off girlfriend Lisa Moorish was pregnant with his first child but, according to Welsh, the prospect of fatherhood 'didn't seem to register'.

It was time for Pete to go into rehab.

Moorish recalls being 'hysterically concerned'. She was just two weeks away from giving birth to Pete's baby, and between her, Banny, Pete's sister Amy-Jo and his mum Jackie, they attempted to persuade him it was for his own good. The foursome conspired with Rough Trade to 'lure' Pete to the studio, giving him the impression he was going there to discuss his new band, but when he arrived, he would be whisked away.

Geoff Travis booked Pete into the Priory – a private hospital long-associated with helping celebrities overcome their addictions. The Priory Group is one of the biggest independent mental health providers in Europe and there are a number of different locations. Farm Place –

where Pete was heading – was a seventeenth-century manor house set in ten acres of parkland, which specialised in treating alcoholism, drug addiction, gambling and eating disorders. It's extremely private and can house only twenty patients at a time.

Travis and his business partner Jeanette Lee drove Pete to Farm Place, near Dorking in Surrey, convinced he needed to sort himself out. 'To try to get this young man's life back on track,' Travis said.

Shortly after Pete arrived, James Endeacott was summoned by Priory staff because Pete hadn't had time to pack a bag, and as such hadn't got any clothes with him. Endeacott nipped to Primark in Lewisham and delivered socks, T-shirts and underwear. Afterwards, driving down the road away from the hospital, Endeacott broke down in tears.

The idea was that Pete would clean up and rejoin The Libertines. But that was easier said than done. Rehab was only going to work if Pete went there on his own terms.

Pete was only in the Priory for five or six days. A 'secret contact' informed him Wolfman and Katie Bapples were about to be married and he made his excuses and left. Of course, it was all a ruse. And it worked.

In a frank account of what had happened to him, Pete told fans reading his discussion forum about the night he was 'helped into a farmhouse with bars on the windows'. He wasn't allowed to make phone calls or use the Internet. But on the 'bright side', he said he shared 'groups' with some of the most perceptive and sensitive people he had ever met. Discharging himself against medical opinion, Pete hitched back to London where he claimed he wandered the streets, penniless and desperate to play guitar and sing. 'There will be an "acoustic" gig this week, perhaps in Whitechapel on the roof again,' he wrote.

Pete's son Astile was born in July. He made it to the birth but went AWOL shortly afterwards for six days – apparently on a drugs binge. His closest fans just wanted him better. 'You know where we are if you need us,' wrote Kirsty and Kirsty – the two 'webmistresses' who looked after the official Libertines site.

Unfortunately, though, Pete was far from OK.

While Carl, John and Gary headed out on the Japanese leg of their tour, Pete didn't sit at home feeling sorry for himself. He wrote songs, gave impromptu gigs, rehearsed with Scarborough Steve and gave interviews. He used one interview, with London-based alternative radio station XFM, to champion new British bands on the scene. 'There's a rich fertile soil shaped like a guitar with a little Union Jack stuck in it right now,' he said.

But that wasn't all he was up to. While the band were away, Pete burgled Carl's apartment.

His mind clearly wasn't in the right place. He was living in Kilburn and was trying to put his own band together – also called The Libertines. His new drummer and bassist were staying on the floor, on the dole, and Pete felt he needed to pay them for helping him out. He had gone over to Carl's flat in Baker Street to ask for money. 'I found myself shouting at [Carl] and it turned out I was arguing with my reflection,' he said to the *Evening Standard*. 'When I realised, I booted the door in. I was engulfed by complete misery and despair.' He insisted, 'It wasn't revenge. It was more: why are you ignoring me? A cry from the darkness. I do feel remorse, I feel sick.'

That afternoon Pete took an antique guitar, a laptop, a mouth organ, a video recorder and a few other items from Carl's apartment.

There was little to suggest Pete was about to hit this all-time low. The night before his arrest he had logged on to his website again and advertised a gig for the following weekend. 'Come one come all,' he had said. The address was Gascony Avenue in Kilburn, and the price,

£10. 'Things are certainly livening up this end,' he said. 'Let me sing to you a while, for new times' sake. The only question is … is London big enough for two bands called The Libertines, and has it really come to that?'

Pete had told Moorish of the burglary. Gary later said he thought Pete was doing it for attention: why had he burgled Carl and not anyone else? Moorish called the police – and it wasn't a decision that she took lightly. Pete had committed a criminal offence, but more than that he needed help. If he was arrested he may be forced into sorting himself out, once and for all.

The police arrived the following evening and discovered the items in Pete's car. He admitted it straight away, but denied taking the *NME* award that the band had won earlier in the year and £200 in cash – both of which he was additionally accused of. At the station he was tested for drugs and they discovered traces of opiates and crack cocaine in his blood.

On 31 July Pete Welsh turned up at Pete's Kilburn house and gave him some 'punches up the bracket', as Pete so eloquently put it on his website. Welsh had heard about the burglary and he was livid. Pete Doherty was a friend and he couldn't believe he'd done it. He was naked when Welsh burst through the door. It can't have been pretty as he chased Pete into the street outside at three in the morning. But in typical fashion Pete managed to make it all sound very poetic the next day. 'Once outside my aching limbs, fresh from a two-day slumber, floundered like a sickly child in the path of this drunken Welsh giant of a hoodlum,' he said, even adding an apology and admitting he'd been a 'c**t'.

'I'm all cut up, unsure,' he told the *Standard*. 'I don't know what I'm doing, I need a good kicking and I need some help.'

On the Monday after his arrest he appeared at Horseferry Road Magistrates' Court and was bailed to appear again on 11 August. The court seemed to attract celebrity cases – even its official government website claims 'celebrities from the world of television and the sporting world have appeared ... as both witnesses and defendants and it is regularly seen in national news reports in newspapers and on television'. As if they were peddling some kind of info-tainment.

By August the name of Pete's new band had changed. It was no longer The Libertines – presumably he finally decided that was too confusing. He had settled for Babyshambles – the title of a recording session The Libertines had started to do in New York and later the name of a song as well. A promoter had mistaken the name of the first song in the set for the band and the name stuck.

The announcement was in the same style as all the previous announcements: in a badly punctuated freeform posting on the Network 54 discussion board. The only difference was that this was the first gig Pete would perform as Babyshambles. 'THIS MONDAY,' it read. 'Free entry to The Gardens club, 188 Broadhurst Gardens, London NW6.' Pete added directions too, and apologised for his no-show at an earlier gig – the night he was arrested for burglary. 'Three days in the cells,' he said, 'with all the torture you could muster to think up for me.' Then came the disclaimer: although it was Babyshambles' first gig, The Gardens only had a 'one-man' entertainment licence, so Pete would be playing alone.

The contrast couldn't have been more glaring. There was Pete, the night before he was due in court again, perched on a stool at the small but pleasant venue in West Hampstead, while The Libertines were headlining the El Rey Theater in Los Angeles, California.

However, on The Libertines' tour some critics were beginning to mourn the loss of Pete. 'The chemistry between Barât and Doherty that surfaced during The Libertines' short Coachella Festival performance this year was clearly missing,' one reviewer noted at El Rey. Another said he didn't like the idea that a band could just replace a member and continue as if nothing had changed. 'I smell the stench of opportunism,' he said, before berating Carl for the way in which he removed his shirt on stage – as if it had become part of the act and was rather contrived. In Atlanta, however, a journalist said The Libertines' show was 'about raw, unadulterated energy; about having a good time and never mind the bollocks'.

In London, Pete put in his scheduled appearance at Horseferry Road Magistrates' Court. The fans were there to cheer him on – most of the boys looking like Pete replicas. In the dock he admitted breaking into Carl's flat and stealing his antique guitar, laptop, video recorder, CD player, mouth organ and books. His case was adjourned until 8 September for pre-sentence reports.

By afternoon the inevitable headlines already started to appear. The *Evening Standard* said: 'I burgled my friend's flat because I'm a crack addict.'

Pete, it seemed, had broken his silence over the issue and had spoken to the *Standard* in the days leading up to his court case. 'Yes, I'm a heroin addict,' he'd said. 'Yes, I'm addicted to crack cocaine, and I don't know what to do.' He admitted first trying heroin when he was eighteen and said there had been times when he'd used it four or five times a day.

The following morning, however, in a now-familiar posting on his Internet site, he remarked: 'The disadvantages of being stitched up by the *Evening Standard* not quite outweighed by tapping the reporter for a few bob towards our own PA system' – referring to the gig he had played a few days previously. 'Thank you to those who turned up in Gascony Avenue the other day – the first gig for a while that you could actually hear.'

The prospect of a prison sentence didn't seem to faze him – at least that's the impression he gave. 'Troubadour Café, Brompton Road, Chelsea, 22nd, 23rd August. Full band,' he wrote on the discussion board.

'Diseased oysters give us the pearls, y' know.'
'I feel drawn to the shadows and country
yards, dusty tracks ... and berry
bramble Arcadian retreats.'

PETE DOHERTY

NINE

BREAKING THE BUTTERFLY

Before each group meeting,

a member of the Priory staff would reiterate why they were there: 'The members of this group all share problems: alcoholism, chemical dependency, eating disorders, personality disorders, character defects, unmanageability.'

Pete recalls being woken by a nurse pulling the sheets off his naked body, saying, 'If you won't get up, this is what we do.'

On his website he gives a unique insight into the time he spent at Farm Place. The entries were copied from the Books of Albion that he had been compiling for a year. He talks about the pain of withdrawal, the hot and cold flushes and the panic; he describes the nurse sitting with him as he sat there crying. 'Is it self-pity? Remorse?' he asks. 'In my heart I know I am still suffering and in shock at Carlos not wanting me in Paris.'

In the Priory he entertained himself by playing songs on a battered old acoustic guitar from music books he'd found in the communal lounge. 'I have been found tearfully strumming away to "Bright Eyes", "Stranger In Paradise" and "Begin The Beguine",' he writes.

He speaks of his frustration at not being able to use the Internet or telephone. When he discussed the agony of drug withdrawal with his nurse, he told her of 'natural agonies, infinite sadness of the soul and melancholy of the heart'. Evidently even in his worst hour he could convey his feelings in poetry. Pete comes across as a tortured soul; as if he is fulfilling that Rimbaldian script that author Jon Savage spoke of: to 'live fast, disorder your senses, flame brightly before self-immolation'.

Elsewhere he juxtaposes his perceived imprisonment against the freedom of nature. As he 'strolls the grounds, playing croquet on the wet grass', he notices ducks swimming across the pond; a butterfly settling on a giant daisy, accompanied by a birdsong chorus. 'The days are long here, and my senses sometimes dulled by the dull scene,' he says. 'The merry chirp of birds and the bright sunshine offer remedy and a giant grand oak spreads itself many armed across the skyline.'

He recounts the emotional drama of group therapy: the swearing and the tears. 'Hello,' he was forced to say, 'my name is Peter, I am an addict and my life is unmanageable.' The Priory practises the same tenets as Alcoholics Anonymous.

He speaks of a profound loneliness, but found solace in the conversation of a Bulgarian man undergoing treatment for heroin addiction. The man, who was once a goalkeeper, told Pete of his 'junk-fuelled days on the streets of Sofia, robbing people for bags, jewellery, cameras or cash for heroin'. Pete told him he'd like to visit him in Sofia one day. He even suggested he could play a concert and the pair of them could take lots of heroin together. 'Half joke,' Pete adds.

Another day his Irish roommate told the group his life story: of his marriage, his harrowing descent into alcoholism, his relationship with a Manchester hooker, rehab, divorce and the blackouts. It must have hit home hard with Pete. He certainly wasn't alone, but his experience had been nothing compared to some of these people. It must have told him what could happen to him if he didn't sort himself out soon.

One woman had smoked crack incessantly and ended up slashing her wrists and becoming hooked on Valium. One said as a baby she had got hold of and drank meths. She ended up on heroin and crack and was rushed to casualty after taking Xanax and Valium and cutting up her arms and legs. Another told the group of her plans to kick the hard drug habit and just smoke weed.

Together with a woman he describes as 'a young, beautiful 38-year-old', Pete came up with a plan to get narcotics sent to them at Farm Place.

The group was asked to write about the damage caused by drugs. Pete's guilt set in. How on earth could he do that when he had just arranged for drugs to be posted to him from London?

He says he was tested positive for cocaine but claims it was a stitch-up. 'The results are nothing more than indicative of heavy crack abuse last Thursday – the night before I came in – I am paranoid they think I'm secretly on the pipey.'

Before his 'escape' from Farm Place, Pete recounts a dream he had. His beloved QPR were in the final. Pete made his way under the stands to the dressing room where the team was awaiting – thinly disguised, he says, as The Libertines. This links up with another recurring dream, in which he would stroll about Loftus Road stealing football kit from the dressing room.

Two weeks before his court hearing – the one in which he would receive his sentence for burglary – Pete broke the conditions of his bail by smashing up a hotel room in Clapham and was promptly re-arrested.

Amy-Jo paid his bail and he moved in with her in south London until the hearing. 'It seems the darkest hour has passed now,' he said.

'Many hours today with my probation officer and liaisons with drug workers with worthwhile results and much clearing of rubbish.'

But whereas publicly Pete was seen to be making efforts to address his drug problems, online the seedy underworld of crack and smack seemed perfect material for his poetic pen, even if he was fiercely against encouraging any of his fans to take up the habit. In an entry entitled 'Cheynes Walk, London NW5', the night before his scheduled gig at the Troubadour Café, Pete describes a visit to the crackhouse where he was shown a huge bag of tightly wrapped rocks of crack. 'The lookout signalled as we turned the corner,' he writes, 'and his needled lover appeared outside the Costcutter, gazing darkly as the car's shadow retracted upon itself and we sped away up the Prince of Wales Road. Fear and hatred do not find expression in tears. They are not worthy of them, best saved for tender feelings.'

The gig at the Troubadour Café saw Pete and his new band together for the first time. The reviews weren't complimentary but Pete came away that night ecstatic, having done what he does best. He later described 'such joy' in his heart and enjoyment at playing. 'The four of us united in some long-lost Arcadian bliss and chaos and embraces, proud of each other,' he said.

Pete was happier playing music in this environment. While his ex-band was on stage at the Carling Festival, garnering reviews like 'we're witnessing the ugly, messy aftermath following the booting out of Pete Doherty' from the *Independent*, Pete was playing the dives again but seemed happier than ever. Although he did wonder aloud how he'd gone from playing in the most important band in Britain to unloading fruit on his friend's stall in Brick Lane. 'How it came to be I'm having to work again (cheers and jeers from he pit),' he said.

The irony was clear. The Libertines' debut album *Up The Bracket* had gone gold, selling over 100,000 copies, and Pete was back playing the 'toilet circuit' again.

But within a couple of days he was advertising another impromptu gig, this time at the Hope & Anchor pub in Upper Street where Roger Morton had first seen The Libertines all that time ago. Pete was also under no illusion about the possible outcome of the sentencing hearing at Horseferry Road Magistrates' Court – now just days away. 'It may be my last gig of freedom if I get a custodial sentence on the eighth,' he said.

When he turned up at the Hope & Anchor on 6 September he was wearing a long Burberry raincoat and a straw hat. Ever faithful, the *NME* were there to record the event. When their photographer asked Pete for a photo, Pete asked that he be pictured with his crack pipe – although the journalist dutifully noted that he filled it with tobacco.

The evening ended after a group of female fans got into a fight. 'Give peace a chance', Pete sang as he walked out of the venue, before heading to the nearby Duke of Clarence pub to continue playing into the night. 'This is Pete Doherty's ideal existence,' the *NME* said in the article that came out the following week. 'A carefree minstrel playing songs where and when he pleases amongst adoring fans.'

Time seemed to fly by and before he knew it Pete was back in front of the beak at Horseferry Road Magistrates' Court, awaiting his fate.

He arrived outside the court, flashing a 'fingers crossed' salute to an entourage that had gathered. His defence solicitor Richard Locke asked the District Judge for a community service sentence, which would give Pete the chance to address his addiction. But District Judge Davies said Pete was likely earning too much money. 'Unlike most of us who have to study and work hard, they suddenly acquire wealth,' he said, to which Pete replied: 'I have worked hard.'

'Domestic burglary is always viewed seriously,' the judge said. 'You kicked down the door to the flat, which was ransacked. What's more, it's against a colleague and a friend. This is a serious offence.'

Richard Locke said his client had carried out the burglary in an emotional and drug-addled state. He said Pete had been evicted from his band because of his habit and that he and Carl had shared a tempestuous relationship. He had felt betrayed by The Libertines.

The outcome was shocking, even though Pete had prepared himself for the worst. He would serve six months in Wandsworth Prison at Her Majesty's pleasure. Pete Doherty was now prisoner number LL5217.

He looked shell-shocked as the sentence was passed, and friends and family sitting in the public gallery broke down in tears as he was led away by two security guards. He left in a Group 4 van just before lunch.

The following day the daily papers carried the story. 'Pop star jailed for burgling friend's flat' one screamed. Another claimed he had had a £200-a-day heroin and crack addiction for five years before the burglary.

Tabitha Denholm, Pete's ex-girlfriend and one half of DJ duo Queens of Noize, said she thought the burglary was a cry for help. 'Something had to happen, otherwise something really bad would have happened to him, though a custodial sentence was a bit harsh,' she said.

Pete found it tough in prison. Understandably he saw a lot of negativity and tension inside. Although he was only a Category D prisoner (those who are considered not to pose a risk to the public and are unlikely to escape), he was taken first of all to Wandsworth and later transferred to an open prison. Wandsworth was built in 1851 and houses long-term prisoners, remands and immigration detainees.

Pete asked the chaplain to get hold of an acoustic guitar for him. He desperately wanted to play music again and resolved to patch up his differences with Carl when he got out. He wanted The Libertines to perform again with him and Carl at the front, in the limelight: two troubadours plying their trade and chasing their Arcadian dream once more. That first night in his cell at Wandsworth prison, Pete strummed along to 'Don't Look Back Into The Sun' and wept.

Pete was both scared and paranoid in prison. He even described how standing in the dinner queue made him feel vulnerable and that the prison officers – or 'screws' – took it upon themselves to make life as difficult as possible for the inmates.

His lawyer was probably right: if Pete had been given a community punishment those around him could have ensured he got help – and stuck to it. But inside he had access to heroin and marijuana. 'I managed to make connections pretty quickly,' he said.

Of course, it wasn't the first time a rock star had been sent to prison, and it undoubtedly won't be the last. In 1988 James Brown was sent to prison for assault and carrying a pistol without a licence. Years before he had been charged with possession of the drug PCP, resisting arrest, possession of an unlicensed handgun and his wife's attempted murder, but those charges were dropped.

In 2000, musician and author Gil Scott-Heron spent ten days in a Manhattan jail before pleading guilty to possession of cocaine and crack pipes, accepting a plea deal of eighteen months of in-patient drug rehab.

Jim Morrison was sentenced to eight months in 1969 for 'lewd and lascivious behaviour', which amounted to exposing himself to the audience at his gig in Miami, Florida, and using profanity.

In the UK Mick Jagger was sentenced to three months for possession of amphetamines. Back then, editor of *The Times* William

Rees-Mogg famously wrote an editorial entitled 'Who Breaks a Butterfly on a Wheel?', in defence of Jagger. 'In Britain it is an offence to possess these drugs without a doctor's prescription,' he wrote. 'Mr Jagger's doctor says that he knew and had authorised their use.' Rees-Mogg said some people resented the anarchic quality of the Rolling Stones' performances, 'dislike their songs, dislike their influence on teenagers and broadly suspect them of decadence ... there must remain a suspicion in this case that Mr Jagger received a more severe sentence than would have been thought proper for any purely anonymous young man.'

The British *Journalism Review* called it a 'single impudent dart that punctured the rhinoceros hide of British jurisprudence – and helped to get the Jagger sentence quashed'. Fast-forward thirty-odd years and times, it seems, have hardly changed. The 'mainstream', represented by the *Daily Mirror*, *News of the World* and the *Sun*, are still gunning for 'Crack Addict Doherty' or 'Junkie Rocker Pete' – as if he poses a threat to the very moral fibre of British society.

By the beginning of October, Pete was given a release date. His six-month sentence had been reduced to two: on 8 October Pete would be a free man.

On 3 October the Babyshambles website announced a 'Freedom Gig' at the Tap 'n' Tin venue in Railway Street, Chatham, for the day of Pete's release. It was everything his fans could have hoped for. 'News just in,' the message read. 'FREEDOM gig for Doherty ex-LL5217 + specially invited guests at Peter's request.'

It also pointed out that the gig was not something thrown together in just a few hours. 'It has been in the planning for the past three weeks without exact knowledge of his release date. At Peter's request a selection of bands and artists were approached to play this gig. More details to follow.'

On 7 October, Carl told reporters that the following morning he would be there to meet his old friend by the prison gates and 'remind him why he never should have got there in the first place'.

The following day Pete walked through the huge prison doors to freedom. The first person he saw was Carl and the pair wept as they hugged before disappearing to the nearest shop to buy beer and cigarettes and then on to a friend's house to catch up.

Arrangements for the Freedom Gig were in full swing and Pete was desperate to sing and play again. Only two hundred lucky fans – most of whom were already making their way to Kent from all corners of the country – were able to buy tickets for the tiny venue.

Just hours after being released from prison, Pete was on stage. Little did the assorted fans, groupies, industry bods and hangers-on that were packed in like sardines know, but they were about to witness the first Libertines gig with Pete in tow since May. Pete had sent a message to Carl, Gary and John via a fan – he wanted them to play in Chatham but at first they were reluctant. 'If we regroup we will need to talk first,' Gary insisted. 'It's too soon.'

The future was far from certain but Banny Poostchi knew the story was far from over. 'To these boys, playing music is a human need, just like eating and drinking,' she told the *Independent*. 'How can they not carry on as musicians?'

Pete was joined on stage by the rest of the band and the sound of screaming from the audience became deafening. Even their old friend the Rabbi from Filthy McNasty's joined them for covers of 'Sally Brown' and 'Dirty Old Town'. 'Don't Look Back Into The Sun' saw Pete and Carl dancing around each other on stage, their mic-sharing antics back, finally, for all to see. Even Gary, who had been determined not to play, wore a stuck-on grin.

Afterwards the *Independent* said they went on to play perhaps the most emotionally charged celebration of music and happiness of their lives. And five days later Carl and Pete were performing again – this time at an impromptu gig on a bandstand in the middle of Regent's Park, strumming their way through the wartime classic, and highly appropriate, 'We'll Meet Again', followed by 'Death On The Stairs', 'Up The Bracket' and 'What A Waster'.

When a Carl Barât DJ set at the Camden Monarch a week later turned into another full-blown Libertines set, an ecstatic journalist from the website Gigwise was convinced it was all preordained. 'This ramshackle approach to everything they do must be a pretence,' he said. 'They're clever boys after all. They know how rock 'n' roll works.'

At the Duke of Clarence – another 200-capacity boozer – they ripped through an explosive set, the audience shouting along to the now immortal line in 'Time For Heroes' that decried Englishmen that wore baseball caps. It all ended in typically shambolic style after a blown amp caused a power cut.

All their promotional work for *Up The Bracket* was over and talk could now turn to The Libertines' second album. Admittedly, Pete, being back in the band was still in its infancy and they'd all need to adjust, but things were finally looking up.

ON 20 October 2003, Banny Poostchi, who shared responsibility for The Libertines' success to date and had got them signed to Rough Trade and EMI publishing, decided to quit. Her management contract had entitled her to manage the band worldwide exclusively for both the first and second albums. By October they had finished touring and promoting *Up the Bracket* and were now poised to head into the studio and record the follow-up album.

Poostchi had left her job at Warner Records a year and a half before to manage The Libertines, during which time she'd seen them become one of the most important British bands for decades. She had set up the worldwide infrastructure for the band in terms of recording, touring and merchandising. She had seen them pick up the *NME* award for Best New Band, appear on the David Letterman show in the States and top the *Guardian*'s list of best British bands (beating both Oasis and Coldplay).

It was not easy leaving the band she had been involved with since the start, touring with them for more than two hundred shows all over Europe, Japan, America and the UK. But she felt Pete had become unmangeable and would remain so unless he got help. All signs pointed to him being far from ready to take this step.

Pete had been in touch with Alan McGee – head honcho of the now-infamous Creation Records label that had boasted The Jesus and Mary Chain, Primal Scream and My Bloody Valentine; in addition, whenever he was quoted in the papers, McGee was regularly preceded by the words: 'The man who discovered Oasis'. The well-connected Scot was only too happy to take over the reins of The Libertines. It would prove a challenge, but if anyone was up to the job, he was.

McGee owned a huge Victorian house in Hay-on-Wye near the Brecon Beacons, and he suggested it would make a perfect place for

Carl and Pete to get reacquainted and bury the hatchet. But what started out as a perfect opportunity to make up for lost time and lost love quickly turned into a time for bickering. Pete discovered that while he was sidelined from the band for taking too many drugs, Carl had been busy on the crack and smack himself. Pete thought it reeked of hypocrisy.

At McGee's pad, Carl drank whiskey like it was going out of fashion, later admitting the trip had been a 'recipe for disaster'.

One evening after Pete had headed off to bed, Carl stood in the bathroom, inebriated, staring at his reflection in the mirror. He was disgusted and felt the hatred welling inside him. That's when he began smashing his face against the sink; repeatedly he pounded his head until blood was gushing from cuts near his eye and on his cheek. Carl then started crying and blood mixed with the tears as he began smashing up McGee's house.

The next morning McGee walked into Pete's room and asked if he had been responsible for Carl's injuries – none of which had been treated, and all of which made him look like the walking wounded. It was only later in the hospital, when the doctor started mentioning 'police' and 'investigations', that Carl confessed.

From that moment on, Pete says nothing was ever the same again.

Carl almost lost the sight in one eye that night. He was rushed to hospital then later to an eye hospital in Hereford where he was diagnosed with a fractured cheekbone and damaged tear duct. He had to have two operations and suffered a great deal of pain as a result of losing the plot at McGee's house in the hills. The media was told he had drunk a bottle of whiskey and had slipped as he climbed out of the bath, cracking his head on the sink.

Pete later chronicled the events on his website: "'Spend some time together, write some songs," he said … he didn't say anything about

Carlos having to get his eyeball stitched up … sex symbol in an eye patch? Buccaneers indeed.'

McGee simply said The Libertines were the most extreme band he had ever worked with.

BACK IN LONDON Pete moved into a new flat behind the Blind Beggar pub in Whitechapel – quickly rechristened the Albion Rooms, despite actually being the Albion Rooms Mk II. Of course, it wasn't long before Pete could no longer resist the temptation to do an impromptu show: on 10 November he logged on to the Internet, advertising 'A wee housewarming shin-dig of a gig this eventidy'.

This was a new venue and, courteously, he gave extensive directions to Darling Row in East London. Sitting on the wall that runs round the estate, he said, would be 'a man wearing a hat and a frilly, frilly frown'. He promised to perform songs from both The Libertines' and Babyshambles' catalogues 'from his bed in the Albion Rooms'.

Pete would play two sets that night, such was the demand. His notoriety was growing and, with that, his fan base. He strummed through 'Don't Look Back Into The Sun', later released as a single, and the then-unreleased 'What Katy Did'. He even managed a cover of the Bacharach and David classic 'Always Something There To Remind Me' and The Stranglers' 1982 hit 'Golden Brown', finishing with 'We'll Meet Again', which he and Carl had played the month before.

The Libertines, it seemed, were back. And Pete was in his element. He had his side project, Babyshambles; he was able to play the occasional solo gig on rooftops or down at the Albion Rooms whenever he chose; and he was back in The Libertines again. The boys in the band were back in business.

At the Duke of Clarence in November, even old Razzcocks joined them for early Libertines numbers 'You're My Waterloo', 'Love On The Dole' and 'Seven Deadly Sins' before Gary leapt back on stage for more familiar album tracks. And aside from Carl – who was forced to play with a red bandanna tied around his head, covering his eye because of his injuries – they looked fantastic. They had also just sold out three nights at the Kentish Town Forum on 16, 17 and 18 December. And not only that – the support act was confirmed as Chas & Dave.

'The electricity is about to run out, my phone is fucked, is anyone near can lend us twenty quid?' Pete wrote on the website in November. But looking back on what was possibly the worst year of his life was not something Pete did forgivingly. 'Oh my sweet Lord Jesus what a year,' he wrote. 'Not one speck can compare, not my shame and sorrow to my family, and my tears – are they real any more? I'll cry them anyway.'

Towards the end of 2003 Pete's contributions to the Network 54 discussion board were becoming more regular. One particular piece of writing titled 'In The Morning's Store' was particularly revealing – despite a disclaimer Pete added abruptly afterwards.

It appeared at 11.42am on the morning of 30 November. In it Pete described sitting with a friend in a Shepherd's Bush basement where a 'sweet, sickly smell of weed and strong coffee' filled the air. Pete had been handed a foil tube and on the website describes in explicit detail how he chased the dragon, 'inhaling greedily' to calm himself of his recent 'tremors'.

Pete and his friend smoked weed and heroin until midnight before heading to a nearby club. Walking down the Goldhawk Road they went looking for a fight and 'didn't care' if they got killed. They then went to a crackhouse in Kilburn Park Road, where they danced 'unselfconsciously' in a darkened room.

When dawn came Pete sat there recalling a trip he'd made one Christmas in the 1980s to visit his nan. His dad had worn an army-issue tracksuit, which he had then taken off before going swimming in a nearby pond. '[Dad's] disowned me, you know,' Pete told his friend. 'Says I represent everything he despises in the human race. Says I'm a thief, a liar, a junkie.'

'In The Morning's Store' is a painfully honest piece of writing – if, indeed, it is biographical. The disclaimer read: '"In The Morning's Store" is a piece of writing that all came out in one go. It is not necessarily true, and neither are the things that occur to the characters in it: and in no way is it intended to promote or encourage others to do anything at all relating to drugs. I've made my position clear on heavy drugs … so don't start.'

On 1 December Pete and Carl returned to Filthy McNasty's to play a forty-five-minute set at the launch of the pub's 'Busking for Beer' night. A few days later The Libertines were at the Rhythm Factory in their beloved Whitechapel playing to 500 lucky punters. A perceptive reviewer proclaimed: 'In case you hadn't noticed, The Libertines like playing live – a lot … we are left in awe of a great band with so much potential it's scary.'

Pete was fully aware of the increasing media interest in his 'addiction', and said he even thought about prefacing one Internet posting he had made at 5am one morning with a 'friendly protest' at being woken up in the middle of the night, 'so as not to fan the ridiculous flames that "Pete's making a 5am post – he must be smoking freebase".'

In November he helped the YMCA launch a new charity initiative by sleeping rough for the night, joining 'It girl' Tamara Beckwith and the then London mayoral candidate Simon Hughes on the steps of Marylebone Town Hall. The initiative was to coincide with a YMCA TV ad campaign to raise awareness of homelessness over Christmas.

The next day Pete posted the night's diary on the web. 'Before 11pm a rush of flashing bulbs and then we settle down for the night,' he wrote. 'By 5am seven of us remain – including the two fellas that "live" there.'

It poured with rain that night and Pete returned to his home in Whitechapel soaking wet. 'Extended highlights' of the night, he said, included Carl turning up drunk at 2am bearing brandy and garlic bread and entertaining the crowd; and getting abuse from the occasional carload of 'savage wits'.

The Night of the first Forum gig had come around fast. Pete was about to play with his heroes Chas & Dave.

Chas Hodges had first heard of The Libertines after watching the Jools Holland show. He'd heard they were Chas & Dave fans and his wife had videoed the performance. 'I was at a gig and when I came home I watched the video at 2am,' he recalls. 'It was the first time I'd ever seen them, and next minute there was a phone call to our manager asking us to support them at the Forum – in front of 5,000 people.

'Pete saying he was a big Chas & Dave fan done us the world of good so we're on a bit of a revival at the minute. He was being interviewed on Radio 1 and said it was because of us that he picked up a guitar and learned to play. My own hero for the piano was Jerry Lee Lewis. I ended up working for him and he virtually taught me to play the piano. For Pete to say he got into music because of us means everything. We're gigging regularly and now we're gradually getting a younger following thanks to him.

'We first met The Libertines that night at the Forum. I remember having a one-syllable conversation with Pete because I felt he was a bit in awe of us. The Libertines' tour manager used to work with The

Stranglers and my daughter recognised him. He came over and said Carl and Pete were so knocked out we were playing with them so Dave and I went over and introduced ourselves to them on the stage while they were doing their soundcheck.

'Someone told me Pete wanted to join in on a couple of songs but was afraid to ask. So during our set he came on stage and we played a medley of old songs I'd learned off my grandad – old Victorian singalongs.

'My daughter told me about Pete burgling Carl's flat. That was all very rock 'n' roll and weird. Jerry Lee was a bit like that – he had been through a lot and was into the drugs too, but managed to sustain himself. I got to know him pretty well. He was only seven years older than me but you'd have thought he was twenty or thirty years older. He's continually on methadone now. I can relate to Pete's wildness: I used to like a drop of booze but packed up six years ago. My doctor said I wouldn't be around the following year and that I'd drunk enough for three lifetimes. Once I decided to pack up drinking I knew I was going to stick at it.

'It's a terrible shame about Pete but a lot of fans think he's cool for being into drugs. I like to think he'll come off it and straighten himself out.'

The crowd punched the air as Chas & Dave played their hits 'Rabbit' and 'Snooker Loopy'. The Libertines' fans had become instant Chas & Dave converts. Three nights at the Kentish Town Forum and the pair had notched up another few thousand fans on their wall.

It was to be an eventful series of gigs. The Rabbi gave a rousing rendition of 'Sally Brown'. Halfway through The Libertines' opening number, 'Horrorshow', Pete kicked his mic stand into the crowd of fans baying for his body, for the spectacle, for him to launch himself into their midst.

The band ploughed through new songs 'Last Post On The Bugle' and the incendiary 'Arbeit Macht Frei'. The *Evening Standard* called it an hour-long set of exhilarating punk rock. The *Guardian* said unpredictability was what kept rock alive, and that The Libertines had it seeping from every pore. The *Independent* noted that, between verses, one minute Carl and Pete were hugging, the next they were running at each other 'like rutting stags'.

As the eventful year drew to a close, Alan McGee reflected on his new protégés. Earlier in the year the band had released their single 'Don't Look Back Into The Sun', which had made the Top 30 and which immortalised McGee's club, Death Disco, in its lyrics. Six months later he was managing the best rock 'n' roll band in Briain. 'I don't know what will happen,' he said. 'Anything could happen – they could break up, they could write their [next] album, they could record their album, they could all die.'

What McGee did know was that The Libertines were at the top of their game. He also knew Pete had become a folk hero. 'I've not seen this level of devotion since The Clash in 1977 or Oasis in 1994.'

TEN

ALBUM TWO

Early in 2004 Alan McGee introduced Pete to Douglas Hart, who had played bass in the Creation Records band The Jesus and Mary Chain. Hart had followed The Libertines to the North of England on the train with his Super 8 camera with a view to making a music video for the band. Hart would later fly out to Paris to direct the 'For Lovers' video to accompany the single Pete was on the verge of releasing with Wolfman in the spring.

Pete was still playing solo gigs, advertising them on his website a day or two before they took place. He'd already recorded 'For Lovers' and was desperate to record the B-side; it was a beautiful song and he was convinced it would be a hit. He'd also finished recording the debut Babyshambles single.

But Pete and Carl still wanted to write together. They needed to collaborate and bond after the debacle of their trip to the Welsh valleys, and they had a second Libertines album to write. So they decided to head to Paris. Pete wanted to be alone with Carl in the French capital and renew their friendship; Carl wanted to get away from the crowd that had attached itself to Pete and the drugs. They both wanted to play guitar and write songs.

Having spent the best part of a week in Hay-on-Wye witnessing the destruction caused when Pete and Carl got together, Alan McGee decided to hire security guards – more as a means of protecting his charges from each other than, say, rabid fans. Nicknamed the Twins, these men had a lot of form. It seemed a little over the top but in retrospect it was worth it. Carl and Pete's relationship was volatile at the best of times and even a trip to the romantic city of Paris was unlikely to throw water on the fire.

They would be staying, appropriately enough, at France's Albion Hotel on the Rue Notre Dame de Lorette. Pete claimed he and Carl would be 'returning to friendship, oblivion'. He didn't bargain on McGee heading out as well to keep an eye on his protégés. It wasn't quite what Pete had anticipated, and as a result Carl was lured away most nights to restaurants and parties while Pete preferred to stay in the hotel room, writing.

That's not to say the break didn't do the pair good. There were fun times. One night Carl and Pete disappeared to a local strip club but ended up seeing 'some old bint pulling her clobber off'. But it wasn't long before Carl got sick and went down with a fever, delirious. Pete couldn't recall ever seeing him this bad – one night Carl began ranting about how it was 'all over' for The Libertines, simply because Franz Ferdinand had topped the charts.

With Carl bed-bound, Pete wrote songs and strolled the streets of Paris alone. It had always been a haven for free-thinkers – its Left Bank cafés a magnet for artists, poets, revolutionaries, bohemians and philosophers. In the 1830s and 1840s, Romantic artists had lived in the Nouvelle-Athènes area in the ninth arrondissement. Pete felt right at home.

In a posting on his website entitled 'The moon elegant over Paris and I', Pete described walking the 'magical streets'; of 'theatres, tin cans, moustaches and pedal scooters'. He wrote endlessly in his latest volume of the Books of Albion; he hung out with a band called The Parisiennes. He encouraged readers of his postings to head out to Paris 'on a grand debauch', while Biggles, aka Carl, was forced to head back to London due to family problems.

After Carl had headed home, Douglas Hart flew out to Paris to direct the 'For Lovers' video. Pete was happy pursuing projects like this, and his mind was wrapped up in his new love, Babyshambles, which he felt was far more than a sideline. While in Paris, Pete decided to do a couple of impromptu gigs; one, which he billed as 'Acoustic Shambles', took place in the Café Bergerac next door to the Albion Hotel. But he was glad to be in The Libertines again and was looking forward to heading back to London, playing live again with Carl and working on the follow-up to *Up The Bracket*.

While Carl and Pete's relationship may have been fraught, love for The Libertines was growing. On 21 February the band picked up the gong for Best British Band at the annual *NME* awards. 'It's the best thing you can win,' Pete said.

On stage, Carl and Pete leaned into the mic and proceeded to recite the First World War poem 'Suicide in the Trenches' by Siegfried Sassoon taking turns to repeat lines until the final, scalding denouement.

It wasn't the usual 'thank you' speech that the event saw year after year. But it emphasised their discontent at Britain's questionable military involvement abroad and underscored Pete's love of poetry.

Seemingly against all the odds, in March the band finally began recording their second album. And McGee's hired 'minders' were there to make sure Carl and Pete didn't spill each other's blood over the recording desk. Mick Jones was at the helm once again and planned to record the album as quickly as possible. This would not only result in the raw sound of a rock 'n' roll band at their peak, but would also help him pin Pete down a little more easily – or so he hoped. Making a new LP was going to be anything but easy.

Meanwhile Pete's prolific songwriting was finding another outlet via the Internet; he asked Kirsty and Kirsty to upload his demos to the Babyshambles website, claiming 'McGee'll turn a blind eye or play act there's a buzzing horsefly distracting him'.

The Libertines were on their second album. Their first had sold well over 100,000 copies. But they were still playing smaller pub gigs to satisfy their core fan base – and because it was more intimate. Pete was also holding last-minute get-togethers at which he promised 'Arcadian revelry'. Even the premiere screening of the 'For Lovers' video – a song that would reach number three in the charts and gain an Ivor Novello nomination for Best Contemporary Song – took place at the 'Wolfden', Wolfman's Gunter Grove flat.

The contrast couldn't have been greater when they played the Birmingham Academy on 29 February followed by three consecutive nights at London's Brixton Academy on 5, 6 and 7 March. Neither The Strokes, White Stripes nor The Darkness managed to fill that 4,000-capacity venue three nights on the trot. At Birmingham one reviewer commented that the electricity between Pete and Carl left the audience wondering whether their relationship was one of love or hate. The gig finished with Pete throwing the band's rider of whiskey bottles and beer cans into the audience, to which Gary added his drumsticks for good measure.

'No sign of their recent troubles, The Libertines played a seventy-five-minute-long session of thrash guitar,' one paper noted. Another said Carl and Pete had emerged from a year marred by violence, drug abuse and imprisonment 'with their mystical vision scarred but still intact'.

Brixton represented the pinnacle of their success on the London scene specifically, and in the UK generally. But it was inevitable that the three-night stomp couldn't possibly pass without incident. It was on the last night that the shit hit the proverbial fan. All the audience saw was Pete storming off halfway through a song and returning ten minutes later with blood daubed across his chest.

The band had been playing 'Can't Stand Me Now' – the Pete-penned paean to his and Carl's soured relationship. And that night on stage at Brixton, whether it was due to love lost between them, paranoia from drug use or simply tiredness, Pete took offence at how emphatic Carl had been while singing the words to the song. 'It had taken six, seven years for him to say it, to say the truth,' Pete afterwards told journalist Betty Clarke for the *Guardian*. 'He sang it to me and I thought, you're right. We've used each other, got here, but underneath it all, you're not my mate. So I kicked his amp over, smashed up his guitar and cut myself up.'

Pete disappeared back stage, out of the exit door, round the side of the huge imposing venue and into the dark alleyway outside. There he'd taken a razor blade and slashed a cross on his chest. Ten minutes later he was back on stage sporting the dramatic markings, like some tribal scar. 'Sorry about that, I had a bit of a strop,' he told the audience before the band launched into a slightly ironic rendering of 'The Good Old Days'.

The *NME* review was typically praiseworthy. They had heard from The Libertines' 'inner circle' that the band's second album could very well be their last but in spite of the inherent problems this series of gigs was, they said, 'taut and supercharged with emotion'. There has, they decided, never been a British band like The Libertines. 'It's like Morrissey and Marr hired a Motown rhythm section and decided to form a Sex Pistols cover band.'

The truth was, however good they were, however much the music press loved them and their fans adored them, The Libertines were on the verge of imploding and there was nothing anyone – not the record company, not Alan McGee, not even The Libertines themselves – could do about it.

In what would turn out to be a particularly ominous posting on 14 March, Pete said Carl was a 'difficult man to love' and gave him nothing in return. 'The one true horror is that if I was to be true to myself as an artist, as a man, as a Libertine, I would not work with the band as it stands any more.'

'Cracks appear,' the headline in the *NME* read. 'The future of The Libertines appears to be hanging in the balance once again.'

Pete's online writing was spontaneous, stream-of-consciousness stuff. Unfortunately, as his star had risen, more and more people were logging on for a glimpse into his mind: including his friends, family, record company – and now his manager. Alan McGee was understandably slightly concerned that this latest post was predicting a swift end to The Libertines.

The following morning Pete had a call to say McGee was worried. To compound this, Pete was on the verge of releasing the 'For Lovers' single – a song that would reaffirm what he'd been saying online, that he wanted to concentrate on his solo work and Babyshambles. If the 'For Lovers' single, released on 12 April, was the outcome, this wasn't a bad thing. Although written by Wolfman, it was not only a brilliant piece of songwriting, but a wonderfully performed and produced song that would immediately silence Pete's detractors. Anyone who thought he'd never have a life outside of The Libertines was clearly wrong.

But despite his drug problems, his love/hate relationship with Carl and his other projects, Pete was throwing himself into working on the new Libertines album. On 23 March he reported: 'One punch-up, lots of live tracks recorded, Mick dancing a lot (good sign).'

Three days later Babyshambles released their debut single on both James Mullord's indie label High Society and Rough Trade. It was a limited-edition release: 2,000 CDs and 1,000 copies on seven-inch vinyl, but that would also ensure it immediately became a collector's item.

Gigs continued with The Paddingtons and Thee Unstrung and in April a second Babyshambles single was recorded. 'Killamangiro' would prove to be a chart breakthrough that would send out a strong signal that this band was far from just a side-project.

It was also in April that Pete decided to open up the discussion board, on which he'd written so prolifically, to his fans. For almost a year the site had provided a glimpse into Pete's mind. He had revealed his thoughts, advertised last-minute gigs and used it as a forum for his poetry. Now it was essentially a free-for-all, and some readers were wondering whether that was a good idea. 'The opening of this forum leaves me with a metallic taste near my molars,' one fan wrote.

Another put it more explicitly: 'A community will develop here and if it closes up again in the morning, we will have all these beautiful missives and troubled musings from Pete, selected offerings from talented others and a bunch of dross. To which I'm now contributing.'

Nevertheless, as the forum grew – and indeed started to fill with a rather large amount of dross and lame offerings from wannabe poets – Pete continued to use it in just the same way he always had.

At the beginning of May the second Babyshambles single went through the final mixes. On first listen Pete knew 'Killamangiro' was destined to revive the British charts. Pete seemed to be flitting from one studio to another; one day working on Babyshambles, the next finishing his vocals on the new Libertines album in the studio with Carl, John, Gary and Mick Jones. Reports had been rife about the tense atmosphere between Carl and Pete but Mick Jones was quick to dispel the gossip. 'If it was as stupid as people are making out – security guards to stop them fighting and that crap – do you think I'd be mug enough to stick around and put up with it? They've grown up.'

Jones said the events of the previous year could have finished any band but that they had made The Libertines stronger – reinforcing their love for each other. Their record company, management, family and friends lived in hope that Jones was right. That summer the band had several European festival dates scheduled and an appearance at the Royal Festival Hall for the Meltdown event, curated by Pete's hero Morrissey.

Unfortunately, Jones had spoken too soon. The Babyshambles gigs of the past few months had revealed a paler, skinnier Pete Doherty, prone to unpredictable outbursts, tales of backstage fights and new, dangerous levels of drug-taking. He couldn't go twenty-four hours without a hit. It was time for him to get help.

Pete was soon back in rehab – sent to the Priory in London in a final attempt to kick his addiction. Writing on his website he revealed: 'I'm fine … they've whacked me on loads of medication. 16 different colours of pills like Hundreds & Thousands or Basset's Jelly Babies.' This idea of 'getting help' was what he would later describe as a 'shot-gun' experience. People visiting him would tell him he was doing incredibly well, encouraging him to keep it up, but he knew inside that he never could. Threats of 'it's prison or rehab' didn't make sense.

The tabloids resurrected rumours that the impromptu guerrilla gigs that Pete had organised for so long were just him 'hiring' himself out to fund his drug habit – a claim that pissed Pete off a lot.

Pete's spokesman Tony Linkin remained tight-lipped about his charge's latest visit to rehab. 'None of the other lads in the band are commenting,' he said. 'We don't know how long he'll be in the Priory.'

Carl, Gary and John, meanwhile, took up residence in the studio with Jones, putting the finishing touches to their album. But the follow-ing weekend Pete had checked himself out of the Priory. He claimed he no longer 'pined for the pipey' and was bombarded with messages from well-wishers.

'I know it's probably been harder for you than we can ever dream in a million dreams,' one wrote, 'but I know your strong spirit will show through.'

Another said: 'The Libertines with you are the most endearing, exciting and beautiful band but without are merely exciting … it is for the good and glory of the world that you get better.'

Gerry O'Boyle, manager of both the Boogaloo on the Archway Road in Highgate and of Pogues lead singer Shane MacGowan, even sent a message. 'The rewards are too great not to try and sometimes try again, keep your faith and all will be fine, steady as she goes, Good luck and God bless you,' he said.

An anonymous message read: 'You've so much to give, so many hearts and souls to affect, so many smiles yet to paint.'

Inevitably there were going to be some sections of the media at least that weren't so sympathetic. It was only a matter of time before the obvious, tedious headlines, nicked from The Libertines' debut album, would appear: 'What A Waster'. Even the *Independent* newspaper, which had championed the band from early on, had harsh words to say. 'Pete Doherty is an example of what can happen when a rock 'n' roll musician really goes off the rails,' its media editor wrote. On the cusp of international success, he claimed Pete was watching it all 'go up in smoke'.

And Pete wasn't doing much to help his cause. On 26 May a headline appeared in the *Sun*: 'Libertines Split ... Addict Pete On Why He Quit The Band.'

Pete had sold his story.

In the interview he claimed he was leaving the band and that his relationship with Carl Barât was falling to pieces. 'I feel like I'm seeking the ghost of a former friendship but Carl gave up on me years ago.' However, he evidently hadn't given up hope on The Libertines. 'If Carl comes and grabs me by the hand, maybe we can reclaim the empire together,' he said.

'I spoke to the *Sun*,' he admitted on his website afterwards. 'How much for the exclusive Doherty Junkie Thief Scum Quits Libertines With Broken Heart?' In the same brief posting, he also told his fans he had chucked his laptop in the Thames, thrown his crack pipe over the wall and buried the foil he used to chase the dragon under some earth.

For those concerned about Pete, the two Kirstys had spoken to Jackie on the phone and found out he was OK. Jackie had taken him to a clinic in France to get well and the following day the news had made the *NME* website. 'The announcement comes,' it said, 'at a time when those close to the star were getting increasingly concerned for his health.'

The Libertines had been scheduled to appear at the revival of the Rock Against Racism concert on 6 June but with Pete in rehab in France they had to pull out, and as a result, the organisers cancelled the entire event. A statement said: 'Peter is making great progress and will be home soon. The band continues to support Unite Against Fascism and Love Music, Hate Racism.'

Pete had badly wanted to play the gig. The reason he'd started a band in the first place was because it represented a feeling of community and equality. 'Any kid who's gone to a state school knows what it's all about – bullying, racism. And you've just got to make a stand,' he had said when the gig was first mooted a few months before. In the 1970s, Rock Against Racism ignited a fire within a new generation of youth. 'As well as being anti-something, you've got to be pro-something,' Pete said. 'So I'm anti-racism, pro-community.'

Despite pulling out of the concert, The Libertines, only a couple of months away from the launch of their second record, insisted they weren't splitting up. Alan McGee admitted times were not happy but that the band were still very much together. 'It's day-to-day as we are trying to make Peter well,' he said.

'They called in the heavy troops, i.e., my mum,' Pete joked. 'She gave me a good walloping and then a cuddle, took all my shoes, all my stashes of drugs.'

The *Daily Mirror* reported that *EastEnders'* star June Brown had even offered to help. Brown said she would fly Pete to a Thai monastery known as Thamkrabok to help him kick his addiction. Her godson Tim had been hooked on crack and she had set up the charity TKB to help others like him. Tim had returned clean; Thamkrabok's methods of detoxification had proved incredibly successful.

Thamkrabok has treated over 100,000 patients since it was built in the late 1950s and it is still the world's most extreme drugs rehabilitation programme. Every year hundreds of young people – mostly Thais – arrive at this remote outpost in the hills of Thailand to go through a gruelling system of detox. Seventy per cent stay off drugs for good. Forty per cent of the monks are themselves former addicts. Patients swallow a glass full of a herbal concoction made from seeds, leaves and bark, which forces them to vomit into concrete gutters in the monastery compound. Drinking large amounts of water afterwards helps purge the body of all the impurities. The dorm rooms are sparse: just a single bed and blanket, cold tiled floors and a patchy mosquito net. Mobile phones are forbidden, and at Thamkrabok there are no second chances: once you leave, that's it.

Much to Jackie's delight, Pete agreed he would give it a try. 'Part of me will never be coming back,' he said the morning of his departure on 8 June. 'I want to live, and want to be fit for the second album's airing. I saw Mick Jones, Carl, John and Gary last night and I know I can mangle out all the creases and live out further my grandly Arcadian dreams and dear divine adventures.'

'If he's going to get clean permanently anywhere it's in this place,' McGee said. 'To say we all jumped for joy last night when his escort texted me and said they were on the plane and all systems were go would be the understatement of this year. He may even reject the West and not return. Who knows? All I hope for is he kills his demons and gets better.'

Inevitably, with Pete in Thailand battling his demons, The Libertines were forced to pull out of festivals scheduled for June. They cancelled their appearance at Meltdown, The Isle of Wight Festival and Glastonbury. 'It has obviously been a very painful period for the band and we wish Peter better more than anything,' a statement said.

Pete later described his lumpy mattress; the whir of the fan in his tiny cell-like room; the 'prison camp aesthetics' of the monastery; his vivid dreams of bats and smoking crack. 'Fifty pence a gramme of heroin in the north of Thailand,' he said. 'Gulp.'

He met a man called Lee who was positive about his new life free from drugs. Pete wondered whether he had it in him to achieve the same thing. He knew there were cold sweats and painful withdrawal ahead and deep down he knew he couldn't hack it. He knew he'd leave this place: it was just a matter of when and how.

The day would begin with a swim as the early morning Thai sun beat down on his body. 'The vomiting was relentless,' he wrote. 'The thick muddy medicine followed by a bucket of water and then it all comes up through the nose and the eyes. I wanted to come home so badly.'

Pete had a breakdown at Thamkrabok. The next day he demanded his bag, wallet and passport, and left for Bangkok.

On the evening of 13 June Pete was in the heart of the city. He'd found a shabby Internet café and logged on to the discussion board. What he wrote hardly made any sense: 'Bangkokfill; thy lust in the shadows swaddled then in still why? only because you don't want to know reversing blunt time's sudden change of face.'

But it was obvious to everyone he wasn't in the monastery any longer. The following day the press carried the story: 'Pete flees rehab'.

A swiftly written statement from Thamkrabok read: 'Having vowed to senior Monks "never to take drugs ever again" upon registration, Peter refused to take even his third dose of medication, and has finally today rejected the sensitive and compassionate care offered by the Nuns and the Monks there.'

Phra Hans, a spiritual counsellor working there, said he was unwilling or unable to let go of his dark side.

On 18 June, Pete flew back to London.

A day later he was sitting in a police cell.

'[Babyshambles are] good enough to make me want to not take crack. There's never been a band good enough to make me give up crack. Babyshambles are better than crack.'

PETE DOHERTY

ELEVEN

THE LAST POST

Just hours after he'd stepped off the plane, Pete was pulled over on the Hackney Road for a suspected driving offence, asked to step out of the car and searched. It was then that they found the flick-knife.

As if things couldn't get any worse, he was arrested, charged with possession of an offensive weapon, driving without a licence, without insurance and dangerously, and was duly sent a date to appear in court. After the ordeal he'd just been through in Thailand, this wasn't the best day Pete could have had.

Pete had been on his way to see one of the Kirstys, who was ill in bed with the flu, when he was 'rudely interrupted by our friends in uniform' as he later put it. His early return from Thailand meant all eyes would be focused on him. Had he 'recovered' enough to continue with his music career? Had the drugs beaten him? The press were desperate for the next chapter in Pete's soap-opera life and happily reported this latest instalment.

In truth the answer was that he hadn't recovered, and to some extent the drugs had beaten him. Pete had had no idea what he was letting himself in for in Thailand, and the few days he was there were some of the toughest he'd ever had to endure.

When he left the monastery he headed straight to Bangkok and into a world of cheap drugs and temptation. He was offered heroin in the hotel he was staying in, splashing out £300 in three days – considerably less than he'd have paid in England, but by Thai standards a fortune.

Back in London he threw himself into rehearsals with Babyshambles, contacted Carl and said he'd do anything to help promote the new Libertines album. 'I'm healthier and more together,' he insisted. 'Maybe we can do the festivals after all.'

He had also become friends with the Scottish singer Dot Allison – former frontwoman of ethereal dance act One Dove, and a one-time vocalist in Massive Attack. The pair had talked of a collaboration and an acoustic tour at the end of July. 'I think he is a very competent musician and we have a common love of music and can empathise with each other musically,' Allison said. Pete's fans also began to suspect a romantic link.

But returning from rehab in Thailand early and now with another court case looming did not impress the rest of The Libertines, who had had enough. Gary, John and Carl decided to resume their touring commitments without Pete. A statement said it was with regret they had to make the announcement, but blamed his 'well-known addiction problems, specifically with crack cocaine and heroin'.

Carl said Pete would always be a Libertine and when he cleaned up he would be welcomed back with open arms. It was a tough decision to make, but Carl said the band had come to the conclusion after three failed rehab attempts, 'all of which the Libertines have funded'. He also said Pete's 'erratic mental state' worried the band and that the pressure of touring would add to his problems.

It was a huge blow to Pete. He felt ready for the festivals. Shortly after Carl and the rest of the lads had announced he was officially out of the band, they confirmed they would be playing both T in the Park and the Oxygen Festival in Dublin in July. Pete desperately wanted to go.

Worse still, there was speculation he would play no part in the promotional campaign for the new Libertines album, and to compound his misery, the tabloids were about to step their coverage of his plight up a notch. The *Sunday Mirror* announced that his 'friends' had claimed he was back on drugs and would die unless he got urgent help. It also said he had begun selling song lyrics in exchange for £150 fixes of heroin.

Even Razorlight's Johnny Borrell threw his twopenn'orth in: 'It's hard to talk about Pete because I've known him for eight years so I know him as the person, not the caricature,' he told one paper. 'When it comes to drugs and stuff I got all that out of my system years ago. It's just boring.'

Perhaps a little contentiously, considering Pete's now widely publicised dalliances with hard drugs, the *Observer* ran a story earmarking eighty young people it believed would shape our lives in the early twenty-first century. It had published a similar list in 1979, and many of the people on which it had taken a punt had gone on to become household names. Twenty-five years on, Pete Doherty found himself sandwiched between scientists, novelists and architects, actors such as Chiwetel Ejiofor and politicians such as David Cameron.

'The last real rock and roller?' the *Observer* asked. 'Unlike other contemporary bad boys, he has the talent to match his personal troubles.'

Dressed in a grey suit and accompanied by Alan McGee, Pete was early for his appointment with the beak at Thames Magistrates' Court at the end of June. That morning he pleaded not guilty to possessing an offensive weapon and the case was adjourned for a pre-trial hearing on 10 August.

Shortly afterwards, in an interview with the *Sunday Mirror*, Pete vocalised what everyone around him had been thinking – that for him, rehab programmes tucked away in the middle of nowhere just didn't work. A mountaintop in Thailand wasn't going to help.

Pete knew that if he was to get clean he would have to do it in the world that engulfed him. 'I am always going to be surrounded by drugs when I'm making music,' he said. 'I've just got to find the inner strength to control it.' He also insisted he didn't take enough drugs to kill him. 'It isn't drugs that I need to get rid of,' he told one reporter. 'It's the demons that fill my head.'

Pete's mum Jackie was distraught. Her son was such an intelligent boy and had made her so proud, not just at school while he was growing up, but also when his band had first signed to Rough Trade. To see him on such a downward spiral was heartbreaking; she felt he was throwing it all away. And as if the truth wasn't bad enough, the tabloids had also begun exaggerating the story and compounding the family's problems. One thing was sure, she would always be there for him.

Carl publicly voiced his support for Pete, too, saying the band missed him and were willing him to get better, but The Libertines had already begun to rehearse with a new guitarist, Anthony Rossomando.

T in the Park was the first Libertines gig without Pete since he'd been to Thailand and the huge audience seemed to be showing their support to the remaining members, encouraged perhaps by Carl who dedicated the first song to his 'best friend, Peter'.

Just one month away from the release of the new Libertines album, it was announced Pete wouldn't be involved in the touring or promotion for the record. Clare Britt, head of marketing at Rough Trade

Records, told *Music Week* that Pete's difficulties had complicated the album's launch. 'It can be challenging,' she said, 'but many great artists are unpredictable. That's part of what makes them special.'

Pete was understandably upset that The Libertines had vowed to continue without him. He didn't think they had any right to play T In the Park if he wasn't in the band, and that as a result he could never go back. And his relationship with Carl was a mess. He also denounced suggestions in some sections of the media that he was spending £1,000 a day on drugs. 'You can't take that much heroin,' he said. 'You'll die.'

Admitting to a drug problem was hard enough. Add to that the impact it had on his family – and now the jeopardy in which it had put his place in The Libertines. But the media in Britain were intrigued by Pete, the 'junkie rock star', and they seemed intent on twisting the knife.

The trouble was that the pressure of the press was relentless. At the end of July, Pete's old flame Katie Lewis sold her story to the *Daily Mirror*, claiming he had encouraged her to take crack and heroin. 'We were young romantics and would write each other poetry,' she told the paper, adding that one night after a drug binge Pete had slashed both their arms with a razor blade and was 'out of control'.

ON 24 July NME photographer Roger Sargent, who had known and photographed The Libertines since 2002, launched an exhibition of 150 photographs of the band at Camden's Proud Galleries. Just a week before, he had taken some of the final pictures for the show including one of Pete standing alone under a railway arch near Brick Lane. One journalist described it as a 'fitting image of isolation'.

The exhibition, entitled 'The Boys In The Band', included a picture of The Libertines taken at their first ever photo shoot – on Pete's bed at the Albion Rooms in Bethnal Green Sargent said, 'Their flat looked like it was styled by Mötley Crüe,' The images included the infamous 'red military jackets shoot' that produced that iconic image, so synonymous with The Libertines.

Pete had agreed to perform at the opening of the exhibition. Tom Green was responsible for PRing the event, and before the show he challenged Pete to a game of pool. 'I was upstairs in the office when Pete turned up with his cronies,' he recalls. 'We had a pool table up there and Pete was drinking JD and smoking a cigarette. I asked if anyone wanted a game and Pete volunteered. I beat him twice; he potted the black the second time. We had a chat about music and he said he was really into ska. I told him I liked Radiohead and he said he'd never heard their album *The Bends*.

'Every so often Pete would nip into the kitchen to do a line of coke. He asked me what I did for a living but he didn't have a particularly large attention span.

'After the game of pool he disappeared into the kitchen for an interview. This journalist was holding a mic to his face and Pete kept turning away, mumbling and taking a drag of his cigarette. I think the guy was annoyed he couldn't hear anything Pete was saying.

'Just before the gig Pete went into the lift to go downstairs to the gallery and I don't think he knew I was inside. As he came in he said, "I can't believe it, the bloody PR guy beat me at pool." I was quite chuffed about that.'

Pete came on stage wearing a retro brown suit and his trademark pork-pie hat. A cigarette hung out the corner of his mouth. 'It was like a garage gig,' Green recalls. 'Just Pete and a drummer, and he seemed a little bewildered by it all; everyone wanted to meet him.'

Pete strummed his way through a half-hour set, playing classics 'What A Waster', 'Don't Look Back Into The Sun' and 'Boys In The Band', but throwing in surprises like a cover of 'Always Something There To Remind Me'.

But the biggest surprise of the evening was when he welcomed Gary on stage halfway through to provide handclaps on 'Don't Be Shy'. It was a show of solidarity that had some of the audience in tears.

'The quality of the music wasn't brilliant,' Green says, 'but people still loved it.'

Christian Livingstone, guitarist from New Zealand rock band The Datsuns, was also in the audience that night.

'The organisers set up a marquee out the back of the gallery,' he remembers. 'The stage was in there and the tent could only hold 200 people but it was just rammed: there must have been 300 people and there was a huge line stretching around the corner. People were squashed in like cattle, downing tequilas and Cokes.

'I was hanging around talking to people behind the marquee when Pete turned up. It was way past his stage time and he was off his tree – on who knows what. I sat on the side of the stage. Everybody was going nuts; it was like Beatlemania. I've honestly never seen anything like that sort of pandemonium up close. Playing Japan with The Datsuns was the closest thing I've ever come to it. But this was different. There were people crying – and not just the girls. They were hysterical. I just didn't realise that level of adulation existed. Everyone was trying to get on the stage and he was just being Pete. He stood there for a few minutes while his roadie was plugging his mic in, just wandering round the stage, smoking a cigarette, and people were going wild – he didn't have to *do* anything.'

Livingstone says Pete played some Libertines songs and introduced some new numbers, then sat on the front of the stage and lurched shambolically through a few more. After that he broke a string, which it took his roadie fifteen minutes to change. Meanwhile, the crowd continued screaming as if he was still playing. 'If it was anyone else, they would have got pissed off and left or gone to the bar,' Livingstone says. 'But their enthusiasm didn't diminish.'

In between each song Pete would yell 'stage invasion' and watch as everyone attempted to jump on. The security guards tried to drag them off but in the end the stage was crowded with people singing and jumping up and down, hanging on to Pete. 'There was such devotion to him,' Livingstone says.

'The Libertines and Babyshambles songs are so English and that's something their fans can identify with. The tabloids want to know everything about Pete – more so than musicians from other countries. He's a brilliant career strategist without even realising it. People are fascinated by him; they don't want to look but they can't look away. When is he going to destroy himself? Is it going to be this gig? When is he going to implode? But that's part of the appeal and to some extent I think he plays up to that. Other stars do lead excessive lives but Pete does all of it in the public eye and he's done that right from the get-go. I don't think you can maintain that sort of self-destructive behaviour unless that's really who you are.'

One day, during a tour of Australia in 2004, The Datsuns had been preparing to go live on air for a radio interview when the DJ told them he'd had The Libertines in the studio a few days before. 'Apparently Carl was completely out of it,' Livingstone says, 'so much so that just before the interview their tour manager was giving him shots of whiskey to perk him up; he thought it would somehow make him coherent enough to get through it. But it was ironic considering Pete had been told not to come on the tour because he was so "out of it". The show was being pre-recorded to air the following day and the DJ told the band: "We're going to talk to you as if the show's tonight," and The Libertines were saying "The show's tonight?" They had no idea what day of the week it was.'

But Livingstone says drugs and alcohol can be a by-product of fame. 'Before you make it there's a good chance you're probably broke, on the dole and can't afford to be self-destructive. It's a lot easier once you've got a record deal. You don't even have to worry about getting up in the morning – someone else will get you up and throw you on the tour bus. If you were into drugs or alcohol before, being in a band just accelerates and exaggerates that.'

The Libertines were still touring as July drew to a close. Pete felt his old bandmates were rubbing it in his face, particularly when they performed at Carl's new club night Dirty Pretty Things in London with the Charlatans' Tim Burgess and Har Mar Superstar stepping in for guest appearances.

With Pete and Carl's relationship in tatters, it was a case of wishful thinking when Gary said in an interview he'd prefer it if the press concentrated on the music. It was far too late for that.

Gary also admitted that jealousy had possibly entered into the equation; The Libertines wanted to play with Pete again, but they also wanted Pete to want to rejoin them. But while Pete resented Carl for effectively throwing him out of The Libertines, he seemed to be enjoying playing in Babyshambles and working on solo projects – something that must have irked Carl.

'Pete likes to have a lot of control, so he needs his own project,' Carl said. 'On a more negative note, everyone [around Babyshambles] is more tolerant of his drug abuse.'

Pete thought Carl was selling out. He didn't see anything wrong with playing venues like the Forum one day and a spur-of-the-moment show in his flat the next. One thing he didn't want to do was go on the road for a year to America to promote an album. 'Carl wants to sell a million records,' Pete said. 'Good luck to him.'

While Carl and the rest of the band were gearing up to tour the new album and meet all their press and promotional commitments, Pete was the one making all the headlines. In Glasgow he provoked a small riot when he leapt behind the bar of the Stereo club mid-gig and handed out free beer to his fans. It was funny – and the story made the music press – but he was becoming more and more erratic. On 3 August Babyshambles were due to play at the Camden Monarch. Pete turned up at 11pm but the doorman refused entry to his guitar technician, and as a result, Pete refused to play. Not to be deterred, he then headed home to his flat and put on an impromptu show for eighty of his fans that drifted on into the early hours.

'I let them write on the walls, put on records, flick through books, make cups of tea,' he said. The next day Pete explained the events of the previous night and apologised, but of the fans who didn't get to see him perform, many were disillusioned.

The following night he was due to play at the King's Cross Scala, supporting his friend Wolfman, who was celebrating his birthday. Again Pete failed to turn up and the Wolf was left to placate a rather irritated crowd, who began screaming 'Where's Pete?' after each number.

This time Pete was furious. 'I apologise to all those who lost out,' he wrote on his website, 'but given some of the reactions, I'm glad that a few of you have been inconvenienced. In fact, I'll eek [sic] out all of the gits until I can be sure I'm playing to a crowd who trust me, believe in me, and don't turn on me at the first chance they get. You want clockwork, amoral live music? There's plenty of that about.'

The media circus went into overdrive in the run-up to the launch of the new Libertines album. The column inches Pete alone was ratcheting up were incredible. Stories such as a 'blood-spattered drumskin' for sale on eBay, used by Gary at a Libertines' gig in 2002, and Pete's 'love child' with Lisa Moorish (Astile had just been 'outed' by the press). Pete even made the *NME* news columns simply for *turning up* for a gig in Bristol.

The *Independent* said The Libertines were 'Britain's most talked about rock band – but for all the wrong reasons' and that the pictures of Pete that had been appearing in the music press revealed a 'stick thin, boggle-eyed and swollen-faced' singer, 'his boyish good looks twisted into an unsettling, doll-like puffiness'.

The Dotmusic website carried an interview with Carl that revealed just how much his relationship with Pete had soured. Asked whether any new band photos were planned, he said, 'Probably not with Peter at the moment.' The last time the pair had spoken was before Pete had reluctantly got on the plane to Bangkok. 'Does he hang out with a bad crowd?' Carl was asked. 'In my opinion, yeah, but I don't really wanna talk about it,' came the response.

Finally he said he couldn't see The Libertines writing or recording another album unless Pete sorted himself out. Ironically, a week later the band's single 'Can't Stand Me Now' – documenting Carl and Pete's fractured relationship – entered the charts at number two. It was their biggest ever hit.

Meanwhile the line-up of Babyshambles, fairly fluid up until now, had finally taken shape, with Patrick Walden on guitar, Drew

McConnell on bass – both from the rock band White Sport – and Gemma Clarke on drums.

Pete's court appearance for possession of the flick-knife came round quickly enough. He was warned that due to his previous form he faced another prison sentence. The case was adjourned until 1 September but one magistrate emphasised that a custodial sentence couldn't be ruled out. Pete was petrified. There was no way he could stand another stint inside.

A few days before the launch of the new album, Pete was attacked by thugs in east London. He had been walking along the road with a friend when a man in a baseball cap recognised him and began shouting abuse. 'He called me a crackhead,' Pete recalls, 'and said he was going to break my nose and stick a knife in my neck.'

In an attempt to get away, Pete ran across the road but was hit by a car. Luckily it wasn't very hard, but by this point he was on the floor and his assailant had begun to kick him in the head. His ears throbbing, Pete climbed onto his feet and managed to flag down the nearest car and make his escape.

The album was finally released on 30 August but fans had been able to download it two weeks before after someone with access to an early copy put it on the Internet. Illegal downloading was becoming a problem for record companies. It didn't worry Pete.

As for the tracklisting, Carl said 'Can't Stand Me Now' was the most self-explanatory song in pop after 'What A Waster'. 'Arbeit Macht Frei' translates as 'work liberates', he said, and was inscribed above the gates at Auschwitz. 'It's an adage to a benchmark of ironic hypocrisy,' he said. In 'The Saga', the *NME* said Pete spun a tale of lies and self-deceit in what it termed the 'album's most harrowing moment'.

ON 1 September Pete arrived outside court an hour early, perched himself on the top of a car and began playing his guitar to the ensemble of journalists gathered to faithfully report his fate. Once inside the courtroom, Pete awaited that same fate patiently, albeit nervously.

Judge Malcolm Reid told Pete he thought he was a successful, intelligent young man. 'Knives,' he said, 'are only made for one reason.'

Pete put his face in his hands as the judge deemed him unsuitable for a community service penalty and sentenced him to four months in prison. He looked up in disbelief as the judge continued: 'But the sentence will be suspended for twelve months. Consider yourself fortunate.' This meant that as long as Pete didn't get into trouble with the law for a year, he wouldn't be going back to prison.

The contrast couldn't have been more striking. On 5 September, just four days after Pete had escaped a prison sentence by the skin of his teeth, The Libertines' second album entered the UK charts at number one.

Shortly afterwards Pete announced another Babyshambles tour, this time with eighteen UK dates.

In Liverpool Dot Allison joined Babyshambles on stage for a rendition of 'I Wanna Break Your Heart', which had appeared on the Internet as an unreleased demo. The band finished with 'Wolfman' – a song Pete had written in tribute to his friend, an intense, howling Doors-esque jam that worked the audience into a frenzy as Pete hugged the mic, swearing and staring out into the crowd. This was what he lived for. It was worth all the pain he'd been through.

In Aberdeen the police were called after 500 fans surrounded the band's tour bus to stop it leaving after they failed to appear on stage. Grampian police later issued a statement saying the gig was cancelled due to a 'problem' with Pete.

Meanwhile, The Libertines were on a tour of the US to promote the new album. Carl said he was only continuing with the band because he was sure what he was doing was right.

Back in London Babyshambles began demoing new songs at Odessa studios in Clapton, working for twenty hours solid. Pete said he hoped that by the end of September they would have 'the foundations of a great album'. Their new single 'Killamangiro' was earmarked for a November release, and in what must have been a huge blow to Carl, Babyshambles were about to make the hallowed cover of the *NME*. As if that wasn't enough, the *Guardian* decided that 'without Pete, The Libertines have lost their mojo'.

Finally, as Babyshambles announced a headline gig at the London Forum on 13 December, the inevitable happened. The *NME*, which had championed the band since 2002, was forced to report that Carl was to 'retire' The Libertines from playing live for the 'foreseeable future'. He told the magazine it was due to 'an ongoing problem' with his health, but everybody knew there was more to it. The band just wasn't the same without Pete. Carl said he still loved his friend and hoped he would return after combating his drug problems to take on the world with The Libertines 'and put the *Albion* back on course'. But reconciliation looked unlikely.

Although intent on taking Babyshambles to the top, Pete's health was suffering. One journalist noted his eyes were pink, his voice husky. 'There are open sores around his lips,' he said. 'His teeth are ruined.' Some of this, of course, could be attributed to heavy drug use. But a 26-date tour with little sleep didn't help either.

Inspired by Pete's success with Babyshambles, Carl also wanted to do something different. He had written a lot of songs and wondered whether he should start a new band as well. He went into the studio with the electronica duo Client, co-writing their single 'Pornography', and Alan McGee revealed that fans could expect a 'great Carl Barât solo album' some time in late 2005.

Pete's professional relationship with McGee had petered out after his permanent split from The Libertines. He felt the manager had put the band on a conveyor belt of touring and promotion. Instead, Pete had teamed up with James Mullord, a like-minded impresario who ran 1234 Records from a small office in London. Mullord had already issued the seven-inch release of the first Babyshambles single. He had the contacts in the industry, but most importantly he was passionate about the band and saw Pete as a poet and a genius. Pete thought he'd make a fine manager.

In late November Pete joined former Blur guitarist Graham Coxon on stage at his gig at the Forum to play 'Time For Heroes'. It was as if Carl and Pete's infamous on-stage battle for the mic and much-publicised bickering was to continue even when they were miles apart. Although not a conscious one, there remained a battle of wills: whose solo project would be the more successful; who could notch up the most successful collaborations.

But if journalists had written Babyshambles off with throwaway headlines using the last two syllables of the band's name, it was all a bit premature. Towards the end of 2004 Babyshambles had become a force to be reckoned with and boasted more than a few hit songs in their arsenal, including the anthemic 'Fuck Forever' and Jam-esque 'Killamangiro'. 'Logic would dictate that Doherty was finished without The Libertines,' one journalist wrote. 'Now it seems the reverse is likely.'

Pete claimed he wouldn't even play live with Babyshambles unless it bettered anything he'd ever done previously. In order to exist, he thought, Babyshambles needed to be better than The Libertines – an almost impossible task. Unfortunately, while the songs the band had recorded were good, live they were hit-and-miss back in 2004. In December Pete had to be forcibly pulled off the stage at the Empress Ballroom in Blackpool after he started forgetting songs and had trouble standing up straight. Babyshambles were scheduled to play two gigs in a row that night and headed straight to the Zanzibar club in Liverpool where fans said the performance was just as bad. Back in London Pete started a fight with a member of the audience while filming *Top Of The Pops* at the BBC's studios in White City.

Three days later, without their unpredictable frontman, The Libertines played their last ever gig – an hour-long set in front of a crowd of 350 fans in Saint-Denis, northern Paris, the location kept secret until the last minute. The gig was tinged with sadness as rumours that the crowd were witnessing the end of The Libertines quickly spread through the venue. Carl, Gary and John put the smiles back on their faces as they ploughed their way magnificently through hits from both albums, ending on 'Boys In The Band' and 'I Get Along'. It was a noble exit.

But as The Libertines came to a dignified end in Paris, Pete failed to show up to a Babyshambles gig at the Astoria in Charing Cross Road, sparking a riot by 200 of the crowd who had waited until two in the morning to see them.

Pete's new manager James Mullord concluded: 'Pete is unmanage-able ... you cannot coerce him into doing anything he doesn't want to do. He is totally a free spirit.'

Connor McNicholas, the editor of the *NME* – a magazine that had stood by Pete and The Libertines for so long – was worried that the Astoria gig could have marked a turning point. It was difficult to see where Pete would go next, he said. 'God willing, he will sprinkle his magic for years to come.'

But he would need convincing.

TWELVE

THE ROAD TO EXCESS

Pete was adamant he would never glamorise drugs. He even went on record saying that crack and heroin were an 'epidemic'. He also said he thought drugs could ruin some people's lives but dramatically improve others. 'Anything that's going to move them from the fucking middling state they're in,' he said. Either way, drugs had become inextricably bound up in Pete Doherty's own myth.

This wasn't new. Drugs had been linked with popular music for decades; drug use could be traced back through the years to the seedy jazz clubs of 1930s America. In his book *Waiting For The Man*, author Harry Shapiro says that drugs developed their own air of mystery, encompassed in the 'outlaw myth' of the wandering musicians of the 1930s and 1940s. One jazz artist said the reason musicians got into drugs so heavily back then was to get closer to each other; it was an intimate form of communication. 'And at that time, shooting up seemed the best way to do this,' he said.

In the 1940s, just like in the hedonistic 1960s, doing heroin symbolised the move away from the 'straight' world to the 'hip'. In the words of author Paul Willis, writing in *Resistance Through Rituals*, once you'd taken heroin you had 'burnt your boats and could not return'. The dangers of the drug were widely known, but in the world of hipsters who took it for their art there was no fear. If anything, the sheer revulsion with which mainstream society regarded heroin only served to improve its image as a conduit for travelling as quickly as possible to the margins of society – a place hipsters were quite content to be. According to Shapiro this confirmed the status of black musicians who, being black, were already on the margins of society. And if, for black musicians, taking heroin represented the move as far away from white society as they could get, for white musicians it symbolised the flight towards black society.

Shapiro adds that back in the 1940s it was common knowledge that if you wanted to find the best band you had to go to the Public Health Service hospitals at Lexington and Fort Worth, 'where many narcotics offenders were sent, supposedly to clean up'.

Twenty years later, while in drugs terms the dawning of rock 'n' roll was associated with speed, marijuana and – later in the decade – LSD, if you were a serious rocker you'd get obliterated on the heavy stuff: opiates. In his book *The Triumph of Vulgarity*, Robert Pattison says speed, cocaine and hallucinogens may have sufficed as 'an appetiser or side dish', but the 'main course on the menu of rock mythology is likely to consist of narcotics, the drugs that obliterate consciousness'.

Pattison says the premier drugs were morphine, opium and heroin. And heroin was the drug of choice for far more musicians than most people think: from jazz musician Miles Davis, singer Billie Holiday and sax player Charlie Parker (a life-long heroin addict), to David Bowie and Jerry Garcia of the Grateful Dead (who most people think just smoked pot and dropped acid), and, famously, Kurt Cobain.

The drug was immortalised in song too. From the obvious – The Velvet Underground's 'Heroin', The Rolling Stones' 'Sister Morphine' and a line from The Mamas And The Papas about being a straight-shooter – to the songs that were probably lost on anyone over thirty: The Stranglers' 'Golden Brown' and Lou Reed's 'Perfect Day' in which he claimed drugs made him forget himself.

In 1967 the BBC even banned The Beatles' 'A Day In The Life' from the airwaves, claiming it contained explicit drug references. Two years later concern over allusions to drugs in an album by Jefferson Airplane caused their record company to delay its release (the band simply left the label and formed their own). In 1970 MGM Records cancelled the contracts of almost twenty of their stars because they believed they were promoting hard drugs in their songs; in the same year President Nixon called for all songs that referenced drugs to be outlawed.

Times haven't changed much. A recent American survey found that 20 per cent of pop songs referenced illegal drugs. At a high school in St Louis, a school band was forbidden from playing the Jefferson Airplane hit 'White Rabbit' because of drug references. This was in 2005 – 38 years after the song's release, and despite the school band's version being entirely instrumental. Drugs – even soft drugs – are still seen as a blight on society. In the mainstream media there is rarely a distinction made between recreational use and addiction; they are one and the same. Drugs of all varieties have gone hand in hand with rock 'n' roll since its inception. That's not to say there shouldn't be legislation but there is seldom any debate when it comes to disparaging anyone who has used drugs, be it cannabis, ecstasy or crack. The *Daily Mail* runs headlines like 'Experimenting with cannabis led teenager into a tragic decline', 'Cannabis-dealing shame of a maths teacher's son', 'Smoking cannabis could kill 30,000 people a year', and 'Extra-strong cannabis is putting the young at risk'.

According to Paul Willis, back in the 1960s heroin was as far removed from acid as acid was from marijuana. He says heroin wasn't talked about much on the scene. 'If you were using it, even occasionally, only your closest associates would know.' Heroin is still one of the most effective painkillers ever made and it makes the user feel detached; some people says it's similar to being wrapped in a ball of cotton wool – a safety blanket from the outside world. With this in mind, Willis says it gives users a feeling of indestructibility; that nothing can harm them when they're high – even being arrested.

So although the 'establishment' in the form of the British tabloid press likes to portray Pete as a pariah figure, what he's doing isn't new. In the 1960s there was pot and acid; in the 1970s punks wanted drugs that gave them energy: glue-sniffing, amphetamines; in the late 1980s and early 1990s it was ecstasy. But throughout – from the opium dens of the late nineteenth century and the dark, smoky jazz clubs of 1940s Chicago to the 1960s rock 'n' roll counterculture, Sid Vicious and beyond, heroin has always been the ultimate narcotic. Pete Doherty is simply perpetuating a legacy of 'doomed intoxication'.

Towards the close of 2004 Carl believed Pete was being led astray by crackheads and hangers-on. 'Bad people,' he said. Some of Pete's friends, however, were keen to romanticise his predicament: he was a poet experiencing the 'other side'.

James Mullord, who was managing Babyshambles by this point, said the more people claiming Pete was heading down the wrong path, the more successful he was to become. 'He's the anti-hero, the outlaw,' he said. 'Pete is real. He's living it. People ask if it's a stunt. That's Pete's life.' But Mullord wanted to see Pete get clean; he claimed he was a happier person when sober.

Pete's booking agent Matt Bates has said Pete would rather see his drugs go than his guitar but adds that history has shown us there have always been wonderful musicians who happen to be drug users. 'He's not destined to die just because he's a heroin addict,' Bates said.

For his own part, Pete doesn't see that it's anyone else's business what he does. 'When they see an individual who's free they can't deal with it,' he says. 'I wouldn't encourage anyone either way. Choose your own path. But tread carefully on this drifting ice.'

The fact remains that by the end of 2004, drugs had driven a wedge not just between Pete and The Libertines, but between Pete and his family and Pete and his friends. Again, history could have taught him a lot. Jazz musician Art Pepper claimed to have lost the love of his family due to his heroin addiction; he committed robberies and notched up a criminal record. 'I was terrified and completely alone,' he once said.

A distance developed between Pete and his father because of his increasing drug use, but Jackie, although clearly worried about her son, was there for him and wanted to help. Through the hype, the distorted press reports and the pain of watching someone plunge into the depths of despair as his addiction took hold, was her son. Even when he was in a really bad way, Jackie said Pete would cling to a copy of Bertolt Brecht or Shakespeare's sonnets; that however messed up he was, he'd always have a book.

But while she could still see Pete and not a 'junkie rock star' standing in front of her, there was no denying that Pete's drug-taking only served to bolster the myth of Pete Doherty, Romantic Troubadour. His fans, the media, in fact anyone who wanted, to could live their life vicariously through Pete. He could live this excessive rock 'n' roll lifestyle and we could read about it, watch it and immerse ourselves in it. And it was fascinating.

There has always been something mesmerising about the rock star who burns out rather than fades into obscurity. In their song 'Live Fast, Die Young' Los Angeles punk band The Circle Jerks didn't want to reach the age of 34. Just over thirty years before them, The Who were hoping they died before they got old.

In 1979 Neil Young wrote 'My My, Hey Hey', which dealt generally with the fleeting nature of fame and perhaps specifically with Sid Vicious's self-destruction. Later, in another nod to romantic fatalism, Kurt Cobain's suicide note contained the line: 'It's better to burn out than to fade away.' The one thing that perhaps the tabloids, the music press and Pete Doherty's fans share is a belief (harboured secretly in some cases) that he too is on this path to self-annihilation.

In song Pete claimed he couldn't tell the difference between death and glory and some people think he meant it literally. In a random posting on his website he said you should defend your own liberty to the death. 'Death,' he said, was 'the ultimate liberty'.

Back in the heady days of 2002, just when it was all beginning (or ending, depending on which way you look at it) for The Libertines, the *NME* asked Pete: 'Do you see a glorious and illustrious career ahead?' Pete replied: 'Personally I think two of us will be dead by Christmas.' He was joking, of course; this was followed by an inane comment about ghosts having good voices, but in view of what happened later – the path his life took in the years that followed – one could be forgiven for thinking it was strangely ominous.

In some quarters, however, not everyone was buying into the notion of Pete as a romantic figure just following in the footsteps of a long line of rock 'n' roll icons.

Artrocker, the underground website and magazine devoted to rock 'n' roll, was bemoaning the demise of the London rock scene. 'What has happened to make it so unappealing?' an editorial asked. 'Decadence,' it concluded. *Artrocker* claimed the city had fallen prey to 'poseurs who piss on the music in favour of column inches ... who think that Sid Vicious is the rock and role model de jour'. Vicious, it said, was simply an idiot with an addiction and no musical talent. And it blamed it all on 'orgies of cocaine' in which young London bands were indulging, and on their obsession with celebrity.

It was a fair point. Bands that appeared in The Libertines' wake seemed to be just poseurs. They tried the guerrilla gigging that Pete had pioneered, they had the swagger and the attitude, they'd attempted the drugs. But they just didn't have the intelligence to galvanise a generation like Pete did. Pete was an enigma, a one-off. He didn't look up to Sid Vicious's pompous attempt at self-immolation. Pete didn't want to rip off the attitude and ideology of musicians who had gone before him just so he could improve his currency as a rock star. He understood what some of these romantic figures had been through, how they ticked. He shared the same belief system, which meant that when he took drugs it was for himself, not to further his career.

Indeed the *Observer* published a comment piece about Pete headed: 'Annihilation beckons the dark star of rock'. He was, it said, 'spiralling towards the classic rock 'n' roll ending ... hurtling headlong toward self-annihilation'. It quoted Tony Gaskin, general manager of Filthy McNasty's, as saying Pete was 'fascinated by the dark side', and that he wondered whether The Libertines' huge fan base was due to the fact they went to every gig as if it was the last – that Pete could have 'popped his clogs' before the next time.

The paper also quoted a 'source' as saying The Libertines' second album would stand as a 'testament to what they could have done and what they might have been'. Anthony Thornton, the *NME*'s reviews editor, said Pete had hit depths he didn't even know existed.

Katie Lewis, who sold the story about her relationship with Pete to a tabloid, said he had devastated his family and that he was 'reduced to scrabbling around for cash for his next hit'.

Interestingly, producer Simon Bourcier thinks Pete has been encouraged to be too wild. 'And the wildness – the demon – has almost overpowered the person as opposed to the person controlling the demon,' he says. 'Pete has an incredibly creative mind. He's an intelligent guy who has a good spirit and a good heart, but he has been encouraged to be more dangerous than is good for him. These "businessmen" behind his career are probably thinking: Well, if we let this guy do loads of drugs he's going to get in the press and then hopefully we'll sell some records. They're thinking it's like The Sex Pistols with Malcolm McLaren, but let's not forget that McLaren was a fucking clever guy who knew how to capitalise on every situation moments after it happened. These guys just let it happen and hope for the best. And that's the trouble.

'It's a shame he's being taken down a dusty road where other people's egos are influencing the situation. Pete is a naive minstrel who is listening to these people because he admires and respects what they've done. But ultimately he is better than they are.'

Bourcier also claims that in the past Pete has been paid cash at certain times in his career, which he says is a deliberate attempt to encourage him to spend it on drugs. 'What's he going to do with that cash advance?' he says. 'These people are fucking arseholes. They're just thinking headlines.'

Could it be that somewhere along his career trajectory Pete has actually been encouraged to be decadent? At some point did someone who held any sway over his recording career actually think that the drugs and excess could be used as some warped marketing tool, his own addiction exploited for commercial ends?

'Thank goodness for Pete Doherty – that he has the talent to be able to not give a shit *and* make a difference,' Bourcier says. 'I'm not interested in what the press is saying because frankly that's not about music and what Pete *is* about is the music. His extra-curricular activities are neither here nor there to me.'

But to some, Pete's drug-taking sets him apart from other more benign rock stars. He is dangerous, unpredictable, and above all playing out a fantasy of the rock rebel skating so close to the edge his life has become a story: Jon Savage's Rimbaldian script.

Some thought he was the new Sid Vicious. Bourcier agrees but says it's not hard to do. 'The media have such an appetite for it – they're hungry for someone to play that role. But it detracts from the music; you become a celebrity and then the celebrity quickly becomes bigger than the music.

'But I think Pete is probably the only person creating a momentum within music at the moment and that hasn't happened for a long time. He's got the balls to do it – maybe he's too fucked up to give a shit. But he's definitely not given enough credit for his intelligence.'

According to Robert Pattison, both rock and romanticism share a 'heroism of excess'. But rock's heroes don't need to be brave or even good. 'They are those whose emotions have broken out of the prescribed limits; who have accomplished the highest degree of novelty, whose selves have achieved bizarre and unexpected definition.' He cites 'the extrovert, the hedonist, the madman, the criminal, the suicide or the exhibitionist' as people who can rise to the status of a hero in rock.

Pete Doherty, therefore, is simply fulfilling a romantic myth – one that has been around for centuries, but it's a path that is rarely trodden now. It's hard to maintain that level of excess: to live outside society's tight constraints is almost impossible, particularly if you're doing it for effect. Pete Doherty is real – this isn't a show, put on so he can seem more dangerous or more 'out of it' than he really is.

It's 'the suicide' that gives the biggest cause for concern, and unfortunately popular music is littered with souls who died young. Even the jazz age had its victims. In 1947 trumpeter Sonny Berman died of a heroin overdose; in 1979 Sid Vicious overdosed on heroin in New York after being accused of his girlfriend's murder. INXS star Michael Hutchence hanged himself in 1997, and the Manic Street Preachers' Richey Edwards disappeared in 1995, believed to have thrown himself off the Severn Bridge between England and Wales. Kurt Cobain was only 27 when he died. He had problems in his relationships with both his wife and heroin. An electrician working on his house found him dressed in jeans and a shirt, lying on his back with a shotgun across his body. He'd fired a bullet through his left temple.

Then there's the accidental overdose – something about which both his fans and those close to Pete are perhaps most worried. In 1999 a coroner ruled that Bobby Sheehan, the bassist for Blues Traveler, accidentally overdosed on a combination of heroin, cocaine and Valium; thirty years before him country rock star Gram Parsons died of an overdose of morphine and tequila in the Joshua Tree National Park in the middle of the Californian Mojave Desert.

Famously, Jimi Hendrix choked on his own vomit after ingesting a cocktail of alcohol and drugs; sultry rhythm and blues siren Janis Joplin died of a heroin overdose in Hollywood, and a year later The Doors' inimitable frontman Jim Morrison died of a heart attack in Paris, also related to drugs.

Dying had become a swift and easy way to ensure you'd go down in history as a legend. That status would be virtually guaranteed if you died young – and left a catalogue of good music behind. That was the real key to immortality.

Soul singer Otis Redding didn't enter into mythology until he died young. 'Dock of the Bay' – perhaps his best-loved song – came out just a couple of months after he died in a plane crash in 1967.

Pete's favourite poet Emily Dickinson had written over 2,000 poems at the time of her death in 1886 aged just fifty-six. But she only sold seven during her lifetime. Folk singer Eva Cassidy died of cancer at the age of thirty-three and her posthumously released LP *Songbird* sold more than a million copies. Singer Robert Johnson had already put 'Sweet Home Chicago' down on tape, but he died a pauper and it wasn't until the 1960s that he became recognised as one of the legends of the blues.

There were some who felt that by the end of 2004 Pete was heading down the same sorry road – and fast. His life had taken a turn; some said for the worst, but Pete felt more content than he had done for ages. He was playing music to people that wanted to hear it. Yes, he had a record company to consider, but he wasn't forced to tour America when he didn't want to and to attend endless press interviews and radio appearances. He could also play those smaller gigs he liked putting on so much.

The trouble was, those around him were worried. Pete's drug-taking was getting worse, regardless of whether the rumours and the press reports were accurate. And the ghosts of people like Berman, Sheehan, Vicious and Hendrix had begun to haunt Pete – the names of stars that died young reeled off by the media in a rather morbid attempt at a warning.

'Do you recognise a self-destructive impulse in yourself?' Pete was asked.

'Yes, I do,' he replied. 'Each man kills the things he loves. I recognise that in myself, in relationships or beautiful things that I've had, then wilfully destroyed.'

The author, pundit and ex-*NME* hack Tony Parsons had some advice for Pete: remember Johnny Thunders. Thunders was in both The New York Dolls and The Heartbreakers. Parsons, a friend of Thunders, said he was 'bright, charming, a brilliant performer and a total babe magnet ... he was also the most hopeless junkie I have ever met ... doomed from the start because too many people got their kicks out of watching his long, slow, sensational path to an early grave.'

But he said there was no one there to applaud Johnny when he died in a cheap New Orleans hotel room fifteen years ago. By then, he said, everyone had abandoned him.

In December Pete appeared on the BBC's current affairs programme *Newsnight*. He was interviewed by presenter Kirsty Wark, and the *NME* claimed it marked the point at which he was 'finally accepted by the mainstream'. Others were more sceptical. On one Internet discussion board, fans thought it was a crass attempt by the BBC to store footage of a youth icon who seemed hell-bent on self-destruction. But there was something rather tasteless and patronising about being interviewed by Wark on *Newsnight*. 'I've spoken to your mum,' she told Pete, as if she was about to tell him off like a naughty schoolchild. It was just impossible to suspend your disbelief that this middle-aged woman was ever a fan of The Libertines. Yes, she was a journalist, but this interview was masquerading as a serious exploration of Pete's music and talent as a lyricist. If that was the case, surely an experienced music journalist would have been better placed to speak to him. Instead it came across as a crass attempt by *Newsnight* to look cool. Was the only reason they wanted to interview Pete because of his notoriety as Britain's own 'junkie rock star'? Surely *Newsnight* wasn't stooping as low as the tabloids?

Either way, the interview was frank and Pete came across rather well as Wark quizzed him about the break-up of The Libertines and his drug abuse.

'I know where the self-destruct button is,' he said. 'I just have to resist the temptation to push it.'

Kirsty Wark had contacted Jackie Doherty prior to the interview and Jackie had written a letter to be read out on air. Jackie liked Kirsty. She thought she was very professional and was as far removed from the tabloid hacks who had blighted her life as you could get. 'He is a sensitive soul and he has many good points,' she wrote.

When Wark read this to Pete he looked touched, if a little bemused. 'Of course it matters to me that my family are worried about me,' he said, adding that his previous attempts at rehab were solely because 'there's a heartbroken lady somewhere'.

'History has shown there's only one conclusion – and that's the blackout, the great void,' he said. 'But I'm not a nihilist – I don't want to die.'

'If you don't want to feel Time's
load on your back when it weighs you
down and your shoulders crack,
stay high; never come down.'

CHARLES BAUDELAIRE

THIRTEEN

THE LAST OF THE ROCK ROMANTICS

Pete Doherty couldn't very well advocate drug use

to his legions of fans, but in being so public about his own drug consumption he inadvertently did. Likewise, in public he claimed he wasn't a nihilist – that he didn't seek death – but in private he felt death was the ultimate freedom. 'I can't tell between death and glory,' he sang. It didn't mean he wanted to die – just that he recognised it as the greatest form of escape; perhaps better than any drug, and perhaps he fantasised about exposing himself to this ultimate challenge.

In both his lyrics and in interviews, Pete had revived the notion of the rock star as intellectual and as romantic troubadour. And this was no simple task. In the twenty-first century the media is quick to put down anything it sees as pretentious posturing or delusions of grandeur.

Simon Bourcier says the word 'pretentious' should not be included in a conversation about Pete. It's simply 'about not having any boundaries in your thinking', he says. 'Where you can actually transcend into any situation.' Bourcier believes that anyone who thinks this is pretentious doesn't have the imagination to go on that journey to the same place Pete is heading.

The Romantic poets of the early nineteenth century, such as Byron, Shelley, Coleridge and Wordsworth, emphasised the importance of the imagination over rationalism, and this prominence given to emotion proved irresistible for Pete. Plus he had a limitless imagination. He said himself he was always living in dreams.

The Romantic movement stemmed in part from a rejection of the modern, a deliberate move away from the reason and order of the Enlightenment, and it gained momentum as an artistic movement in both France and Britain. The Romantic poets felt that the Enlightenment had drained creativity of its passion. They believed that the intellectual and creative life of the nation had become so sophisticated it had lost its ability to dream, its imagination and its violence. The Romantics wanted to get away from this modernity. They fell in love with the old gothic culture, began rebelling against modern life and embraced nature in all its unpredictable power.

William Blake, who was born in Soho and whose love for London and England was shared by Pete two hundred years later, also referred to England as 'Albion'. In his poem 'Albion Upon The Rock', he describes the storms and snows beating around England: 'howling winds … roaring seas … lightnings glare, long thunders roll.' Nature was harsh and nothing could bring it under control.

The Romantic poets also embraced the simplicity of the countryside over the city; the power of the imagination over cold logic. Wordsworth idolised ordinary language and fell in love with people who lived in the country – the simple folk. Writer Robert Pattison says that despite their bourgeois origins, the Romantic artists 'automatically achieved membership of some lower class' and that, by comparison, membership in rock's lower class is achieved 'not by birth or poverty but by purity of instinct'. He quotes the Rolling Stones' song 'Play With Fire', in which Jagger sings about a girl who exchanges the high life in west London for Stepney in the east end.

The same can be said of Pete Doherty. He was born to a middle-class family in Northumberland but he had embraced the streets, idealised the working class and spent time in squats in London, essentially busking for food. He was fascinated by, and had the utmost respect for, those way down the ladder of society.

Simon Bourcier also thinks Pete has looked at all the different strands of society and projected himself into each of them. 'How he might fit in and what that world might be like. Maybe he looked at how he would have operated as a performer, writer and poet living either a working-class existence or a middle-class existence,' Bourcier says. 'He is very much a poet with a romanticised view of life and I can understand how he could get a lot out of being a fantasist, especially exploring genres and film and literature, which he does.'

'I'm interested in William Blake,' Pete told the *Socialist Review*, 'but there are less spiritual, more practical people like Galton and Simpson [who wrote *Steptoe and Son* and *Hancock's Half Hour*], and Joe Orton, who were interested in the fineries of everyday dialogue and puns. In the same way that I immersed myself in The Smiths, I did the same with a lot of aspects of English culture. I was obsessed with certain writers, certain styles of film ... about a pride, a dignity and a respect for people with whom you feel you belong.'

Artists who embrace this 'Englishness' are, by and large, white and male, and write for a genre of rock in which the lyrics are essential. It's true that many if not most British bands have historically tried to recreate American rock 'n' roll rather than come up with a quintessentially English substitute. The so-called 'British Invasion' of the US in the 1960s, by bands like The Small Faces and The Beatles, was one exception, channelling as they did their unique brand of British pop across the pond. As Martin Cloonan put it in the academic journal *Popular Music and Society*, *Sergeant Pepper* was The Beatles' 'most dedicated exploration of a fading English culture of Northern brass bands, vaudeville entertainers and travelling circuses'.

Pete admits that initially The Libertines were trying to be as much like The Strokes as they could. That was their mandate. But with Babyshambles, and his increasingly prolific solo acoustic material, Pete had moved away from that sweaty New York punk shtick. Babyshambles are still a rock 'n' roll band but Pete is more concerned with the subject matter of his lyrics, and in fact he seems more 'English' than he ever has.

Wheras punk was, as Jon Savage claimed, 'a noisy revolt against the slow death and suffocation that is the emotional experience of living in England', Pete's music was a celebration of the best bits of that England. Mark Sinker, writing in the *NME* back in 1988, said The Smiths could only have come from England 'because of their frequent references to towns within it' and their 'unchallengeable parochialism'.

Morrissey's vibrant and hilarious imagination was manifested in lyrics which, if you thought them miserable, you'd missed the point. Mark Simpson, writing in the *Guardian*, summed up Morrissey's love of Englishness thus: 'the grainy black-and-white 1960s iconography of The Smiths' sleeves, the lyrical world of iron bridges, humdrum towns, repression, frustration, and amorphous desire.'

It wasn't an England in which everyone lived or which everyone could even recognise as being England – it was a romanticised vision, and Pete had that vision too. Morrissey was also well aware of the myth of living fast and dying young – burning like that hard gem-like flame – singing, as he did, of the possibility of being mown over by a double-decker bus with his lover as a blissful way to end it all.

Hugh Barnes, author of a forthcoming book on Byron, says the Romantic poets were the rock stars of their day. They didn't want to be part of mainstream society and, as such, toyed with both drugs and death. But the mainstream just couldn't leave them alone. Barnes says these poets played a social role. 'They were ostracised, but this was good for society. It represented something very deep,' he says – a form of 'voodoo'.

Byron – probably the greatest poet of his age – was hounded out of England in 1816 and driven into exile, thus fulfilling an idea of the 'cult of the outlaw'. The outlaw myth was later appropriated by Hollywood: the loner, the wanderer, the adventurer. Byron's private life was scandalous but Barnes says many of the allegations were untrue. The same goes for Pete Doherty. The media likes to exaggerate his drug-taking; stories have abounded about promiscuity, gay sex, time spent working as a rent boy, living in drug-fuelled debauchery. And much of that is probably untrue as well. But it's a form of exorcism for mainstream society.

Barnes says there is something 'shamanistic' about acting out what he calls the 'drama of ostracism'. 'There's something tribal about a newspaper's need to vent these inarticulate feelings of rage. It's not tangible or real. The fascination with these figures has something to do with feelings society has repressed deep beneath the surface.'

The media's demonisation of Pete reeks of hypocrisy as well. Alcohol intake is legendary in Fleet Street and it's no secret that some journalists have a penchant for cocaine. It's almost as if the papers are fulfilling a role they assume they ought to be filling; that the mainstream doesn't want to even attempt to understand Pete and his art. How many *Sun* readers – all too familiar with 'Junkie Pete' – can name a song by either The Libertines or Babyshambles?

Over thirty years ago, when Mick Jagger was charged with drug possession, *The Times* newspaper – that bastion of conservatism; the voice of middle England – leapt to his defence. After the austere 1950s, perhaps *The Times* was swept along by the tide of liberal thinking. After all, abortion had just been legalised. This was the permissive era. Apparently not so in 2005.

Pete is fulfilling the role of the 'outsider' – a character society has branded immoral, but which society needs far more than he needs society.

IN 1770 the poet Thomas Chatterton – a key influence on Percy Shelley and John Keats – killed himself when he was just seventeen years old by drinking arsenic, driven to despair, according to author Robert Pattison, by the apathy shown to him by the London literary world. In death, Pattison says, Chatterton became a Romantic martyr; 'a hero of sleepless energy, slain by the world's exploitation, but triumphant in annihilation', and rock was quick to adopt this theme of victimisation. By the same token, the mainstream was happy to fulfil the role of vilifier.

In Henry Wallis's 1856 painting *The Death of Chatterton*, his subject lies draped over a bed, beautiful in death. According to Hugh Barnes, the Romantic poets fetishised death as a return to a purer state. Pattison compares the painting of Chatterton to photographer Annie Leibovitz's iconic image of Keith Richards of The Rolling Stones. Richards, he says, instinctively reproduces Chatterton's pose – 'eyes shut in languorous self-annihilation, one arm limply falling to the ground while the other lies across a chest exposed by an open shirt-front revealing the pale, erotic flesh of beleaguered youth'.

Death featured prominently in the work of the Romantics. In his play *Cain*, Lord Byron wrote: 'I have look'd out in the vast desolate night in search of him (death) ... for with fear rose longing in my heart ... but nothing came'. In 'Ode to a Nightingale', Keats writes: 'My heart aches, and a drowsy numbness pains my sense, as though of hemlock I had drunk ... That I might drink, and leave the world unseen ... I have been half in love with easeful Death ... To take into the air my quiet breath.'

And so to endure the living, the Romantic poets turned to drugs. But their use of narcotics – particularly opium – was not solely for anaesthesia. Drugs took them back to a purer place of unsullied emotion. When they were high on opium they were fully awake. It stripped away all the dismal reality of modern life and left them with the only thing that mattered – the imagination.

In adulthood this purer place could only be reached, so the Romantic poets thought, through drugs or death. Other than that, the only pure humans were infants. While Shelley was studying at University College, Oxford, he grabbed a child from its mother's arms on Magdalen Bridge, repeatedly asking her: 'Will your baby tell us anything about pre-existence, madam?' Children, Shelley claimed, came from a place where everything was known, good and right.

In the late eighteenth century, Samuel Taylor Coleridge began using opium to relieve toothache – something that would later become an addiction. Wanting to be around like-minded poets such as Wordsworth, Coleridge moved from London to the Lake District and the pair collaborated on a book entitled *Lyrical Ballads*, which included 'Rime of the Ancient Mariner'. One writer described the poem as 'a story of ghosts, omens, sailors lost at sea, hallucinogenic visions, transgression, and redemption'. The same year that *Lyrical Ballads* was published, Coleridge wrote 'Kubla Khan' – the story of a mythical paradise called Xanadu, which he penned in a drug-induced coma.

Coleridge's friend Robert Southey joined the poets in the Lakes and soon the three of them began discussing setting up an alternative community on the east coast of America – in which they would share not just their accommodation but their wives as well – but the dream soon fell apart. The nearest they came to their utopian dream was homes a few miles apart in the Lake District; they never made the move across the Atlantic. But it's interesting to note the comparisons with rock 'n' roll.

One of Pete's friends, Pogues singer Shane MacGowan, once lived in a London street with his fellow band members. 'We were living in various houses on Burton Street,' he recalls. 'It was a great time.' Burton Street contained what were known as 'short-life houses' – effectively licensed squats. Through the 1970s and 1980s, these artistic ghettoes, operated by Acme and Space, thrived, letting artists, musicians and writers live and work while paying rent in the region of £25 a week.

'It was amazing,' says Jem Finer, the Pogues' guitarist and banjo player. 'It was such a varied community in that street. But Ken Livingstone, in his wisdom as boss of Camden's Housing Committee, decided to move us all out.'

'Me, Jem and Spider were stuck in the last house left standing at one stage,' MacGowan says. 'Scenes like that usually produce good art.'

When Carl and Pete first hit London this was exactly what they had envisioned – and to some extent the Albion Rooms embodied this Arcadian fantasy. It was only one small flat but its open-door policy and creative environment spawned much of The Libertines' – and later Babyshambles' – output.

Pete has always acknowledged the influence great art has had on his music, much of it subconscious. 'It's not like we sit down and think, well, this dead poet has inspired the whole of the band – but anything can tantalise you, and make you think: shit, how did I ever live before hearing that sentence?'

Sex and rock 'n' roll have always gone hand in hand. Sex and drugs and rock 'n' roll were all Ian Dury needed. Pete Doherty is fairly explicit in his depiction of sex. 'Fuck Forever,' he urges his fans. Pete even liked to allude to a sexual relationship with Carl; when they were vying for the mic, they would almost kiss. On stage their sweaty, lithe, shirtless bodies had homoerotic overtones.

In their book *On Record*, Simon Frith and Angela McRobbie identify two kinds of male performers – those who perform 'cock rock' and those who play 'teenybop'. Cock rock performers are, they argue, 'aggressive, dominating and boastful', exemplified by 'male bodies on display' and the 'rampant destructive male traveller, smashing hotels and groupies alike'. The teenybop performer's image 'is based on self-pity, vulnerability, and need'; it's 'the young boy next door: sad, thoughtful, pretty and puppylike', singing songs about loneliness and frustration.

Interestingly, Pete positions himself in between. He is dangerous, sexually prolific (so we're led to believe) and has been seen to be aggressive in public. But he can also turn on the doe-eyes, that 'little-boy-lost' charm. And it's quite a coup because he can count on fans of both. Aside from those who simply like the music, there are the girls who want him as a 'sensitive and sympathetic soul mate', and the boys who like the image and aggression.

Whether consciously or not, Pete plays up to this incredibly well. On stage he is at once vacant, staring and unpredictable, and at the same time alive, energetic and entertaining. He's the consummate rock star. But why does the image of a rocker in the throws of self-destruction appeal to us? Are we really living our lives vicariously through him? Is Pete Doherty the person we all wish we could be?

Pete has the attitude we secretly wish we could have – sticking two fingers up to society. Where we come home from our nine-to-five jobs and bemoan the bills piling up before settling down to watch the latest episode of *Lost*, Pete, we assume, is out of his head somewhere – the day-to-day mundane stuff we are forced to endure is alien to him; it doesn't feature in his world. At least, that's what we like to believe. It's the myth we have built around him. In fact, in November 2005 Pete was flat-hunting near Brick Lane. It made the news – just – but we don't want to know that about our rock 'n' roll stars: that they can and do lead normal lives as well.

Yes, Pete's excessive behaviour is real; his drug-taking is not an act, but he still watches TV occasionally.

FOURTEEN

|WHO|THE|F!%$|IS|..|

By the beginning of 2005

the British media's fascination with Pete hadn't waned in the slightest. The tabloid press still cursed him; the broadsheets tried to deconstruct him and certainly pretended to understand him; the music press – by and large – adored him, and television had begun to show an interest in his self-destructive image. It could make 'good TV' after all. By and large though, the media had single-handedly failed to grasp what Pete really stood for. Whether it was the music press or the tabloids, they all seemed absorbed in the soap opera; even the music press weren't really interested solely in the music. It had all become secondary to the dramatic events in his life.

The fact that he was about to begin dating a supermodel wasn't going to help him stay out of the public eye. And it wasn't going to make the media start focusing on the music. Kate Moss was a superstar. Since the dawn of reality TV the 'celeb count' had risen dramatically in the UK, but most of these were just chancers. We didn't really have too many genuine A-listers. There were a few actors; Madonna had chosen to live over here; but a good deal of them had disappeared to find the tax breaks. Kate Moss was of a dying breed. And now she was going out with a rock 'n' roll hellraiser.

In addition, an eccentric media studies lecturer and one-time documentary maker by the name of Max Carlish had been showing an interest in Pete and had begun to assemble a documentary of this fascinating character – this musician-cum-poet that he'd discovered. The truth was Carlish wasn't too familiar with the world of rock and pop; he had produced a Bafta-award-winning TV series about the Royal Opera House but since meeting Pete at a gig in Leicester he too had become fascinated by the myth of Pete Doherty. 'I was intrigued by him,' he admitted to the *Guardian*. 'Perhaps part of it was because I'm a former crack addict myself.'

Carlish thought Pete was a 'beautiful, cool, gorgeous guy' and said if he was gay he'd 'have a crush on him'. He thought it would be hard to get access to Pete to make the film he envisioned, but this was prior to Pete's relationship with Kate Moss, and although the tabloids were interested, Pete still wasn't the obsession that he would later become.

Carlish attended Babyshambles gigs religiously and inevitably became, in his own words, a kind of 'court jester', invited on stage by Pete at every opportunity. 'So long as I found new ways of humiliating myself, they let me penetrate their inner sanctum with my Sony camera,' he said. It was all rather embarrassing. Carlish would clamber on stage and start dancing like your dad. For his film he'd occasionally turn the camera on himself and make cringeworthy asides. Sometimes he'd even say them to Pete, commenting on how amazing he was, how he was a rock 'n' roll star.

Carlish recalls spending one night in the recording studio with Babyshambles, watching as Pete chain-smoked heroin and penned the words to the B-side of the single 'Killamangiro'. Carlish knew he was in the presence of genius but he was also fully aware that Pete was in danger of becoming a wasted talent due to his drug abuse. That, Carlish must have decided, was what his film would really be about. Pete thought he seemed harmless and was happy to oblige.

Just before Christmas 2004 Pete had admitted to a journalist that he had overdosed on his tour bus the previous month and that was the reason he'd had to cancel the show. He claimed he'd given up taking crack and was feeling much healthier. He also wanted to spend more time with his son, Astile, and take some responsibility in his life. Lisa Moorish, Astile's mother, had been reluctant to let Pete see their child due to his drug problems. She also felt he was unreliable and didn't stick to arrangements. Pete felt it was about time that all changed.

He also wanted to prove that he was committed to Babyshambles. The cancelled gigs and no-shows of 2004 were unavoidable but he didn't want to let his fans down any more. On New Year's Eve Pete played four gigs back-to-back in four different cities: Birmingham, Stoke, Oldham and Manchester. Predictably, the gigs were a heady mix of music, screaming and stage invasions. But Pete was on form. One fan compared the Manchester gig to Beatlemania. Some girls, even some boys, in the audience were crying, carried away in the drama of it all.

By January, whispers that John Hassall was about to rise from the ashes of The Libertines to form a new band became fact. It was to be called Yeti and feature John on guitar and vocals, his friends Mark Williams on guitar, Brendan Kersey on bass, Andrew Deian-Jung on lead guitar and Graham Blacow on drums. And their Specials-meets-The La's rock already had the A&R men and women salivating.

Carl was still deciding on his future career. He hadn't firmed up plans to form a new band but Alan McGee had announced that a Carl

Barât solo project would materialise some time toward the end of 2005. There was, it seemed, life after The Libertines. Who'd have thought?

It wasn't until January that Carl revealed one of the reasons he had disbanded The Libertines. The year before he'd simply described it as an 'ongoing problem' with his health. Now he admitted he was to have an operation to remove a tumour from behind his ear.

He also said he intended to contact Pete and rekindle their friend-ship. Could this mean – if not a Libertines reunion – then at least a reconciliation between Carl and Pete?

If the tabloids were running out of clichés to chart the 'demise' of Pete Doherty, they can't have believed their luck when on 18 January it transpired that he'd hooked up with Kate Moss at her thirty-first birthday party. Inevitably the tabloids would begin the labo-rious process of coming up with enough 'Bad Boy And The Angel' metaphors to play this one out. One paper summed it up with the phrase: 'Kate Moss, her thirty-first birthday and a fling with the most notorious drug addict in pop.'

'Close pals' of Kate seemed to be crawling out of the woodwork to spill the beans on how the pair were 'all over each other' when they first met at her party in the Cotswolds. Kate was said to be 'smitten', and 'flirting outrageously' with Pete as Mick Jones and his fellow Clash colleague Paul Simonon provided the musical accompaniment.

The tabloids were also keen to point out the incestuousness of the situation: Pete had an eighteen-month-old son by Lisa Moorish. Moorish also had a daughter, Molly, by Liam Gallagher. Gallagher was married to Patsy Kensit, who was once good friends with Kate Moss. It was pure tabloid media gold. Not quite the story of the year but definitely something that would keep the copy flowing for quite some time. Entertainment editors could put their feet up for a while at least. This one was going to run and run.

A few days after the party Pete confirmed the rumours, telling ITV it had been his best week in a long time because he'd found love with Kate. And then it transpired they'd had tattoos of each other's initials inscribed on their bodies. In the mid-1990s Liam and Patsy graced the cover of *Vanity Fair*, representing the 'face of Britpop'. The pair were celebrated in Tony Blair's new Cool Britannia. But not Pete and Kate. Gallagher's drug-fuelled excess barely registered on the tabloid barometer. Perhaps they felt because he wasn't the sharpest tool in the box, he didn't pose a threat. He was just a typical rock star doing typical rock star things. They'd write about the brawling and mention the drugs but he certainly wasn't a pariah. Liam Gallagher was celebrated as the best of British. Perhaps because Pete was brighter than a lot of the journalists writing about him, he posed a threat. There was certainly a method to his madness.

If Pete's personal life seemed to be back on track, Babyshambles was about to suffer a blow: at the end of January drummer Gemma Clarke walked out on the band after falling out with manager James Mullord. In an open letter to Pete, she said: 'You are a great artist and have been a massive inspiration to me,' but claimed his choice of management had given her no option but to quit. Her letter didn't elaborate.

She was replaced by ex-White Sport drummer Adam Ficek. Apart from Pete, Babyshambles was now made up entirely of former White Sport members. Ficek's inaugural gig at the Brixton Academy was announced for 22 February.

Clarke's goodbye was pleasant compared to the poisonous missive Pete's former girlfriend Katie Lewis was about to deliver. Lewis had sold her story to the tabloid press once before. That time it was about Pete's drug problems. Now she was commenting on his relationship with Kate Moss. 'He's evil, twisted and the only thing he loves is her money,' the *Mirror* quoted her as saying. 'They are a match made in hell.'

But Pete had fallen in love with Kate. She understood the pressures of fame; she was familiar with his world; plus she was beautiful. She loved rock 'n' roll; loved gritty bars like the Boston Arms in Tufnell Park where she'd seen the White Stripes play when they first landed in England. But most of all she loved Pete. The tabloids wanted to know all the minutiae of their relationship, and where the facts were hard to come by, they would use guesswork. This was so much more than just another Rod Stewart/Rachel Hunter or Billy Joel/Christy Brinkley. This was Jagger/Faithfull all over again. Kate Moss was a millionaire model from Croydon who had been snapped up by a modelling agency at JFK airport when she was just fourteen years old, and had gone on to become one of the biggest supermodels in the world. Fleet Street's editors knew their relationship would provide reams of copy and sell thousands of papers.

But unlike their coverage of Mick Jagger and Marianne Faithfull, the knives were out for Pete and Kate's relationship. The *Independent* summed up the feelings on Fleet Street with its headline taken from Joe Jackson's song: 'Is she really going out with him?' They couldn't believe it. It was wrong, and it seemed they'd stop at nothing to see it fall apart.

And so it began. Kate had dumped Pete by text message; they were due to get married imminently; she wanted his baby; he'd given up drugs for her; they were moving abroad. If Pete's life was a soap opera before, this was a Hollywood blockbuster – if one that was only half based on a true story.

Pete's close friend Wolfman told one reporter from the *Daily Mirror*: 'Kate is besotted. She adores him. We all do. Pete is a lovable character. When Kate is with him she is natural, childlike. He doesn't treat her as a celebrity. It's as if she's under his spell.'

It seems that everyone who got to know Pete fell under that spell. He is one of the most charismatic individuals, not just in rock, but of his generation.

'He is a successful musician and is going out with the most beautiful girl in the world,' said Wolfman. 'It reminds me of the story of George Best when he was dating Miss World, and someone asked, "George, where did it all go wrong?"'

Thin Lizzy's guitarist Scott Gorham was warning Pete in the pages of the Glasgow *Daily Record* to learn from the mistakes his band had made and not get involved with drugs: Thin Lizzy's singer Phil Lynott died from heart failure as a result of years of heroin addiction.

That was just before the photos came out that would shock middle England to the core. Max Carlish had sold stills from his documentary movie to the *Mirror*. They showed Pete smoking heroin by 'chasing the dragon' at a recording studio in north London. These weren't some grainy snapshots, clinched without Pete's knowledge. They were full-colour, close-up and taken in broad daylight. Pete had known he was being filmed; he had known there was a chance the film could have been televised. He didn't know they'd be sold to the tabloids beforehand but what did that matter? But it wasn't as if he was doing it for attention. If he was making any statement at all, it was that he would never let his freedom be compromised. He wasn't trying to cover anything up: Pete Doherty took drugs. And he believed he should have every right to.

Carlish later claimed a friend of his had seen the footage in the film's rushes and told him to sell them to the press. Carlish soon found himself in the middle of a bidding war between rival tabloids. He insisted he didn't want to sell the pictures – that he just wanted to finish making his film – but in the end he succumbed. Pete called him after the photos had been published. Carlish, somewhat pathetically, suggested continuing with the documentary but of course it was too late for that.

Carlish's 'documentary' wouldn't appear on television for another three months, and even then it would be vastly different from the film he'd first envisaged. *Stalking Pete Doherty*, as it was called, was ultimately more about what looked like Carlish's descent into madness than it was about Pete. But for now, the tabloids had made their latest kill. This was front-page news and would fulfil their insatiable appetite for 'Pete' stories for at least for another week or two. And more importantly it fulfilled their self-imposed remit to pull Kate Moss's new beau to pieces.

'Kate's lover and the heroin fix: he can't live without it,' screamed the *Mirror*. This time its readers were asked to witness 'chilling photographs' of Pete heating a piece of foil with a lighter and inhaling heroin fumes. It called the scenes 'sordid' and went on to catalogue his past misdemeanours.

Carlish, meanwhile, portrayed himself as a concerned 'real friend' of Pete's. But Pete thought Carlish was a joke, and when the film was finally aired we could see why. Carlish displayed an unhealthy obsession with his subject, 'stalking' Pete wherever he went. At first Pete played along, inviting him up on stage like the band mascot. But later Max had clearly become an annoyance.

The film was never repeated, despite the topical subject matter and the publicity Pete had been getting; the *Mirror's* photos would have ensured the documentary could have been re-run on terrestrial TV in a prime-time slot. But no. Something was amiss.

A few weeks after the documentary had aired the producer was happy to hand out Carlish's two mobile phone numbers to journalists wanting to follow up on the story, but she said she'd had no contact with him for a while and didn't know whether the numbers were still working. 'It won't be shown again because we had problems getting some of the footage cleared,' she said.

Was Carlish even in control of the final edit? It didn't do Pete's reputation any harm, but Carlish came off badly.

During the month of February 2005, Pete notched up more column inches than ever before. The media onslaught was relentless. Musically, Babyshambles seemed to be going along the right track. Meanwhile The Libertines had been nominated for four *NME* awards, but in the Best Live Band category they were up against some tough opposition: Babyshambles.

Pete said the nomination meant a lot to him. 'Most of my favourite bands did well in the *NME* polls when I was growing up and I dreamed of being nominated one day,' he said.

Babyshambles played a concert to raise money for the child victims of the South-east Asian tsunami. Pete came on stage wearing a pair of sunglasses and black leather jacket and ended the gig by diving into the crowd, singing 'Fuck Forever'.

It was a typically feverish performance, but music critic Gavin Martin said the crowds were flocking to watch the 'sad, final days of Pete Doherty'. And it was still only February. Martin could have been right. But at the beginning of 2005 it wasn't the drugs that looked set to take Pete out of action. A couple of days after the charity concert, he was arrested for assault and theft.

The sorry chain of events that led to another run-in with the law took place early one evening at the Rookery Hotel in Islington. Pete had gone to meet Carlish but was furious with the documentary maker for selling the photos to the papers and wanted to have it out with him.

Carlish's version of what happened next went like this: everything was 'fine' until Pete began demanding cash. Carlish claimed he wanted thousands but refused to give it to him because he knew he'd spend it on hard drugs. As a result, he said, Pete 'went berserk'.

What is in no doubt is that Carlish was whisked to University College Hospital for treatment on two black eyes and a broken nose, but was discharged shortly afterwards.

Later that night Pete was taken into custody and charged with robbery and blackmail. His friend Alan Wass, a musician from the rock band Lefthand, was charged with the same offences and both were scheduled to appear at Highbury Corner Magistrates' Court.

A doctor said Pete was high when he arrived at the police station and wore the scars on his hands from injecting heroin. Pete had denied mainlining.

Pete appeared in court on the Friday morning. He was given bail but Rough Trade records failed to come up with the £150,000 needed in time and Pete was sent on his way to Pentonville Prison. One inmate said he looked nervous as he was led along by a prison officer.

'Potty Pete in Pentonville' came the *Sun*'s predictable alliteration on the Monday, while a 'jailbird pal' of Pete's told the *Mirror* there were 'a lot of seriously hard bastards who will want to make mincemeat out of him inside'. It was a sweet irony that Pentonville lay on the Caledonian Road – immortalised in The Libertines' song 'Up The Bracket'.

Of course, only Pete could use the experience of a week in that hell-hole for the benefit of his art. Together with a Rastafarian inmate known as General Santana he penned a tasty slice of reggae called 'Pentonville Rough', singing of sleeping on an uncomfortable bed staring at the cracks in the ceiling.

Unusually, it was the *Telegraph* that leapt to Pete's defence on 5

February, claiming he had become 'trapped in a freak show'. The paper said Pete was one of Britain's most talented songwriters, 'with a delightful way with words'. It went further, saying he had an 'instinctive understanding' of the passion and commitment that was required to make a rock band great.

It was an incredible eulogy from the most unlikely source. Welcome, yes, but still very strange.

By contrast, the *Mirror* had found a lap-dancer who claimed Pete had screwed her in a 'disabled loo' after snorting a line of cocaine, and the *Telegraph*'s Sunday sister paper had found an irate ex-neighbour of Pete's willing to regale its readers with stories about Pete 'and his groupies' arriving back at the flat in Bethnal Green for 'impromptu karaoke session following a night of chemical excess'.

It was an old story but who cared – it involved Pete Doherty. And Pete Doherty sold newspapers.

There was no let-up. Pete wasn't doing himself any favours getting arrested for assaulting Max Carlish, but with a high-profile romance and an addiction to try to keep under control, he had become not just fodder for the tabloid press, but a free-for-all for all the media.

Pete was in Pentonville only six days, but when he came out he found himself the subject of a fair amount of excitement in the literary world – due in no small part to his prodigious talent, but in some part to his growing notoriety as well.

Not only had Pete been scribbling poems since he was a teenager, but he'd also been keeping the scrapbooks known as the Books of Albion, publishing scanned copies of some of them on his website, giving some away and keeping others for himself. Publishing houses were more than a little interested and talk was of large sums of money that had the potential to change hands.

But there were other things on Pete's mind. For one he had promised Kate and his family that he'd get help for his addiction. Prison had scared him.

He chose to speak to the *Mirror* on his release. In some quarters it was difficult to comprehend why Pete would choose to speak to the very newspapers that had hounded him for almost two years. It may have been a strange kind of logic, but he felt that if they were going write about him anyway, he may as well get paid for it. James Mullord was more succinct: 'The press here won't leave you alone, but Pete does like the attention, it's true. He's his own worst enemy when it comes to getting the wrong type of attention.'

Pete told the paper it was hell being inside and that his cell stank of vomit but that the thought of seeing Kate again kept him going.

Pete was bailed to appear in court again at a later date and in the meantime was given a 10pm to 7am curfew and ordered to undergo a drug treatment programme. If convicted at a later hearing, he faced four years in jail for the assault.

Babyshambles' appearance at the Brixton Academy was cancelled as Pete, once again, headed to rehab.

Pete's father Peter Sr knew a lot of what the papers wrote about his son was a vast exaggeration, but the pair had rarely spoken since Pete's troubles with hard drugs had begun. Pete had asked Jackie to persuade his dad to visit him in rehab and the pair had an emotional reunion – and heart-to-heart – at the London clinic. Jackie's brother

Philip said it must have been an emotional meeting as they had barely spoken, even at Christmas. 'His dad couldn't get his head around Pete's drug addiction,' he said. Although Pete Sr was a child of the 1960s, his life had taken a vastly different path to his son's. He was a pillar of society – a major in the army – and as such had very forthright views when it came to drugs and drug-taking.

It also must have been hard for Major Doherty, whose son was notorious for all the wrong reasons. It didn't matter whether most of it had been exaggerated. His colleagues only knew what they'd read in the papers.

The same day Pete trundled off to rehab, it was announced the band had sold out a forthcoming show at the same venue they had just been forced to cancel.

Bassist Drew McConnell publicly voiced his support for Pete, saying he was part of a band that was fully behind him and that cared for him. Liberty, he said, was the most important thing, and whatever lifestyle choice Pete made, Babyshambles would be sticking by him.

Chatter in music circles turned to the possibility that Pete and Carl would be forced together at the *NME* awards that both were due to attend. Pete was hoping to leave his rehab clinic for the show and Tony Linkin said if he did he'd have to head straight back to rehab afterwards. Carl was still convalescing after his operation but he too intended to go. In the end, Pete didn't show up, but Carl made a touching tribute to his old friend as he picked up The Libertines' award for Best British Band – presented by Graham Coxon.

Compared to Pete and the attention he had been getting from the media since his split from The Libertines, Carl had been virtually unheard of. At the ceremony he said he'd been working on new material, which he planned to unveil shortly. Carl had tried to contact Pete just before the *NME* awards, to no avail. 'This wouldn't have been the ideal place to meet up for the first time,' he acknowledged, 'but my heart's still with him and I hope to see him.'

There's something faintly amusing about the *Daily Telegraph* purporting to have the 'inside story' on Pete Doherty. Nevertheless, that was its claim on the day of the *NME* awards. To be fair it did contain some interesting comments from Babyshambles' ex-drummer Gemma Clarke, who said Pete needed a strong eye on him to keep control, but that nobody was looking after him. 'There were hundreds of hangers-on. Everyone was on drugs, except me and the road crew,' she said.

It also quoted Jake Fior, manager of Pete's close friend Wolfman, who said junkies were attracted to Pete – a man with a lot of ready cash – like flies, because in a warped way it reaffirmed their 'not particularly glamorous lifestyle choices'. He added that it was a bit rich that despite The Libertines touting songs like 'Skag And Bone Man' – a barefaced reference to hard drugs – everybody then claimed to be 'horrified when it turned out the singer was on drugs'.

Finally, it quoted an anonymous 'ex-girlfriend', who it said summed up the dilemma nicely: 'It is difficult for his friends to tell him he is going wrong in his life because he's been dating one of the world's most beautiful women, he's got a top ten single with his band and he's on the front of every newspaper in this country.'

ON 19 February Pete walked out of the rehab clinic after being clean for two weeks. He'd had a Naltrexone implant embedded in his skin, which is intended to prevent heroin having any effect if Pete ever succumbed to temptation later on.

Pete had a lot of respect for Paul Russell, the man who ran rehab clinic The Smart Treatment Project. The key was trust and the pair clicked. 'Pete said he wanted a clinic where he wasn't treated like a child or a bad person because of his drug use,' Russell said. 'My job is to help clients to make informed choices – which Pete's done really well.'

Then Conservative party leader Michael Howard had earlier made an example of Pete, saying: 'Here you have a man who takes drugs and gets locked up – yet ends up on the front pages ... I think many parents will have been rather surprised by the celebrity coverage given to Peter Doherty over the last month.'

Pete was quick to respond: 'Michael Howard thinks I'm glamorising it – that's not true ... it's the press isn't it? Crack and heroin are an epidemic. There's probably more drugs on building sites than in bands.' That was the irony, and Pete had summed it up beautifully. The tabloids, which turned Pete into a pariah for his drug use, the papers that called him 'junkie scum', were being devoured by people, some of whom were actively taking hard drugs themselves.

Now Pete was out of rehab, he was about to start a twelve-week programme of counselling and therapy. If his physical addiction had been broken, the psychological addiction still needed to be addressed.

'It's become a self-perpetuating horror story,' Mullord told the *New York Times*. 'The drugs, the missed shows, the law, all of it. That's not what it's supposed to be about. But it reached the point where it's just got completely out of hand ... Pete does breed chaos. It's just that simple.'

Pete played a warm-up show at the Garage venue in Islington before Babyshambles' date at Brixton Academy. He walked casually on stage wearing a pinstripe suit to rapturous applause and even tears from some members of the audience. Later, when he took his jacket and shirt off under the hot stage lights at the small venue at the top of Upper Street, you could glimpse the Naltrexone implant. If the stories of Pete's addiction and rehab had all seemed unreal – tonight it hit home that he had been to hell and back.

'Killamangiro' was pure punk pop adrenaline – like The Jam reincarnated. 'What Katie Did' took on a whole new meaning now that Pete was dating Kate Moss. The song wasn't written for her but all his fans knew from press reports that he'd given his new girlfriend a framed copy of the lyrics for her birthday. The gig ended with a glorious version of the beautiful 'Albion' – the song of which Pete was most proud – and a rousing 'Fuck Forever', before the lights went out and the band left the stage. Pete returned home before his curfew.

If the warm-up show ended without incident, the following night at the Brixton Academy was altogether different. The judge had extended his curfew by two hours. Mick Jones came on to announce the band, beckoning them on stage, but towards the end of their set Pete ripped out Patrick Walden's guitar lead. Whether it was an accident or a deliberate attempt to rile his friend mid-set, inevitably Walden was a little frustrated and lashed out at Pete. As the band's roadies rushed on stage, Pete and Walden playfully kicked and pushed each other but ended up brawling on the floor before they were pulled apart and forced to exit stage left. It was predictably chaotic. The assembled throng of fans might well have hoped there would be something to talk about for days after the concert – and now there was.

A series of cancelled gigs followed. It looked like this was the way things were going to be with Babyshambles. The fans were left with two options: desert the band or put up with it. But on 22 March the welcome news filtered through that Babyshambles had headed into a studio in Wales to complete their debut album.

The Twin Peaks studio in the Brecon Beacons, once used by the Manic Street Preachers and Catatonia, couldn't have been more remote.

But the huge stone house with its many outbuildings, set in acres of pinewoods and surrounded by waterfalls, was idyllic and peaceful. It was exactly what Pete needed – an excuse to get as far away from the hustle and temptation of the city as possible.

Pete still had his court case hovering worryingly over his head, but the magistrate relaxed his bail conditions in order for him to start recording the album. And in just seven days at the studio, Babyshambles committed an astounding twelve songs to tape, with another six written and ready to record. Pete promised a series of secret gigs to follow.

Carl, meanwhile, had signed a new record deal with Vertigo – the resurrected label under the wing of Mercury Records, which was home to the pop band Texas and jazz/trip-hop band Lamb.

Carl and Pete hadn't seen each other since the previous June, when Pete had flown off to rehab in Thailand. On 16 April they were about to meet again – in an emotional and unplanned reunion at the Boogaloo, in Highgate. Carl went into the bar around 10pm and heard that Pete was due to turn up. An hour and a half later Pete sauntered in, and the pair hugged and sat down on the leather sofa.

Pete had moved his belongings into Kate's house in Oxfordshire. The *Daily Star* ran pictures of them holidaying in Cannes together, and it finally looked like he was sorting his life out. Babyshambles had nearly finished their debut album, which 'sources' were describing as 'groundbreaking'. Hilariously understating it somewhat, drummer Adam Ficek told the *NME*: 'You're going to hear a band playing in a room.'

At the Ivor Novello awards in May, Pete and Wolfman's 'For Lovers' was pipped to the gong by Franz Ferdinand's 'Take Me Out'. Pete was nonplussed. A journalist asked if he was disappointed he didn't win. 'Didn't we?' he asked.

'He is a true romantic with a
God-given gift for melody and verse.'

ROGER POMPHREY, FILMMAKER

FIFTEEN

|POETRY|

Pete had been booked to appear at a Scottish poetry festival in May. Since coming out of Pentonville Prison he'd become potential hot property in the literary establishment and had even said he felt more comfortable writing poetry than being a rock star.

Characteristically unpredictable, Pete had been writing for a free magazine called *Full Moon Empty Sports Bag*, which was distributed in pubs the length and breadth of London. For the March issue, Pete had proposed 'the self-destructiveness of fame' as a theme. In addition to a poem about coming to terms with the fact he'd never play football for his beloved Queens Park Rangers, he had also submitted a painting for the front cover, for which he had used his own blood to denote the destructive nature of fame.

Full Moon Empty Sports Bag encouraged new writers, publishing articles, creative writing and poetry that the mainstream press wouldn't touch. Put together by the creative team behind *SleazeNation*, it worked on the same principle as another London publication, *Shoreditch Twat*, in that it was given away free in bars and galleries around Shoreditch and Hoxton near London's East End. Articles questioning globalisation and power, cutting-edge art and design and freeform poetry seemed to go down a treat with the cool Hoxton crowd. Since The Libertines had moved on from playing the 333 and the Queens of Noize had packed up and left for Camden, the area had lost some of its credibility. It was seen as a little pretentious. But by autumn 2005 the Queens were back at the decks again on Old Street, and magazines like *Full Moon* had breathed new life into the area, trying to rid it of its trustafarian boho image. As there was only a limited number of copies printed, it quickly became a collector's item – particularly the issues to which Pete had contributed.

Some of Pete's wordplay was infectious. In a poem entitled 'Clear as they can make out', Pete wrote: 'There are no clues / Except for a pair of old shoes / A morning full of blues / A brand new bruise.'

Since the poetry trip to Russia some years before, Pete had also read his work on BBC radio, posted copious spontaneous offerings on his website and in interviews regularly cited Emily Dickinson as an influence. Dickinson's poems were divided into 'books' that include life, love, nature and eternity. In one she writes: 'If I should die, And you should live, And time should gurgle on, And morn should beam, And noon should burn, As it has usual done.' Her niece, Martha Dickinson Bianchi, wrote in 1924 that she had a profound intuition; that Dickinson was 'the part of life that is always youth, always magical'.

The Burns An' A' That festival to commemorate the life and work of Scottish poet Robert Burns takes place at the Gaiety – a turn-of-the-century theatre in south Ayrshire – every year. The similarities between Pete's life and Burns's weren't lost on some of the newspapers reporting his invitation to speak at the festival. Traditionally Burns Night includes haggis, whisky and poetry 'and a special toast to the lassies' – women and alcohol were Burns's big weakness.

In addition to looking at the impact Burns had on literature, incredible new works are given a platform at the festival as well. Eddie

Reader, singer with folk band Fairground Attraction, collaborated with the Royal Scottish National Orchestra to record an album of Burns songs in 2003 and the resulting disc had entered into festival legend. Reader, for one, was glad Pete was attending. 'Maybe the idea that poetry can be radical and something really important to young people's lives has been lost a bit,' she said, emphasising the reason Pete was invited. She added that Burns wrote poetry 'about being dumped or just loving a bit of countryside' and insisted Pete was showing other young men that poetry can be important at these times.

Rock 'n' roll hadn't seen anything like The Libertines for too long. Pete knew his poetry and his literature, but he gave it an edge – he made it cool. And the truth was, thousands of kids were getting inspired. Pete's love of language; his passion for England and Englishness; his quest for Arcadia; his love of literature, all rubbed off on his audience. Rock 'n' roll had been injected with intelligence.

Suddenly Internet message boards – thought of as time-wasting and even dangerous by parents – were alive with chatter, but fans were discussing where the terms 'Albion' and 'Arcadia' had cropped up in British literature. They were talking about Oscar Wilde, quoting Blake, Yeats, Coleridge and Byron. They knew Pete loved The Smiths – perhaps there was some connection between the Romantic poets and Morrissey's lyrics; perhaps there was a link between Romanticism and rock. It was inspiring stuff. And beyond that these kids were themselves beginning to create; they had been inspired to write their own poetry and post it on the message board. They were congratulating each other on their work. Christ, their English teachers had been trying to get them to do this for years. But this wasn't something they wanted read out from a school exercise book. This was private – solely for the eyes of those who understood.

Pete encouraged them by posting his own poetry. And it was remarkable – they could see that. It was freeform all right – misspellings, bad grammar and all – but beyond the mistakes was a beauty; a beauty in the words that was so clear, anyone reading it couldn't help but be moved. Were they witnessing the germ of a song to which Peter would later add drums and bass and an indelible punk-pop guitar riff? Would it go in his Books of Albion? Would it end up in published form – in *Full Moon Empty Sports Bag* or in a future book? Or were they being given exclusive access to something that would be lost forever if the message board was ever taken down or deleted? Just a sketch of an idea; a flicker of genius only to be extinguished after it had served its purpose.

At the Burns An' A' That festival, Pete would also be hooking up again with Tam Dean Burn, with whom he'd travelled to Russia on the British Council poetry trip. Lou Reed showed up at the festival too – a major coup for organisers wanting to bring the work of Robert Burns to a wider audience. His presence gave the festival considerable cachet. Pete was a fan of The Velvet Underground, and their contribution to popular music was huge. Reed had also been one of the most famous heroin addicts in rock 'n' roll and had lived to tell the tale. Quoted in Michael Wrenn's book *Between the Lines*, Reed said: 'You do a lot of terrible things that are put together by pharmacists, because they don't have your best interests in mind.'

Suited and booted, Pete took to the stage attempting a Scottish accent before reading poems and playing songs on his acoustic guitar. He made a vain attempt to ignore a crowd chanting for Libertines songs, but it didn't take him long to give in. Pete gave a rousing performance of 'Can't Stand Me Now' and journalists there described him as 'sober and focused'.

Before leaving he asked someone in the front row for a light before removing his black tie and throwing it into the audience. With that, he was gone.

Finally the New Babyshambles album

was complete. Pete confirmed the first two singles would be 'Fuck Forever' and 'Albion'. One title mooted for the LP was 'Up The Morning' but in the end it became the far more appropriate *Down In Albion*.

Pete also admitted the album was 'terrifying' for him to listen to. 'There're a lot of really sad songs on it,' he told radio station XFM. 'Listening to those voices again and again and hearing those lyrics, but it's too late to turn back.' It was very personal. Pete hung his dirty laundry out in public on the album: dealt with his relationship with Kate, with his drug demons and with his run-ins with the law. This was different from the tabloids running regular and sensationalistic commentaries on the seedier aspects of Pete's life. On *Down In Albion* Pete was in control; and it was art. For Pete the album clearly marked a new era. The Libertines could, finally, be consigned to history – at least for now. Of course, he'd never entirely rule out a reunion.

On May Day Pete played a solo gig in Trafalgar Square to 40,000 people in aid of the Unite Against Fascism campaign. Its aim was to bring to attention the worrying rise of extreme right-wing political parties in the country, particularly the BNP's disturbing electoral successes.

'Never Again' was its motto – they wanted the threat of fascism removed from the country – and Pete joined a host of performers including Estelle, Metro Riots, Roll Deep and Lady Sovereign to highlight that aim. An ecstatic crowd cheered as the veteran Labour

MP Tony Benn took to the stage, followed by a host of other political figures.

Considering the reason for the event, the most significant moment of the day was not when Pete was singing his heart out to his adoring fans. Nor was it when he crowd surfed to find a way out of Trafalgar Square. It was when ninety-four-year-old Holocaust survivor Leon Greenman congratulated Pete at the end of his performance and told him and Alan Wass about his experience in Hitler's death camp Auschwitz.

An unforgettable picture was taken of Wass, Greenman and Pete, capturing the moment when Greenman revealed the numbers '98288' tattooed on his forearm. It was his prisoner ID at Auschwitz. His eyes are closed as he explains what it was for. Pete is staring at Greenman's arm, apparently horrified to be faced by the reality of it. Greenman told Wass and Pete that he was in Trafalgar Square because he was determined to help galvanise a new generation to oppose fascism at every turn.

Pete had also been approached to play at the Live 8 concert set to take place in London's Hyde Park on 2 July. Twenty years on from Live Aid, Sir Bob Geldof was back with a rallying cry to the leaders of the world's richest countries to cancel third world debt and make trade fairer for the poorest people around the globe when they met for the G8 summit in July.

'I was a bit ignorant as to the extent of world poverty,' Pete said. 'To think that 50,000 people a day are dying – it puts it all into perspective.' Rumours abounded that he was to take part in an extremely unlikely collaboration – with Elton John.

Before that, though, there was the Glastonbury Festival. The UK festival season always kicked off with Glastonbury at the end of June, and the festival's ethos seemed to suit Pete to a tee. It was vastly different from the corporate-sponsored live events that bands are usually forced to play. At Glastonbury you could rejoice in creativity in a communal environment rarely seen in Britain in the twenty-first century. That said, it certainly wasn't all about hippy idealism – and that was underscored by a chaotic set by Babyshambles which verged on punk-rock mayhem, ripping through tracks like 'Killamangiro', 'Black Boy Lane' and 'In Love With A Feeling'. Backstage, Kate Moss and Mick Jones were looking proudly on.

Streams had burst their banks, and once more – as had been the case in both 1997 and 1998 – the weather was relentless. Mud everywhere. Tents were swamped, some irretrievably, and any paths that organisers had laid out had turned into rivers. It was Woodstock without the need for aid from the American army choppers.

The *Independent* said 'Killamangiro' got the crowd 'skanking' and Pete, bravely, dived into the 'mud-spattered crowd … somehow making it back with his Panama hat'. Their set had turned, the journalist decided, from a freak show to a celebration, with 'Fuck Forever's 'death-or-glory sentiment perfect for the occasion'.

The *Sunday Telegraph* said the performance was typically chaotic, and the *Evening Standard* said that at close quarters Pete's 'stumbling, incoherent performing style' was exhilarating.

If Glastonbury had been a resounding success, Pete's performance at Live 8 was about to be slightly different.

Stumbling on to the huge stage in Hyde Park, Pete and Elton launched into a cover of T-Rex's 'Children of The Revolution'. It was an appropriate enough song; the trouble was Pete seemed to forget the lyrics and some members of the 210,000-strong crowd took it upon themselves to vocalise their disapproval. Pete appeared slightly dazed and staggered around the stage with a lighter hanging dramatically from his lips; his eye make-up was smudged and he looked like he was in a narcotic daze.

Pete didn't think his performance was bad at all. There were some suggestions that he was high but he hadn't taken any drugs beforehand. Yes, he was nervous – it was the biggest crowd he'd ever performed in front of – but he loved being up there. He'd gone back to Kate's afterwards to watch the performance on video.

A few days later Pete playfully told a journalist that Sir Bob Geldof's daughter Peaches had squeezed his bum just before he went on stage and whispered sweet nothings in his ear, which had put him off. That was the reason for his slightly controversial performance, he said.

It wasn't long before Peaches responded to Pete's allegations. And she chose the *Sunday Telegraph* in which to vent spleen and outline her version of events. Peaches said she was excited to meet Pete as she was a big fan of both The Libertines and Babyshambles. Her sister Pixie had apparently convinced their father to include Pete in the line-up, 'but not because I have an all-consuming lust for him that makes me, in a fit of passion, "squeeze his bum hard" before he performs,' she wrote.

Babyshambles had been gearing up for the release of their new single 'Fuck Forever' and a UK tour to precede their debut album. Unfortunately there were 'artwork issues' and the single had to be delayed for two weeks. Their previous single 'Killamangiro' had gone top ten and Pete wanted this to do the same. But it had to be perfect. When it finally came out, 'Fuck Forever' went in at number four.

When Babyshambles previously played the song live, the *Evening Standard* had described it as their 'nihilistic anthem' and Pete's first claim to greatness. The *Mirror* called it 'half-hearted and ill-formed', blaming the drugs. No surprises there.

If their fans had to wait a little longer for the single, the tour still seemed to be shaping up nicely. They added a date at the Iceland Airwaves festival in October, joining The Zutons and The Fiery Furnaces, but just when things were looking up, they had to pull a show supporting Oasis in Southampton. Pete was stuck in France at fashion designer Hedi Slimane's birthday and couldn't make it back in time.

Never shy of speaking his mind, Liam Gallagher said Pete had blown his chance of ever supporting Oasis again – Babyshambles were due to support the band again in Milton Keynes shortly after but as a result of Pete's no-show another band was found. 'This is the greatest group in the world and what we're not going to do is let anyone, Pete Doherty, Liam Gallagher or Elvis, fuck it all up,' Gallagher said. A month later, when Oasis appeared at the V festival in Chelmsford, Gallagher pointed to a large inflatable penis in the crowd that he'd noticed someone was waving aloft during Oasis's set on the main stage. 'Look,' he boomed into the mic. 'It's Pete Doherty.'

He wasn't the only celebrity to have a pop at Pete. Earlier in the year Blur's Damon Albarn said in an interview he'd like to start a new move-ment: 'Make Doherty History' – a play on the 'Make Poverty History' campaign.

The irony was that in Britpop's mid-1990s heyday, Albarn and Gallagher were famously at loggerheads, exchanging insults almost weekly in the pages of the *NME*. It came to a head with Blur and Oasis vying for the number one spot, 'Country House' vs 'Roll With It'. Now two of rock's old guard – some would say has-beens – were united in their attack on Pete Doherty. But Pete didn't want to get embroiled in what he thought was immature name-calling. If people didn't like him or what he was doing, that was fine; he'd do it anyway because there were plenty of people who did enjoy his music and fans who hung on to his every word.

Pete's media image was far from favourable; the tabloids made him seem arrogant and pretentious. It looked like he was hogging the limelight and had created this nihilist rock 'n' roller image for effect. That just wasn't true. Pete didn't like the lies that were written about him, but in a perverse way he was finding it increasingly difficult to live outside of the limelight – his myth had become bigger than him. James Mullord had said that Pete was his own worst enemy because he liked attention. The problem was he couldn't help attracting the wrong sort of attention.

Pete's appearance at Hedi Slimane's birthday party was telling. Paris-born Slimane had worked with Yves Saint Laurent before becoming the chief designer for men's clothing for Christian Dior in 2000. In 2002 he was named International Designer of the Year. And he was fascinated by Pete – so much so that he had spent a year documenting Pete's life through photographs for a new book called *London: Birth of a Cult*. Focusing on the city's thriving rock scene, the book would portray Pete as its leading light – a rock 'n' roll legend.

Pete had effectively become Slimane's muse and was often sent the latest samples from Dior's collection. One journalist noted Pete had been given a bag stuffed with designer suits just before he took a flight to Scotland. Another said his image – drainpipe jeans, black suits, dirty white shirts – was typical Slimane. But that was missing the point somewhat – Pete's sense of style was influencing Slimane, not the other way round.

The style-writers, in turn, had coined a new term: 'skank chic'. 'You're probably loaded, you love mud on your wellies, the occasional brawl, and oh yes, you're probably gorgeous,' wrote Polly Vernon in the *Observer*. Kate Moss and Pete Doherty were the obvious doyens of this new look, described as a 'trashy subversion of glamour and civilised celebrity behaviour'.

Other protagonists were Lindsay Lohan and Kelly Osbourne. It was, according to the fashion features editor at *Vogue*, 'the antithesis of flawless plastic Hollywood'.

Rock 'n' roll has always influenced fashion – from The Beatles' moptops and suits, the Teddy Boys' long coats with velvet trim, to Jim Morrison's leather trousers, and the 1960s incarnation of The Rolling Stones with their leathers and jeans.

In the late 1970s, punk fashion matched the lifestyles of its fans: being students or unemployed, they had a limited income, so punks personalised – usually meaning 'cut up' – old clothes from charity shops, and accessorised with black steel-toe-cap Doc Marten boots, chains, safety pins and body-piercing.

Just as Vivienne Westwood had inspired and become inspired by punk fashion in the 1970s, so Slimane was looking to Pete for inspiration. There was nothing new about that.

In the 1950s, the 'teenager' – a new concept – wore tight trousers and T-shirts and black leather jackets. But for middle-class adults, dressing like a rock 'n' roll star was unthinkable. After The Beatles, all that changed.

If Pete's fans weren't able to dress exactly like him, either because of the expense (the suits Slimane gave him were worth thousands), or because it was a little bit too over-the-top (on stage Pete has worn a woman's military-style jacket, 'cropped' well above the waist and T-shirts cut to shreds), they can make do with the high street. Not one to miss a trick, Top Shop swiftly began stocking Libertines-style military jackets complete with silver buttons up the sleeves.

Back in the 1960s, London represented high style – centred on

Carnaby Street – while San Francisco defined the charity-shop hippie look. Almost forty years later, Pete had managed a combination of both. Shane MacGowan once berated a journalist for turning up to an interview looking shabby; MacGowan may have been the butt of tabloid jokes for his wayward appearance but this was usually to do with his teeth, puffy face and propensity to polish off a bottle of white wine on his own each lunchtime. What he regularly did was make sure he always looked the part – usually donning a shirt and jacket or a full suit. It was the old-fashioned notion that if you went out, you should make an effort. Pete's love of 1950s England taught him the same; Hancock would rarely be seen without a tie on and his enduring image is one in which he wears his trademark trilby. The same applied to Sid James – photos always showed him wearing a tie or bowtie and a jacket of some description.

If Pete's sartorial well-being was taken care of, the same couldn't be said for his band. In July Babyshambles were forced to postpone their summer tour so they could complete *Down In Albion*. It was rumoured that Pete had sacked the remaining members of the band after an argument over a remix of 'Fuck Forever'. The usually faithful *NME* even asked: 'What do you think about Babyshambles' week of crisis? Can Doherty turn it around or is it the final letdown for the band's fans?'

It transpired that Babyshambles had never split but that it was decided they all needed space away from the public eye after months of intense attention. The cancelled gigs were, apparently, an effort to avoid the spotlight – if only temporarily.

Keeping out of the spotlight was never going to be as easy for Pete as it was for the other members of Babyshambles. He found he was constantly being hounded. One night he was having a drink with his friend Alan Wass at the Boogaloo when he was approached by Laurie Hanna, a reporter from the *Mirror*, asking for 'a quick chat'. Pete let Hanna buy him and his friends a drink before shouting: 'What is it your paper calls me – f***ing junkie scum?' and punching him in the head.

On 2 August Babyshambles were back in the saddle again, performing a gig in Stoke which the music press decided was a sign that the 'band had re-formed'. It was the first Babyshambles concert since postponing their UK tour so the reaction was no surprise.

A gig at the Oya Festival in the Norwegian capital Oslo was scheduled for 12 August, and the night before, Babyshambles played an impromptu gig at Islington's Duke of Clarence pub as a warm-up. It was typically shambolic, particularly as it was last-minute, with the audience – rammed in like battery hens – having to avoid a huge electric cable running the length of the pub floor. Kate Moss was in tow that night and joined Pete on stage for a duet on two of his songs.

The police were called towards the end after residents complained the noise levels were unacceptably high, and together with environmental health officers from the local council, thirty officers raided and took equipment away. By the time the boys in blue had entered the pub, Kate had slipped out the back, Pete through the front door. Photographer Danny Clifford, who was there that night, remembers Pete ambling down the road, 'the entire crowd following him. It was an amazing Pied Piper scene'.

The band decided to press ahead with the trip and arranged to borrow equipment in Norway. Pete dutifully boarded the plane to Oslo, but the next day the headlines told a different story to the one he had anticipated.

'Pete Doherty Fined For Drug Smuggling,' they screamed.

Customs officers at Gardermoen Airport in Norway had discovered crack cocaine and heroin on Pete. He was held for four hours and fined 8,000 Norwegian Krone – around £700 – before being freed. He had escaped a court appearance, and, after festival organisers paid £1,400 for his release, he finally arrived at the festival five hours after he was due to perform.

When Pete finally made it up on stage he puked up in front of 4,000 people before telling them of his ordeal. 'They strip-searched me and threw me in a cell for three hours. I got really mad,' he said. A festival spokesman was less than impressed when asked what he thought of the performance by the story-hungry media. 'Pete also threw vodka bottles into the audience and, at one point, told the crowd his singing was supposed to be out of tune,' he said.

Strangely, considering the debacle that was the Max Carlish documentary, Pete had agreed to let the BBC follow him round for a documentary, eventually titled *Who The F*** Is Pete Doherty?* Pete's manager James Mullord was still interested in getting a documentary made and a mutual friend introduced him to the BBC journalist Roger Pomphrey.

As well as directing comedies for the BBC and Channel 4 and promos for Massive Attack, REM and UB40, he had also directed a documentary on Jimi Hendrix's classic album, *Electric Ladyland*, in 1997.

Mullord was adamant that anyone working this close to the band would need to gel with them. They would need to effectively become part of their crowd in order for them to open up – and for a BBC documentary this was essential.

Pomphrey was determined to get to the bottom of who Pete really was; what made him tick. He wanted to discover the inner workings of the boy 'writing obsessively in his journal at the back of the tour bus'; the boy with the 'razor-quick wit', who did those hilarious 'impressions of Tony Hancock'. And he was willing to go the extra mile to find out.

Pomphrey admitted Pete was a tough subject. His phone would ring in the early hours of the morning demanding he turned up to some impromptu gig or stunt Pete was about to pull. Often, he said, when he arrived Pete was asleep and the event had been 'postponed'.

Unfortunately, in a peculiarly familiar turn of events, some screen stills were 'leaked' to the tabloids after filming on the documentary had wrapped. The shots were graphic and showed Pete cutting his chest with some broken glass before destroying two film cameras by kicking them across a patio. The scenes were deemed to be too explicit for BBC executives after mental health charities warned it could encourage copycat behaviour, and they were cut from the final edit.

As journalist Paul Morley commented, 'Roger and his crew had entered Pete's world, where logic was slashed with broken bottles as regularly as wrists. He hopes a version of his film will be shown in the cinema, a reward for the way he's [Roger] bravely, foolishly chased down the scoop, the glamour, the experience, the dragon.'

Ultimately, Pomphrey concluded he had rarely met anyone with such a desire to live life for the moment, accepting the consequences 'with no fear of criticism or scorn. He is a true romantic with a God-given gift for melody and verse,' he said.

And what the man with the God-given gift needed was a literary agent. The man he recruited for the job, however – Paul Roundhill – would end up alienating some of his fans.

Roundhill lived on the third floor of a council flat in Whitechapel. Inside it was stuffed with vinyl, books and various ephemera. The walls were covered with posters and graffiti, and a woman who went by the name of Mrs Rabbit lived there too – or at least was round there the majority of the time.

Roundhill decided to set up a website for Pete. For a start there was the name – Bala Chadha – which is street slang for crack cocaine. Roundhill claims Pete came up with it. Roundhill promised the website would be a 'living biography' to which subscribers would have access. They could watch home videos of Pete, listen to song previews and demos, read his poetry, and read updated extracts from the Books of Albion. The trouble was, for the past three years they'd been able to do that for free via the discussion board and Babyshambles and Libertines websites.

Roundhill had shot four hours of footage of Pete performing and talking with friends. In one scene Pete describes what happened when Roger Pomphrey was filming him for his BBC documentary. 'He asked me how I felt about things at the moment,' Pete says. 'I didn't think it was appropriate in the interview so I broke a glass, cut my chest, booted the camera and beat the cameraman up.'

Roundhill is heard chuckling loudly in the background. In another scene Pete asks for a razor blade before jabbing at the 'K' for Kate tattoo on his arm. Blood pours from the wound. Roundhill told the *Guardian* it was staged with red ink.

Pete, he claimed, wanted to use the site to 'communicate more closely' with his fans. But the reaction of his fans to the site was mixed. One questioned Roundhill's intentions. Some accused him of things far too libellous to print. Others expressed annoyance about a gig Roundhill had supposedly organised but at which Pete had failed to show. Some claimed Pete had succumbed to a version of 'reality TV'.

Most of Pete's fans, however, knew that ultimately he wouldn't let them down. When it came to the music, Pete would deliver; everything else was irrelevant. The Babyshambles album was a few months away from being released and they were desperate to get it home and put it on the CD player.

SIXTEEN

FANS

Back in 1965 psychedelic country rock band The Byrds were asked by a journalist to comment on the 'teenage revolution'. David Crosby told the interviewer: 'Over half of the people in the country are under twenty-five. The country isn't being run as they know and feel it should be and the wrongness and the corruption disturbs and upsets them. They're interested in the possibility of love as opposed to war … in trying to learn, trying to grow, and they're resentful of the situation they've been handed as their lot.'

Not much has changed. The difference was that in the 1960s protest was politicised; in the 1970s punk rock was, as Jon Savage says, 'an explosion of negatives … and a rejection of most values', but The Libertines and Babyshambles – and by extension their fans – chose escapism as their form of protest.

If you look at the social situation it makes sense; according to music writer Nik Cohn, in England teenage rebellion had always been something good-natured and formalised. 'It starts fashions, sells records, makes fun for the people, but it doesn't change much,' he said. 'It doesn't start revolutions. Put succinctly, England simply isn't ugly enough to make white kids feel passionate.'

In 1960s America it was very different. Like Woody Guthrie before them, American musicians found there was plenty to sing about. Folk singer Odetta, who so inspired Bob Dylan, sang about her struggle for civil rights in the early part of the decade – using negro spirituals like 'I Shall Not Be Moved' to emphasise the point. And the civil rights struggle garnered support among other American musicians and artists. At the end of the decade the country's involvement in Vietnam gave the same generation even more to sing about. Folk singer Joan Baez refused to pay the portion of her taxes that subsidised the war.

British punks outraged society with their safety pins through their noses, outrageous hairstyles – the Mohawk being the most popular – drug use and attitude. Punk self-consciously bastardised regular clothing and objects. Trousers and T-shirts were snipped apart, wrapped with gaffer tape and defaced. Safety pins were used to hold the otherwise rags together or as jewellery – often through the septum. Rubber clothing resembling fetishwear was also popular – all to subvert the idea of what clothing should be about and most of it simply designed to shock.

Punk fans brought hooliganism into rock 'n' roll but it rarely meant full-scale fights. It usually consisted of gobbing at one another in the mosh pit, throwing things at the band – often glass beer bottles – and a penchant for pogoing. All of which may have seemed violent to the untrained eye, but it was largely there for effect.

The Libertines – and to a larger extent Babyshambles and Pete Doherty – drew on elements of all these protest movements, though their style is closest to 1970s punk in its subversion. Occasionally Pete's appearance was undistinguishable from Sex Pistol Sid Vicious's. There's an iconic image of Vicious standing on stage, his hair messed up, vacantly staring into the audience. He's holding a microphone in one hand but looks like he's got no intention of using it. In the other he holds a cigarette, and his naked torso is surrounded by smoke. Pete has taken the punk-rock image of the washed-out nihilist sticking two fingers up to authority, and made it his own. He's also borrowed the idea of subverting clothing, but he has injected the image with a healthy love of literature – an intelligence rarely found in 1970s British punk rock. And by the same token his fans have appropriated his image, watered it down slightly for use offstage, and made it their own. There's no way they could go to school bare-chested, high on narcotics, wearing a ripped T-shirt. But they could take elements of his style – and particularly his attitude – and use them.

For The Libertines, their protest was to take their audiences on a journey to Arcadia, their dream of a utopian England found in the back alleys of London, and to find a beauty in its crowded East End markets and in its history.

'*Albion* is our vessel, Arcadia is our destination, and our starting point,' Pete had said back in the very beginning. 'We're going to jack it all in and throw ourselves into eternity.' And to join them you only needed an imagination. It was about freedom; it was about not being constrained by society, by the nanny state; it was about being a libertine. Carl and Pete were protesting against mediocrity. Anything just to pull people out of the mundane and the ordinary. Challenge the status quo. They were champions of the dream; soldiers of the imagination.

In their book *Starlust: The Secret Fantasies of Fans*, authors Fred and Judy Vermorel quote one fan on her passion for David Bowie: 'I thought the man was an absolute poet. I used to analyse his lyrics from here to kingdom come and try to get some meaning out of them … he was so stylish and so completely different from any other pop star of that time that he was lost in his own isolation.'

This fan could have been talking about Pete almost thirty years on.

Fast-forward to 2005 and Pete Doherty is two hours away from taking the stage at the Brixton Academy in London. A 16-year-old girl stands at Vauxhall underground station waiting for the tube. She has two-tone black and blonde hair and is wearing a Libertines-style military jacket, short skirt and green pixie boots. Her boyfriend looks like a hooded-topped hooligan. As their train arrives he conjures up some phlegm from the back of his throat and spits on the tracks. 'Are you ill?' she asks him. They both reek of alcohol as they climb aboard.

When they arrive at Brixton, crowds of teenagers are flooding onto the platform. Two soberly dressed lads waiting to get on the train look bemused.

When Pete takes to the stage later on, he too is wearing a black military jacket with silver buttons and epaulettes. Halfway through the concert a succession of teenage girls run to the side of the venue and puke on the carpet before heading back into the throng, desperately trying to get closer to their idol.

After the gig has drawn to a close, crowds of teenagers flood onto the street; many of the boys bare-chested, their hair dripping with sweat. Some are wearing pork-pie hats. Some talk in fake cockney accents. A girl who looks 12 years old stands outside a bar, barefoot. She's wearing a 'Fuck Forever' T-shirt and has a glittery scarf tied loosely around her neck. Two boys who look even younger try to negotiate the busy main road.

A fat boy moans that the T-shirts for sale are 'one size fits all'. 'I don't happen to be that one size,' he says.

Back on the tube a boy wearing a black shirt, black jeans and Converse boots sings a verse from 'Fuck Forever' repeatedly, and out of tune. It's a rallying cry. Soon twenty other people have joined in. Just

like Bowie back in the 1970s, Pete Doherty has inspired a new generation of teens in the twenty-first century. And it's a religious experience.

IN 1975 author Sheryl Garratt wrote that part of the appeal for
a fan was a desire for comradeship with their hero. Garratt was a Bay
City Rollers fan. 'With the Rollers at least,' she said, 'many became
involved not because they particularly liked the music, but because they
didn't want to miss out. We were a gang of girls having fun together,
able to identify each other by tartan scarves and badges.'

In other words, being a fan was – and still is – like being part of
a club.

Many of the boys who like Pete Doherty mimic Pete Doherty: pork-
pie hats and bags of attitude. Of course, no matter how much they tried,
they couldn't *be* Pete Doherty. The rock critic Greil Marcus said popular music has a constant need for 'weirdos' – people 'who in pre-rock
times would have been inconceivable as public icons'. Nik Cohn said it
was due to the simple fact that 'Anarchy has moved in'. In his book
Awopbopaloobop Alopbamboom he wrote: 'For thirty years you couldn't
possibly make it unless you were white, sleek, nicely spoken and phoney
… suddenly you could be black, purple, moronic, delinquent, diseased.'

One fan, talking to Fred and Judy Vermorel for their book *Starlust*,
said she always imagined pop stars in physical pain. In some ways this
'mothering instinct' is bound up with the obsession of being a fan.
'They're really time-consuming, my fantasies,' she said, 'because once I
get involved with them I'm just obsessed with that person for ages.'
Fandom is a kind of fetish. As writer and philosopher Edgar Morin said
in 1960, 'The worshipper always desires to consume his god.' And fans
collect anything they can get their hands on. Elvis biographer Jerry

Hopkins says that fans took leaves from the Tupelo trees, grass from the lawn outside Graceland – even tumblers Elvis drank from.

As for Pete Doherty – in just one day on the Internet auction site eBay these items are for sale: limited edition Pete Doherty pop art; a 'Pete Doherty is innocent' T-shirt; leather jackets, Pringle polo shirts, rosary beads and pork-pie hats 'as worn by Pete'; a used drum-skin from a Babyshambles concert, and rare demos.

According to Morin, the star is a total item of merchandise. 'There is not an inch of her body, not a shred of her soul, not a memory of her life that cannot be thrown on the market.'

But surely that's a good thing. Before The Libertines the British music scene seemed stagnant, stuck in a quagmire, clawing at the sides to get out. Then along came Pete Doherty – to some, the saviour of rock 'n' roll; to the red-top tabloids, just a junkie; to Coldplay fans, perhaps someone who simply confirmed they were getting old. The closest they had come to having somebody like Pete was Richey Edwards from the Manic Street Preachers. As Nicky Wire rightly said in his laconic, faintly arrogant way: 'Every generation has its defining moment. We are yours.'

The Manics hailed from Blackwood in the Welsh valleys. Richey Edwards joined the band in 1989 on rhythm guitar and, together with Wire, wrote the lyrics. While there were overtly political jabs – in 'Spectators of Suicide', democracy is seen as the big lie – there were also nods to disaffected youth like The Libertines ten years after them. In 'Little Baby Nothing', frontman James Dean Bradfield sang about rock being a teenager's epiphany – something that could address their alienation and boredom.

Edwards was different from the rest of the Manic Street Preachers. That was clear from only a brief glimpse at the band. He looked like a tortured soul, lost in his lyrics and seemingly bent on self-destruction.

He was anorexic and prone to self-harming. In 1991 he famously carved the words '4 Real' on his arm with a razor blade in front of the then-*NME* live reviews editor Steve Lamacq, needing seventeen stitches. It compares with Pete's self-mutilation in front of the BBC cameras fourteen years later. Then, on 1 February 1995, Edwards left his flat in Cardiff and disappeared – never to be seen again. His car was found near the Severn Bridge and he entered into rock mythology.

As Alex Petridis wrote in the *Guardian*, 'the notion of the rock star as an alienated, self-destructive and mentally unstable tragic hero is one of the most pervasive myths in pop music'. He cited Pink Floyd's Syd Barrett, tortured singer-songwriter Elliot Smith, and Vines frontman Craig Nicholls, who has Asperger's Syndrome. Petridis said that the myth's 'stock ingredients' included drug-taking, bewildering behaviour and reclusiveness – none of which has prevented their fans wanting more.

But kids could do a lot worse than adopt Pete's lust for life, his romantic vision, his passion for England and Englishness. They could also do worse than to absorb his 'two fingers up' attitude to the establishment, questioning mediocrity and trying desperately to change the status quo – at least for themselves if not everyone else. There are few bands doing that today. Most are caught up in the gravy train – the comfort zone that the music industry creates for them. They'll do the required number of press interviews; they'll climb aboard the tour bus and turn up at every date on their scheduled tour; they'll sign CDs and they'll happily add to the air of mystery that is accorded to rock stars by keeping a low profile at all other times. Most importantly they won't rock the boat. Someone like Pete Doherty, who upsets the cart and is the antithesis of this, comes along once in a generation.

The Vermorels note in their other book, *Fandemonium*, that the 'magic of stars is the work of fans'. But if that fan back in the 1970s thought David Bowie was a poet, analysed his lyrics and followed his style, that was where the comparisons with Pete Doherty ended. Mayhem didn't follow Bowie around like it does Pete. Bowie's career trajectory seemed far more staged. Pete's seems to be totally unplanned – as if not even he is aware what will happen next; he lives each day like it's his last. And that's what makes him such an enigmatic and engaging figure. But Pete isn't another Sid Vicious: he has intelligence and talent that set him apart from those who have gone before him but who have been better known for their destructiveness than their ability as musicians.

Likewise, Pete's fans share a level of intelligence seemingly higher than most teenage rock fans. They have latched onto that lust for learning in Pete and have developed a passion for literature, for poetry, for self-expression. Libertines fans were and are intelligent. The same applies to Babyshambles fans and Pete Doherty fans.

'I used to be terrified of dying,' wrote Kate, one Babyshambles fan, on the Internet discussion board. 'Then I read something Socrates said about the fear of death being an arrogant assumption – that we know enough about it to fear it – and for some reason I stopped worrying about it. I'd like to think dying meant going to some kind of idealistic heaven-type place. I don't want my soul to be at peace and be nowhere, I want to end up somewhere physical: a heaven that's a reflection of paintings of England as it never really was – the kind of hilly landscapes with people walking around in totally unsuitable clothing just quietly getting on with life. Peaceful but still real.'

It's this level of thinking – this poetic vision – that Pete seems to inspire in his fans, and that's what sets him and them apart from all the rest.

Journalist Michael Holden interviewed Pete for the men's magazine *Arena* and said he acknowledged that Pete's life had been a living nightmare for the past year or so and accepted that the one thing Pete really needed to do was make a truly great record. Holden observed: 'The other components of the myth are already there – they arrived ahead of time. All he needs to do is to stay alive and let his work catch up with his character.'

That was easier said than done. At the end of August Pete attacked Razorlight's singer Johnny Borrell backstage at the Carling Festival in Leeds.

Babyshambles and Razorlight had both been booked to play the final date of the weekend festival that takes place annually in both Reading and Leeds. Pete had walked straight to Borrell's dressing room after his performance and headbutted him before security guards intervened and escorted him to his tour bus.

Former Libertines manager and current Razorlight manager Roger Morton explains: 'After the fight happened, Babyshambles' tour manager was very apologetic. At Reading they had trashed loads of their hired equipment. I know how tough and complicated it is getting a band on the road – even when you've got vaguely together people. And there are a lot of sensitive issues like insurance – it's a vital part of the touring process. So how the fuck a band like Babyshambles can ever get booked or do anything, I'll never know.

'We'll see how long it carries on for. They certainly didn't endear themselves to the Mean Fiddler organisation [which organises the Reading and Leeds festivals]. At Leeds they were highly apologetic to us. Johnny's stance was: "This is my workplace so how can they allow people into my dressing room who are highly unstable, dangerous, potentially violent psychopaths?" He said security should have been tighter. The organisers said there is nothing they could have done about it as it was another artist who attacked him.'

Rock 'n' roll always had attitude – and that has sometimes inevitably meant violence. Punk liked to tout itself as dangerous– more to frighten the older generation than anything else – but it amounted to little more than gobbing in the mosh pit. In an article for the *NME* in 1977, Charles Shaar Murray said people got violent when they lacked the power to 'articulate their rage'. The hardcore punk scene in America, however, began attracting aggressive fans to shows in the early 1980s, who trashed clubs and caused the police to make regular appearances. Mods and Rockers famously battled in Brighton in the 1960s, and, likewise, Pete's occasional propensity for violence does nothing to harm his myth. If anything it makes him more intriguing. There's no real evidence he is a dangerous person, but the myth that has grown around him – and taken on a life of its own – has decided that he is.

Murray said Johnny Rotten had become a 'national scapegoat'. 'MPs and journalists rail at him, broadcasters refuse his advertising and ban his records ... and he gets attacked in the street.' To adults, punk was strange and scary. But Murray said in fact punk violence was largely metaphorical. The same applies to Pete. If Pete lashes out at a journalist – which he has done in the past – it is highlighted and becomes a central theme in the newspaper article. The sub-editor will take the paragraph that mentions Pete's supposed propensity for violence and use it as a 'pull quote' – in bold, larger letters. The reader is drawn to this before he reads the whole article and it reinforces the belief that this rocker is dangerous.

As Murray said, 'Media that love scandals have turned punk rockers into a national scandal, made them a larger and larger target simply in order to have the pleasure of seeing them shot down. John Rotten is

Public Punk Number One.' Today, Pete Doherty is Public Punk Number One.

By the beginning of September, Babyshambles had announced details of a new nineteen-date tour, including dates to compensate those who missed out on the cancelled summer tour. Things were hotting up in the run-up to the release of their new album and there was even a rare respite in the press from the 'Junkie Pete' headlines.

Two weeks later Carl unveiled the line-up for his new band. Dirty Pretty Things, as it would be known, would include Gary on drums, Anthony Rossomando (who had filled in for Pete in the past) on guitar, and Didz Hammond on bass, who had left his band Cooper Temple Clause specifically to join Carl.

If it finally looked like things were back on track for Pete, the soap opera was about to surprise everyone with a cliffhanger.

On Thursday 15 September, George Bush told the United Nations that the battle for democracy in Iraq was being won. Freddie Flintoff had been photographed a little worse for wear after a night on the tiles to celebrate England's Ashes victory, and Prince Harry gave an unprecedented interview to mark his twenty-first birthday.

On the front page of the *Daily Mirror*, however, was a large, grainy picture of Kate Moss chopping out a line of cocaine on a CD case. There was a smaller photo of her snorting the drug through a rolled-up five-pound note. Below that was the headline: 'Cocaine Kate'.

Inside were a further four pages of exclusive photos accompanied by the headline 'High as a Kate'. Somehow, somebody had secretly filmed her at the Metropolis recording studios in Chiswick, where Pete and the rest of Babyshambles had been recording their album. Of course, Pete snorting a line of coke wasn't news, nor anyone else in his entourage. But Kate Moss – this was different. She was a supermodel, and more importantly she had a two-year-old daughter. That was the clincher as far as middle England was concerned.

Picking up the story, the *Evening Standard* focused on the fact that Kate had insisted two years previously that she'd given up drugs for good. Back then she'd said she didn't do any class A drug; she also had a stint in the Priory, saying she'd been doing 'too much partying'.

The *Mirror*'s story explicitly described everything that happened that night in the studio, claiming Kate had 'five lines in 40 minutes'. Mick Jones was also taking the drug, it said.

Kate and Pete were in New York at the time the story came out, for fashion week. Her spokesman told journalists she never discussed her private life, but inevitably reporters had tracked her down to the hotel she was staying at with Pete. When confronted she said: 'A video? What video? F*** off, I don't want to know,' before launching into a tirade of swearing.

But the news 'revelations' didn't stop there. The following day the same paper ran a story claiming Kate smoked 'too much "skunk" cannabis' on holiday. It also published pictures of a 'seeping wound' around Pete's Naltrexone heroin implant, saying he'd complained of being in pain. They were taken from the same footage as the cocaine sting.

The night after the first story broke, Kate's friend, advertising mogul David Lipman, visited her at her hotel in New York. Initially Kate was still seething – she felt the papers had overstepped the mark this time and both her and Pete wanted blood. But Lipman told her the story wasn't going to go away. He knew the papers back in England were going to have a field day with this one and if she handled this wrongly it could have serious repercussions on her career. He told her to think of her daughter, Lila Grace, when coming to her decision.

Although Kate is clearly an A-list celebrity and therefore some sections of the media see her life as a free-for-all, in some corners there were cries of 'hypocrisy'. It was an open secret that Fleet Street and cocaine went hand in hand, almost as much as its association with alcohol in years gone by. The pop star Robbie Williams told the *Independent* he'd even taken cocaine with some media figures who were now saying that Kate shouldn't take drugs. He said Kate's private life should remain private – it had no bearing on her work as a model.

Talk soon turned to outing the mole who had taken the pictures in the first place and been paid by the *Mirror*.

Pete had his suspicions. At one point Kate was looking directly at the camera, laughing and joking. Surely it was the person sitting in front of her – but who was that? Did they use a concealed camera? Was it a cameraphone?

It wasn't long before Babyshambles manager James Mullord came into the frame. He had been questioning Mick Jones's production style and that had irked Pete. He'd also bought audio surveillance equipment two weeks before, but claimed later it was because he seriously questioned the loyalty of some of the people surrounding Pete.

In the past Mullord had said, 'You wouldn't believe the sort of money I've been offered for pictures of Pete and Kate – it's hundreds of thousands … but I've told Pete I don't want him to do any press for anything but his music.'

For a few days after the photos were published, Mullord helped in trying to out the culprit. He then flew to France and on to Scotland – and that was when he was outed as the possible culprit.

Mick Jones's wife Miranda Davis was a close friend of Kate Moss. She was convinced Mullord was to blame, and sent him a barrage of text messages accusing him of double-crossing not just Kate, but Pete and Mick as well. In addition his name was sullied over the Internet. But Mullord told the *Evening Standard* that he wasn't even in the studio when the film must have been taken. Initially he was accused of heading back to the studio the following day and collecting the footage to pass on to the *Mirror*.

James Mullord was in awe of Pete Doherty. 'He's a genius,' he would say. 'He's a poet.' He truly felt he'd landed on his feet managing Pete. 'I've never met anybody as charming or charismatic as Peter.' Yes, he wasn't the easiest person – Mullord admitted as much – but what did it matter when you were looking after someone so talented?

But Mullord also, perhaps naively, saw the close-knit 'gang' surrounding Pete as central to his charge's creativity. The very suggestion that an 'outsider' should make a film or write a book about Pete was alien to him; as far as Mullord was concerned, it couldn't and wouldn't happen unless that person was from their inner sanctum, from 'Pete's group'. But there were an increasing number of 'druggy' hangers-on surrounding Pete since he'd formed Babyshambles, and some of his closest friends and family were concerned. As far back as the Gunter Grove gig in Wolfman's flat, Gary had turned up willing to play the gig with Pete but had left as soon as he'd clocked the 'druggy crowd' that had started to assemble. Carl had said in an interview some time before that he felt everyone 'around' Babyshambles was more tolerant of Pete's drug abuse.

In truth it was hard to believe Mullord had anything to do with the Kate Moss incident. He was far too loyal to Pete, far too in awe of his talent to stitch him up. He was an inexperienced player among the music industry big league – even less experienced in management. It made far more sense that it was an 'acquaintance' of Pete connected with the East End drug world.

The video for the 'Albion' single had already been made – by Roger Pomphrey who had filmed the documentary for the BBC. It had contained a segment in which Pete and Mullord walk together around Trafalgar Square. By the time the video was released, Mullord's face had been digitally erased from the final edit.

The decision had been taken by Rough Trade. Mullord felt they were doing it just to keep Pete happy and that Pete would never have pulled such a petty move himself.

It was trivial, but a tide of paranoia was sweeping over Pete's once tight-knit 'family'. They still didn't know who had betrayed them and, until the culprit was found, some people were treating Pete with kid gloves. He'd been through a lot.

'I have been clean on this tour. It's libellous
to call me a smackhead - it's a good job
I am too disorganised to sue.'

PETE DOHERTY

SEVENTEEN

|DOWN|IN|ALBION|

Kate's publicist issued a statement saying she took full responsibility for her actions. 'I also accept that there are various personal issues that I need to address and have started taking the difficult, yet necessary, steps to resolve them,' Kate said. 'I want to apologise to all of the people I have let down because of my behaviour, which has reflected badly on my family, friends, co-workers, business associates and others.'

She then booked herself into the Meadows Clinic in Arizona. Whether she thought she really had a problem with drugs or not is irrelevant. It was seen as a necessary exorcism in the eyes of the public – or at least the media. It was a rite of passage that every celebrity admitting to a 'drug problem' had to go through, whether or not it was the best thing for them to do. If Kate was just a recreational user, an expensive rehab clinic in Arizona was probably not even necessary.

After all, according to Guy Trebay, a columnist on New York's *Village Voice* newspaper, the modelling world is rife with class As. Backstage, apparently, models snort coke out of empty lipstick cases, and 'Do I smell Chanel?' is code for 'Got coke?'

But if heading to rehab was necessary to revive her career then that's what she'd do. It was a very public way of addressing what society deemed as a 'wrong'. There was also the issue of her daughter. If the press are to be believed, Lila Grace's father, the publisher Jefferson Hack, wasn't too enamoured with Kate's choice of boyfriend in the first place. Now with the world looking on to see how he'd react to the pictures, he was left with little choice but to back Kate's decision to attend rehab.

The Meadows is owned by a woman called Pia Mellody, a former alcoholic who runs the centre with her husband, Pat. Nestled in the high Sonoron Desert north of Phoenix, it offers treatments for alcoholism, drug addiction, sex addiction, eating disorders, post-traumatic stress disorder, bi-polar disorder and even love addiction.

Kate was certainly not the lone celebrity among its patients. Alumni (the word the Meadows uses to refer to former patients) include Elle McPherson – who was treated for post-natal depression – footballer Paul Gascoigne and Ronnie Wood of the Rolling Stones – who both went to address their alcohol problems – Drew Barrymore and Whitney Houston.

Peaceful walks in the centre's vast and beautiful gardens, combined with a strict twelve-step programme based on the tenets of Alcoholics Anonymous, are designed to cure patients of their addictions. The central component of the twelve-step programme is to meet regularly and share both problems and triumphs. The most widely cited of the steps is to admit to your addiction, but elsewhere in the programme the philosophy is that addicts should place their faith in a higher power who could 'restore them to sanity', make a list of all the people they had harmed and promise to reconcile, and to enjoy a spiritual awakening.

Back in London, the recording studio in which Kate was filmed snorting coke was raided by police and it was revealed that she would be interviewed on her return to London.

Lucrative modelling contracts with H&M, Chanel and Burberry were withdrawn, but while Kate was getting treated in Arizona her agent revealed she was on the verge of signing a contract with a 'prestigious perfume brand'. It was later announced she'd been approached by a major fashion house and offered movie roles. After she left the Meadows, Kate flew to Ibiza to shoot photos for Italian fashion designer Roberto Cavalli's 2006 collection, due to appear in *Vogue*. She was also reunited with Lila Grace.

Pete, meanwhile, had to deal with even more feverish press attention than usual. The *Sunday Mirror* managed to find a twenty-one-year-old Swedish drama student who claimed Pete had once asked her to marry him and that he had cried when they first had sex.

It was easier to ignore this sort of story. Nothing could hurt him more than the photos that had been published a couple of weeks before of Kate in the studio. He must have felt responsible. And now the love of his life was thousands of miles away and he didn't know when he'd see her again.

ON 21 September Babyshambles were back on the road again, playing the first gig of their highly anticipated UK tour. With the media still baying at his heels, this tour was going to be a little different – the first time the paparazzi would be jostling for position by the backstage door, and tabloid hacks would be willing to pay four or five times the value for a ticket on the black market.

Nevertheless, Pete was just Pete and tried not to let it get to him. He was also characteristically open with the press in interviews. He told the local paper in Carlisle this was the 'first time in years I've come on tour not being a heroin addict'. In an interview with a Dundee radio station he said, 'A lot of people basically are obsessed with the missus and I don't know really ... she's just a bird from south London.'

The tour bore all the eventful hallmarks of the usual 'Pete Doherty experience': scuffles with fans, inter-band arguments, police stop-and-searches – in Dundee Pete was pulled up for drinking in the street – and in Scotland the tour bus was raided after a 16-year-old girl fan disappeared with the band. But it did seem Pete was being unfairly targeted because of his notoriety.

The worst came on 2 October. Babyshambles had just finished an incendiary set at Shrewsbury's Music Hall when their tour bus was again raided by police – this time drug-squad officers and sniffer dogs. Pete was arrested for possessing class A drugs and detained overnight. As a result, a gig in Norwich the following evening had to be cancelled.

After his release the next day Pete told waiting reporters the law was an 'arse' and his arrest had been an inconvenience. He also said they'd got it completely wrong – that they'd mistaken his Naltrexone implant for hard drugs. Pete claimed his implant had gone septic and was 'spitting pills'. It was frustrating for Pete. Every day of the tour Babyshambles had been warned they could be subjected to raids by police. But Pete insisted he'd been clean on the tour. 'It's libellous to call me a smackhead,' he said. 'It's a good job I am too disorganised to sue.' Adam Ficek called it a witch-hunt and Pete was bailed to appear again in Telford in December. Pete was later vindicated when the police said no further action would be taken.

As the tour drew to a close journalists were beginning to get sneak previews of the new Babyshambles album, *Down In Albion*. And by and large, they were impressed. The problem for the record company was that it had been available to download on illegal file-sharing networks over the Internet for four weeks already, so hardcore fans were already listening to *Down In Albion* on their iPods. According to one newspaper, as illegal downloading has thrived, the record industry has lost about one-third of its sales in the last three years. Another said the British Phonographic Industry would be continuing its crackdown on those illegally uploading the music.

Pete was philosophical, saying, 'If you're a fan, you have to have the downloads.' Pete had never been in it for the money anyway. If anyone was going to get annoyed about the album being leaked, it would be the men in suits. Pete knew what it was like to be skint – he was just happy he had people out there wanting to listen to the music he was making. However, his attitude didn't necessarily apply to everyone. When, mid-interview, a Japanese journalist admitted to downloading the album, Pete put the phone down on her.

Meanwhile, Carl's new band debuted their material at some low-key gigs in Italy. In addition to playing acoustic versions of some Libertines crowd-pleasers, new songs 'Dead Wood', 'The Enemy' and 'Pirates' seemed to go down well.

Babyshambles played the final gig on their tour at the Brixton Academy. When Pete took off his jacket he revealed a T-shirt sliced to pieces underneath, and black sleeves up his arms – not actually attached to anything – that looked like ladies' gloves from the 1920s.

Emblazoned across the skin of Adam Ficek's bass drum were the words 'Pipe Down' – a cheeky reference to crack. (The song 'Pipedown' on the album was, Pete said, actually anti-drugs – it was about 'telling tales' on himself.) On stage, from behind the speaker cabs, an old guy in a pork-pie hat grinned throughout the performance as he videoed the event.

The first song was a new one with which few in the audience were familiar, but it didn't seem to matter: their idol had taken to the stage.

Things heated up with 'Killamangiro', drowned out at the beginning by incessant screaming. It was a strange, vaudeville performance, coherent and together, yet foreshadowed by a feeling that something was about to happen. It was as if the audience was anticipating something – like they were waiting for a car crash that didn't materialise. It was an unpredictable night.

There was a lengthy gap between the last song and the encore. The band disappeared for over ten minutes; some fans chose to leave, others began booing, loudly and somewhat unfairly – even the Babyshambles faithful turn into a football mob when the star of the show takes longer than they like to reappear. Others began to debate whether Shane MacGowan would make a surprise appearance – after all, he had stumbled out of his cab just minutes before Pete went on stage.

But Pete did reappear and the world was all right once more.

The encore consisted of 'Fuck Forever', and the Doorsy fifteen-minute epic 'Wolfman', accompanied by relentless strobe lighting, and during which Pete stage-dived and lost his shirt. While Pete rode on the hands of the crowd, Wolfman himself, sporting dark glasses, entered the stage and began to rap poetry while the band jammed.

As about ten fans joined Pete back on stage, the security guards seemed confused, and the star of the show, meanwhile, looked like he was relishing the mayhem of it all.

Pete looked relatively composed that night – if a little dazed. How someone can withstand being in the public eye as much as he has is beyond comprehension. The tabloids had managed to watch almost every gig on the tour – just in case something happened. In Southampton an *Evening Standard* journalist was evicted for 'asking too many questions'. Unsurprisingly the last three gigs of the tour had to be cancelled due to 'fatigue' and 'continued harassment from outside sources'.

But the Brixton gig was well received. For the *Evening Standard*'s Andre Pain the onstage chemistry was surprising considering some of the hit-and-miss gigs earlier in the year. 'Babyshambles were tight and even funky,' he concluded, despite Pete's vocals being erratic. 'He is undoubtedly a charismatic frontman … it is impossible to ignore his star quality.'

Fazed webzine said the fact that the mainstream didn't understand Pete or his music was what made him so appealing. 'Tonight Pete doesn't give a damn if he impresses the *Daily Mail* readers, some of whom are here to see what the fuss is about, to see him fall,' the reviewer noted. 'The venues are bigger and Doherty is riding a wave of success.'

The *Mirror* chose to mark the gig by running a story on Shane MacGowan, who 'flashed £20 notes from his taxi as he sped away' following the gig.

The Books of Albion had been a source of media interest for some time. In interviews Pete could be more than cryptic, often downright difficult. But in the Books of Albion it was as if he bared his soul more than anywhere else. The excerpts that had appeared on the Internet contained everything from poetry, lyrics and drug-induced rambling, to red-wine stains, artwork and messages of love. He held nothing back.

In one are half-formed lyrics for a song entitled 'Palace of Bone'. 'I'm going to build me a palace of bone,' he writes. 'High open walls and an ebony throne / and all the broken children from all the broken homes / can all come and dance in my palace of bone.'

Elsewhere there is the telling phrase: 'At the mercy of not very clever people'; on another page someone, possibly Pete, writes: 'I woke up dead a few times / just blacked out / didn't know what was happening.'

It then lists: '30–40 downers, 600mg of Methadone, bottle of vodka.' On the following page is a cartoon of a man blowing smoke from a joint into cut-out photographs of two policemen. On another still there is a photo of Pete kissing an unidentified girl, eyes closed. Above it is the line, 'My heart sings, these days have been joyous.'

Pete had apparently given one volume of the Books of Albion to photographer Jamie-James Medina, who had snapped him since The Libertines days. Medina chose to publish pages from the book in the *Observer* music magazine in October. 'These diaries,' it said, 'reveal a sensitive singer whose poetry is both haunting and emotional.'

One entry is written to a lover, which the magazine presumed was Kate. 'No numbing or narrowing of the mind can strip my soul of its orchestra that pipes up a crescendo when you say you love me,' Pete writes. 'And, in my heart, I am inclined to trust you.'

The book also included press cuttings – there was one scrap glued in with the headline: 'Boss of QPR on gun plot charge.' Elsewhere there was a psychedelic-style drawing of Pete presented to him by a fan. On another page he has written down his concept for the new Babyshambles album – a three-act 'play' on the theme of *Beauty and the Beast*. 'Beast meets girl,' he writes under Act 1. 'Beast re-pledges his love to girl … but his actions result in tragedy … Beast is sent to Penton (ville),' he writes in Act 2. Finally, rehabilitated, 'Beast is released from prison and hailed as a hero.' At the end of Act 3, the beast attempts to lead a normal life but is 'drawn back into things'.

It's the master plan, the entire concept of *Down In Albion*. Clearly biographical, Pete had laid his soul down on tape. It was all there – not just his thoughts and feelings but a factual biography of the past year or so. What Pete didn't realise was that the ending of Act 3 would play out in a slightly different way to that which he intended.

Pete liked the *Guardian* and *Observer*. They were two of the few newspapers he trusted. They often got it right, he thought. And it was to the *Guardian* that he gave a rare and open interview, which was published on 4 November. But it was journalist Simon Hattenstone's observations that made for more interesting reading.

The pair met in a shabby hotel in East London's Brick Lane – one of Pete's favourite haunts. Ficek and McConnell told Hattenstone that Pete was upstairs cleaning his room in preparation for the meeting. But when Hattenstone went up there he was met by what he described as a 'shocking state': for one, there was a motorcycle *in* the hotel room which Pete proceeded to rev while the interview was taking place; drug paraphernalia was lying predictably all over the unmade bed, along with scores of 'blackened, broken miniature bottles of alcohol from which he has been smoking'; and, horrifically, the words ROUGH TRADE had been 'daubed on the wall in fresh, dripping blood'. Pete told Hattenstone that in addition to being the name of his record company, it was a mixed-message expression which meant both 'bum deal kid' and was also a dated word for 'rent boy'.

Pete wasn't the first rocker to self-harm. Sid Vicious famously used to injure himself on stage, slashing his chest before horrified onlookers. He had been cutting himself since he turned eighteen. Photographer Dennis Morris recalled seeing Vicious in Malcolm McLaren's office shortly after he came off tour. Vicious walked in with a knife stuck in his leg. 'We said, "Sid, you've got a knife in your leg." And he said, "Uh, have I?" and pulled it out. He was so doped up all the time, especially on heroin, he never felt it.'

Richey Edwards once said: 'Cutting myself or hurting myself is the way I deal with anger.' Courtney Love famously said self-destructiveness could be a byword for self-reflection and demonstrate a poetic leaning.

'It can mean empathy, it can mean a hedonism and a libertarianism and a lack of judgement,' she said. Rocker Marilyn Manson was hospitalised for self-harm and depression, claiming it was a form of 'wanting to let go – of wanting to get out'. On stage he claimed he was trying to show people his pain, whereas offstage he was simply feeling it.

Hattenstone said Pete was 'out of it' when they met. A young girl called Nuha Razih was filming the interview for posterity – a future 'Pete-produced' documentary perhaps. Razih had been the subject of a *News of The World* article the week before, in which she was 'outed' – wrongly as it turns out – as Pete's lover.

Hattenstone asked Pete whether he was aware of the frequent references to death on the new album. 'You seem half in love with the idea of death,' Hattenstone said, making a veiled reference to Keats' poem 'Ode To A Nightingale' in which the poet writes: 'I have been half in love with easeful Death'. Pete, however, was unequivocal: 'No. No. You either is or you ain't.'

He said that, contrary to press reports, there was no pressure for him to achieve academically when he was young. He said he wasn't into 'chart music and bands' when he was younger. 'Just into songs.'

It's this reinvention of his childhood that has helped form the myth of Pete Doherty. In fact, according to Andrew Asplin, Pete's old friend when he lived on the military base in Germany, they loved American boy band New Kids On The Block, SNAP and the Fresh Prince. But that wouldn't be very cool to admit.

Finally, Pete revealed that Kate was fine and wanted him to go into rehab at the Meadows after she had come out. If he did, it would be the first time he had ever gone into rehab of his own volition.

Kate didn't like Pete talking to the media about their relationship. They'd argued about this before, but he didn't elaborate – even with the

Guardian, which he trusted. Pete couldn't help being honest and in a way he wanted the world to know that things were still OK between him and Kate, despite what the tabloids were saying.

Incredibly, by the beginning of November, the very paper that had exposed Kate and had been the bane of Pete's life decided he was actually a modern-day icon. The *Mirror* article was written by Tony Parsons. Parsons had worked on the *NME* as a young man and was now an author and familiar pundit on TV. He'd also been instrumental in documenting the punk-rock movement in the 1970s along with his then-wife Julie Burchill. In 1977 they'd co-written a book called *The Boy Looked At Johnny* – a history of punk in which they'd taken a jab at American bands like the New York Dolls, who they claimed made better junkies than punks. Pete had borrowed the book's title for a Libertines song.

Parsons described *Down In Albion* as an instant classic, saying Pete would 'take his place among the true greats of British rock music'. He added that he couldn't imagine anyone who had ever loved British rock music not loving the new Babyshambles record. It was some eulogy, but hardly made up for the thrashing Pete had taken from the paper over the past year or so.

The *Independent* noted the album's autobiographical nature and said its ragged quality was an 'improvement on The Libertines formula'.

The Songs On Down In Albion are both confessional and private. They tell stories – something Pete felt was imperative in songwriting. He was also well aware that although his tortured soul was laid bare on this album; the tabloids would largely opt to talk about his drug problems rather than the emotion in the songs, the melodies or their narrative.

Its most recognisable numbers are the singles 'Fuck Forever', 'Killamangiro' and 'Albion'. The first track on the album, 'La Belle Et Le Bête' (Beauty And The Beast), is an ironic and very British ditty about a 'coked-up pansy' that demonstrates not just Pete's lyrical dexterity but also that Kate had a talent for singing as well. 'Is she more beautiful than me?' she asks. And probably knew the answer. 'La Belle Et Le Bête' turns into a dark, vaudeville performance at the end, with sniggering in the background and ad-libbing.

It wasn't the first time Kate had appeared on record – she had joined Oasis at Maison Rouge Studios in London to add vocals and tambourine for a re-recording of their B-side 'Fade Away' on the War Child album *Help*. It also featured her then-boyfriend Johnny Depp on guitar.

Kate and Pete were continuing a lineage of boyfriend/girlfriend, husband/wife collaborations in rock – some controversial – that boasted John and Yoko, Paul and Linda, Mick Jagger and Marianne Faithfull, and recently Rod Stewart and Penny Lancaster. In February 2005 Lancaster claimed they recorded music together all the time but that she knew she'd 'get slated for it'.

With Kate it was different. She was beautiful, mysterious and very cool, and while she didn't add any kudos as far as Babyshambles fans were concerned, she certainly wasn't about to incur their wrath.

There's an unmistakable ska influence running through the entire album. In 'Sticks And Stones' – a response to the hounding he gets from the tabloids, perhaps – Pete plays around with his own lyrics, referencing a Libertines single with the line 'Don't look back into the mother-f***ing sun'. It's a strange affair – acoustic, sparse, and once again it seems ad-libbed in places.

'A Rebours' ('Against the Grain') is a perfect, bouncy slice of pop in the vein of The Buzzcocks or The Only Ones. Its title is likely borrowed from the book of the same name by French author J.K. Huysmans – a novel about decadence, dandyism and overcoming boredom in the late 1800s. It famously influenced Baudelaire, Flaubert and Oscar Wilde.

'The 32nd of December' is a happy-go-lucky Kinksy number; Pete's vocals are occasionally off-key but it sounds as if the song has been recorded in one take – and whatever happened in that take was left on the final recording. If evidence was ever needed that Pete wasn't into manufactured pop pap, this was it.

The press were divided.

The *Independent* and its sister paper the *Independent on Sunday* disagreed over the finer points of *Down In Albion*. The *IoS* said it felt like a bag of half-finished demos. Pete's voice, it decided, 'suggests he was either out of his mind during the sessions, or pretending to be'. The *Independent*, on the other hand, said the album contained 'a handful of indelibly catchy, albeit ramshackle, outsider anthems' and that on the whole it was a 'far better album than we have any right to expect from the tabloids' favourite dissolute folk devil'. The *Sunday Telegraph* said there wasn't enough 'musical meat here to make a sandwich', and the *Daily Mail* called it 'patchy', despite 'Ficek's doughty drumming' and Mick Jones's 'spirited production', concluding though, that the band had potential.

The BBC *Collective* website said Pete revealed 'flashes of touching poetry', calling the record 'a carcass worth picking over'; *Gigwise* decided Pete 'hadn't lost his eloquence and knack for storytelling' but that his attention had turned 'to the darker side' of his imaginary world, 'Albion'. Although the *Drowned in Sound* website didn't really like the album, it said the choruses of 'The 32nd of December' and 'Up The Morning' 'revealed shards of greatness' and that on the album's title track 'Albion' Pete sounded 'disarmingly vulnerable and utterly compelling'.

Incredibly, the best review had come from Tony Parsons in the *Daily Mirror*.

Being apart from Kate was hard. But Pete had found love and he was proud of his achievements on *Down In Albion*. He summed it up in an interview with the *Irish Times*: 'I do believe in love, and I do believe in the album, and I've waited patiently for both. Now that both have arrived at the same time, it's just a question of holding it together.'

He admitted he needed to 'wise up'. For the sake of his own sanity, for Kate's sake, and for Astile.

Pete Doherty had become a living legend – some would say for all the wrong reasons. The majority of his fans, some from as far back as the early days of The Libertines, had stayed faithful, despite all the cancelled gigs and no-shows. And the establishment was beginning to recognise his talent as well. After relentless media coverage of his extra-curricular habits, perhaps they thought they ought to listen to what Pete actually did for a living. Here, finally, there was interest beyond the drugs, beyond the supermodel girlfriend, beyond the onstage brawling. For Pete it was always the music that mattered most. Would it take the launch of the debut Babyshambles album to persuade the rest of the country that he'd been saying this all along?

EIGHTEEN

|BETTER|TO|BURN|OUT|

It was one of life's peculiar ironies when Kate Moss's ex-beau Johnny Depp revealed he was to star in a movie about seventeenth-century poet, naval officer, promiscuous bisexual and brawler, the Earl of Rochester, who lived fast and died young at the tender age of thirty-three. The film was called *The Libertine* and was due for release in November – around the same time as the Babyshambles album.

John Wilmot, Earl of Rochester lived during the reign of Charles II. Rochester's poetry was explicit to say the least. In 'A Satyre On Charles II' he wrote: 'Peace is his aim, his gentleness is such, And love he loves, for he loves fucking much. Nor are his high desires above his strength, His scepter and his prick are of a length.' 'A Ramble In St James's Park' was even more risqué: 'Each job of whose spermatic sluice / Had filled her c*** with wholesome juice,' he wrote.

Pete Doherty's 'Fuck Forever' would hardly elicit the same reaction from society four hundred years later.

Rochester was a member of the Ballers' Club – an infamous fellowship dedicated to imbibing alcohol and debauchery; he lived during the Restoration – also known as the 'libertine' period. The word 'libertine' had been coined a hundred years earlier to describe an offshoot of the church which had decided that, since God had created everything, sin couldn't exist. Understandably, their actions – based on this philosophy – shook the church to its foundations and 'libertine' soon came to mean 'debauched'. Historian A.C. Grayling, an expert on the subject, says the 'louche lifestyles of Kate Moss and Pete Doherty seem positively Rochester-like'.

But it wasn't the last time history would bear witness to 'the libertine'. A century after Rochester there was Sir Francis Dashwood – son of a wealthy businessman who had married into the landed gentry and became an MP. But Dashwood was also a libertine. Together with contemporaries the Earl of Sandwich, the Marquis of Granby and, most shockingly, the then Prince of Wales, he formed the 'Hellfire Club' in which members could take part in mock religious ceremonies and all manner of debauchery. Dashwood and his cronies used masks and costumes to disguise themselves (usually as monks) and indulge in various unspeakable activities, which included boarding barges and taking prostitutes down the Thames from London to act as masked 'nuns' to their 'monks'; inevitably they were accused of devil worship and indulging in orgies. Dashwood didn't help his reputation by building a network of caves near his ancestral home in West Wycombe Hill to be used by the 'monks' for what the locals again assumed was group sex.

The Albion Rooms and Pete and Carl's dream of a libertarian lifestyle were positively tame by comparison. But every generation – every century it seems – has its libertines. It is perhaps surprising that in the twenty-first century those who live what in society's eyes are dissolute lives are still vilified by the establishment – today represented by the mainstream press.

And the Internet – used to such effect by Pete for his musings, impromptu gig announcements devoid of record company control, and poetry – worries some sections of mainstream society who feel they are unable to exert any control over it; they are devoid of power when it comes to the very method of communication and expression today's libertines have chosen as their medium.

In Pete's Arcadian world, death should not be feared. It is the ultimate freedom – nirvana for a libertine – simply because it is the biggest thing of which 'society' is afraid, because it is the biggest thing it can't control.

Of course, society loves to lose control through drinking huge volumes of alcohol each week. But when the libertine chooses drugs as his method of escape, he is seen as a 'junkie' and his brand of 'out of control' is frowned upon.

Pete had inspired debate among his fans. Those who hadn't already devoured literature began to read the Romantic poets, books on the history of London and others that spoke of the concept of 'Albion'. Joining in a debate about liberty, 'KateD' posted a message on Pete's website that said: 'To take liberty to extremes would be anarchy, but that would end up with some people restricting the freedom of others.' She recalled an earlier posting of Pete's which said: 'But let not your actions or desires infringe upon the liberty of others.'

'Obviously not everyone can have the freedom to do whatever they want. It confuses me,' Kate admitted. Morality was relative, she said. 'What's moral this century isn't exactly the same as what was moral last century.'

The name Peter Perrett would persistently emerge in discussions about Pete and about the trajectory his life seemed to be on. Perrett was the singer in punk band The Only Ones, who had disbanded in 1981 – five years after they formed. Perrett was hedonistic, effortlessly charismatic and beautiful. He was also a heroin addict. And like Pete twenty years later, the media were fascinated by him.

There were other, striking similarities with Pete's life. The Only Ones were said to have been falling apart from day one. Pete and Carl had acknowledged the same was true of The Libertines; the minute they signed their deal with Rough Trade it was the beginning of the end for them – opening their lives up to a world in which they could afford all the drugs they wanted.

The Only Ones recorded three albums for CBS, and whereas all the managers involved with Pete – Roger Morton, Banny Poostchi, Alan McGee and James Mullord – had said he was 'difficult to manage', so CBS felt The Only Ones were hard to market: one LP contained a photograph of the band in their dressing room at a gig with Perrett looking like he was shooting up. Definitely one worthy of a 'parental guidance' sticker.

The Only Ones' most memorable song was 'Another Girl Another Planet'. Pete thought it was a classic and would play it acoustically at the Albion Rooms all the time. Back in April 2004, shortly after Babyshambles released their debut single, Perrett joined them on stage to perform his classic, and The Libertines song 'Don't Look Back Into The Sun'. It was a wonderful moment for Pete, but it also got tongues wagging about the comparisons between the two vocalists on stage. An acoustic version of the song by Pete eventually appeared for download on the Internet. Pete and Perrett may have been divided by a generation but their lives had followed incredibly similar paths.

Select magazine called Perrett 'an individual in a twilight of sex, drugs and narcissism'. Like Pete, Perrett had had run-ins with the law, although his were slightly more serious than Pete's: on The Only Ones' last US tour Perrett was arrested for attempted murder after running someone over with a Hertz rental car while he was high on drugs. The California warrant is still in force. When Perrett returned to the UK he made a swift exit from the music scene and spent the next fifteen years

– often called his 'lost years' – heading into narcotic oblivion. Like Pete, he was renowned for living for the moment.

Hard drugs had been around in the 1960s – ten years or more before Perrett, rock's torchbearers were dabbling with the brown. But mostly, as music journalist Charles Shaar Murray put it, they simply 'smoked their shit and sat giggling in their headphones'.

In an article for underground magazine *Cream* in 1972, Murray said for the past few years heroin and cocaine had re-entered their 'hip' vocabulary. The jazz men of the 1940s and 1950s had taken these hard narcotics, he acknowledged, but said hippies in the 1960s had learned from history and hoped that dropping acid and smoking marijuana wouldn't lead onto the so-called 'hard stuff'. Murray says there was a general consensus against hard narcotics, 'until we started losing a few rock and roll stars here and there'.

Pete hadn't read the warnings.

Oklahoma singer-songwriter Hoyt Axton had written 'The Pusher', immortalised by Steppenwolf, about smoking weed and popping pills but warned explicitly against the perils of harder stuff.

Murray summed it up: 'We're going to have to eliminate this poison from our community. Skag ain't dope, it's death.'

Others, it could be argued, glorified its use. Murray quotes Leonard Cohen's *The Butcher* in which the singer describes inserting a silver needle into his arm. The Heartbreakers epitomised 1970s American punk rock, and Johnny Thunders, Richard Hell and Jerry Nolan all had heroin habits to match the aggression of the music. Their then-manager Lee Black Childers told journalist Jon Savage some years later: 'They brought heroin to the punk scene in England. When we arrived it was a very innocent scene, drug-wise, and it changed extremely fast.' Jon Savage notes the group 'scored within twenty-four hours of arriving in the country'.

One of their early numbers was 'Chinese Rocks' – a paean to heroin from the Far East, which had become popular on New York's Lower East Side in the mid-to-late 1970s.

In 1985 rumours abounded that Culture Club's flamboyant singer Boy George was addicted to heroin. Added to that, his relationship with the band's drummer Jon Moss had dissolved and he was on the rocky road into decline. The following summer he admitted his addiction but shortly afterwards a keyboard player who had worked with Culture Club in the past was found dead of a heroin overdose in George's house. Culture Club broke up, George got clean and his comeback single, 'Everything I Own', in 1987 was one of the music industry's most emotional returns.

Eric Clapton said artists needed drugs to free their minds and their imaginations 'from the prejudices and snobbery that have been bred into us … take the drugs away from rock musicians,' he said, 'and you're left with only half a man.' But heroin was something else entirely. It had such a dark, dangerous image – associated with junkies in council blocks, needles discarded on cement stairwells, disease, pallid flesh, violence, dole queues and squats – that it was safer to steer well clear. Pete tended to romanticise the squalid existence of a troubadour but he didn't romanticise heroin. He knew it was junk. And after the 1980s there was also AIDS to consider, which had made sharing needles even more risky.

Charles Shaar Murray's advice was simple: stay away from the hard stuff.

Just after it was announced that Kate Moss had signed a contract with telecommunications company Virgin Mobile for its next advertising campaign, and the company's spokesperson had said they thought she deserved a second chance, Pete agreed to head to the very same clinic in Arizona which his girlfriend had attended.

He'd always said he'd never go of his own free will, that he'd have to be forced. Pete couldn't go a day without crack and he was well aware of that. But for Kate, he would. It was a brave move and it was done with the minimum of fuss or fanfare. Even the press missed this one at first. 'He is believed to be in the Meadows Clinic in Arizona,' the *Mirror* said.

Pete had kept a low profile ever since the end of the Babyshambles tour. He had moved temporarily to Bath in the Cotswolds – a city that writer Nigel Nicolson said offered 'eighteenth-century England in all its urban glory' – and in a demonstration of just how prolific a songwriter he was, had begun recording a solo acoustic album. Pete only headed back to London to appear on the Jools Holland show. Now he was leaving for Arizona.

Pete was in love with Kate. She had not only inspired his songwriting on the Babyshambles debut but even more so on the acoustic demo tracks he had just laid down in Bath, and of which he was incredibly proud.

On one Internet posting almost a year before he had met Kate, Pete had quoted the lyrics to The Smiths' song 'These Things Take Time'. Looking back it's eerie just how apt those words were, describing as they did the discovery of a place where they could live in anonymity. They were also confessional – admitting to being sick and to a disbelief that someone like her could care about someone like him.

Pete had changed one line to read 'When we piped in your room'. The most ominous line though, was right at the end, where Morrissey predicted his love would leave him.

These words would become prophetic as Pete and Kate's relationship teetered on the brink of collapse – torn apart by his addiction and by the lifestyle he just couldn't leave.

In addition, the opening phrase of the song was an appropriation of the American Battle Hymn of the Republic, 'My eyes have seen the glory of the coming of the Lord' – had been used by Pete's friend Shane MacGowan in his song 'USA'. MacGowan's words – bastardised to include references to shooting up – would also take on a haunting significance in 2005.

But Pete was determined. He'd get clean for Kate and then they'd buy a place together in the States – away from the prying eyes of the British paparazzi. It would be perfect.

Following the success of the first two singles 'Killamangiro' and 'Fuck Forever', both charting inside the Top 10, Babyshambles had high hopes for their debut album *Down In Albion*. Rough Trade records may have been hoping for a higher chart entry, but when it debuted at number 10 on 14 November, Pete was happy.

The album was up against Madonna's latest LP *Confessions On A Dancefloor*, the debut UK release for Swedish rockers Diamond Dogs, a thirtieth anniversary re-release of Patti Smith's classic *Horses*, and the inevitable saturation of Christmas compilations and greatest hits collections in the run-up to the festive season. These included Take That's *Ultimate Collection*, which preceded the band's comeback tour. Hardly in the same ballpark as Babyshambles, but there's only so much space the papers and TV channels can devote to new music.

Alan McGee reported back from dropping in on one of Carl's recording sessions with Dirty Pretty Things. 'The album is turning into a classic already,' he said. 'The sessions are going incredibly well … "Bang Bang" is a massive hit. And so is "Deadwood".'

On the Bala Chadha website 'Mrs Rabbit', one of the moderators, a close acquaintance of Pete's 'literary agent' Paul Roundhill and apparently a 'friend' of Pete's, posted a message wishing him luck in Arizona. 'Peter finally boarded a plane on Saturday,' she said. 'Thanks to all who made the concerted effort to get him to the airport and onto the plane.'

This from the same woman who in a later posting spelled Pete's surname 'Docherty'. If they hadn't smelled something fishy before, some of the fans who had logged onto the site began to question aloud just how close Mrs Rabbit was to Pete – and, by extension, how close Paul Roundhill was.

The website's message board had previously had to be taken down after it was bombarded with abusive messages about Pete's drug-taking. Roundhill said back then: 'It's a mess. We're going to have to take the site down. Kids have got onto it and written all this stuff about Pete and crack-dealing.'

Pete was bored in Arizona. He felt the twelve-step programme wasn't right for him. He thought he'd be able to stick at it but he just couldn't. Five weeks in there and he thought he'd go mad. At one stage he'd been forced to carry a fluffy toy bear around with him to demonstrate how he'd left his 'inner child' behind.

He decided to come back to England, but he needed money to pay for the flight. And money was something he didn't have access to in the middle of Arizona. He had his ticket home but it had been booked by someone else and he couldn't change it. Pete decided to put a message up on one of the Internet discussion boards he occasionally used. According to the *Sun* newspaper, a female fan 'opened up her purse at San Francisco Airport'.

Back home in London, Pete told the *Sun* reporter he had shared a room with two other people at the Meadows and described it as being like a prison. He'd had every intention of seeing it through, for his family and for Kate, but this world was alien to him. He missed his friends back home.

He knew Kate wouldn't come back to England – not yet anyway – because of reports the police wanted to interview her, and because of the relentless media hounding she knew she'd face. He knew that bailing early from rehab would upset her, but he told the press on his return that he'd come back specifically to attend the opening of a new photo exhibition at London's Proud Galleries. It was the same space that had housed Roger Sargent's Libertines retrospective the previous year; this time it was to host an exposition of Babyshambles photographs taken by Danny Clifford, who had accompanied the band on their most recent UK tour. Pete had hoped that Kate would return to London for the opening night of the exhibition in Camden.

He couldn't face rehab again but he promised Kate he'd return to the Meadows after the photo exhibition was over.

Clifford told *The Times* he was sad Pete had checked himself out of rehab. 'His lifestyle is unsustainable,' he said, warning that history has shown us it could all end tragically. Clifford once asked Pete whether he'd ever want to give up. He said no.

Pete threw himself back into London life; he went to the Brixton Academy to watch New York new romantics The Bravery in concert, and he hung out with his friend Wolfman.

Pete claimed he and Wolfman were on their way to his grandfather's grave in west London when they were stopped by police. It was to have been a rite of passage, an act that would symbolise his drug-taking days were finally over. Pete said the pair were going to bury their remaining stash of narcotics by the grave, and this, he claimed, would underline his desire to give up the crack for good. That's what he said. The police didn't believe him.

On Wednesday 30 November, Peter and the Wolf were pulled over in Cleveland Road, Ealing after their car was apparently being driven in an 'erratic manner'. Police said they removed class A drugs from the car and Pete was arrested on suspicion of possession.

He was eventually bailed at six o'clock the following morning, told to report back in January. He was exhausted and was petrified of telling Kate what had happened. On top of that he'd somehow mislaid the demo tape of the acoustic songs he'd been working on in Bath.

The Babyshambles Internet message board was understandably more active than usual. 'Johnnymac' posted a message that simply said: 'Damn, things are going downward lately.' 'Gman' was more abrupt: 'It's getting to the stage where it is embarrassing to say you're a fan,' he wrote. 'I end up defending him vehemently, but the person I'm trying to persuade will frequently have no frame of reference except that fucking 3am page in the *Mirror*. So I sound like I'm defending the act of taking drugs, not the fact there's a brilliant man behind all that nonsense ... I'm proud of Pete, despite it all. He's an inspiration. I wouldn't have the audacity to feel "ashamed" of him.'

Another message read: 'The guy is very talented and I hope he sorts himself out, I really do, but I work with addicts all day and he's no different from any of them ... Pete is a lucky guy to have all this support but he obviously doesn't feel ready at this time to quit the drugs … he's too weak … he's a talented guy who happens to be a junkie.'

It was difficult for the fans to turn on Pete totally. After all, he made music they loved; he spoke to them and they could identify with every lyric. They were also genuinely concerned. Yes, it was difficult defending to older generations what he did – particularly if those generations read the tabloid press. But they knew that, despite the drug-taking, despite the failed attempts at rehab, the Pete Doherty in those newspapers wasn't the same Pete Doherty they loved so much. The papers seemed entirely disinterested in the music – which was the thing that mattered most to his fans.

Although Pete had been appearing in the newspapers on an almost daily basis, he rarely gave formal interviews. Despite the tabloids announcing 'exclusive interviews', most of these were snatched conversations walking down the street or after the reporter had caught Pete off-guard outside his home. Pete's problem was that he could rarely resist the temptation to talk. Maybe it was an attempt to put the record straight, but experience should have shown him that this seldom happened.

So it was no surprise when the *Sun* revealed it had a 'sensational interview' with Pete in which he 'spilled the beans on his shambolic love affair with Kate'.

Pete told the reporter he'd been dumped by Kate after she discovered he'd left rehab and had been arrested by police for drug possession. He said she'd shouted at him down the phone before throwing her mobile phone against the wall.

The *Mirror* claimed to have got the scoop on Kate, quoting her as saying, 'I wish I'd never met him', and that he was a 'user in every sense of the word'. Actually it was a 'friend' of Kate's recounting what she'd apparently told her.

It wasn't long before the story of Pete's arrest had reached America as well, reported everywhere from the *St Louis Despatch* to the *Miami Herald*. While The Libertines were never huge in the America, and Babyshambles virtually unheard of, the name Pete Doherty was familiar and Kate Moss was a superstar. Middle America, it seemed, would also now form an opinion of the 'junkie rocker' Pete Doherty. His notoriety was going global.

But Pete's fans, while openly discussing what they'd read in the papers, would also sensibly reserve judgement. There was a sense in which they never quite believed *anything* the tabloids said. But where else could they get their information, and updates on Pete's life, if the tabloids were the only papers that featured regular snatched quotes from him? Simon Hattenstone's *Guardian* feature on Pete was revealing and intriguing but glimpses like that into Pete's world were few and far between. Being a fan requires being up-to-date with the goings on in the life of the person you're a fan of. Although it left a bad taste in the mouth, it was the tabloids that persistently carried the stories – nearly all bad – about Pete. They rarely demonstrated any knowledge of his music or acknowledged his talent as a songwriter and poet, but at least Pete's fans could find out whether he was in America or England, in rehab or out of rehab, in prison or in his flat, presumably smoking crack.

The question was: would Pete really have chosen to tell one of the red-tops his innermost secrets? Surely not. As one anonymous post on the message board read, 'When the tabloids scream "Nutter Doherty High on Skag-Pipes", we usually sigh and curse the *Sun* and the *Mirror* and *OK!* magazine, fling on one of those demo recordings, maybe "Albion", maybe "I Love You But You're Green", ... and we put on The Libertines and sway along with "Music When The Lights Go Out". But read them they would. It was a necessary evil.

'I like his music a lot. I like the
romanticism of his self-destruction.'

ANONYMOUS FAN

NINETEEN

BURN'D IN A HOLY PLACE

Pete Doherty turns twenty-seven on 29 March 2006. In the BBC documentary *Who The F*** Is Pete Doherty?* presenter Paul Morley turns to camera and says that he is worried, worried that Pete is on the less than salubrious waiting list to join the club of 'rock star casualties'. Morley reels off the names – Kurt Cobain, Janis Joplin, Jimi Hendrix – all of whom died in their mid-twenties. Pete has categorically said he doesn't want to join that club, but if he ever did, Morley quite rightly acknowledges the media would have blood on their hands. 'Every one of us,' he says.

The media had only served to reinforce the stereotype. It had become almost impossible for Pete to live as anything but the drug-addled rock star. Whether or not anyone with any influence in his career had encouraged him in his drug-taking at an early stage is something we'll probably never know. The fact that the media are encouraging him now is indisputable.

In 1975 Lou Reed, having left The Velvet Underground five years before, started to give his close friends and family cause for concern. He looked weaker, paler than usual and seemed on the verge of self-destruction. It was no secret Reed was a drug user. He cancelled a scheduled European tour after collapsing from what his publicist said was 'nervous exhaustion'.

During his *Transformer* era, Reed was tagged the 'Phantom of Rock' by his record label, as if capitalising on his worsening condition, using his addiction and failing relationship (with his transvestite lover, Rachel) as a marketing tool.

Thirty years on, it may not be the record company capitalising on Pete's condition, but it's a sadly all too familiar story. Rough Trade had done everything they could to help Pete when he was with The Libertines. Record sales could wait; the most important thing was for Pete to get clean. But there were a lot of other people who stood to benefit from Pete's increasing notoriety.

The *NME*, which had supported Pete from the very early days of The Libertines and continues to support him now, said Babyshambles had become as famous for cancelling their gigs as they had for Pete's drug dependence.

Pete is his own worst enemy. His managers have said it. His own mother has said it. And it's going to get worse. By the closing days of 2005 it was clear Pete Doherty was no longer really in control of his own destiny; perhaps he hadn't been for a long time. He couldn't stick at rehab and it looked like he'd lost one of the two most important people in his life – Kate Moss. Jackie would always stick by him; that's what mothers were for. But Kate and Jackie were, without question, the two people who mattered most, and now he was down to one.

After Pete had absconded from rehab in Arizona and been arrested for possession of drugs again, those closest to him started to feel the tide turn against him. The tabloids would continue their relentless pursuit and demonisation, but how long would it be before the broadsheets – the papers that had tried so hard to understand Pete – began to turn on him as well? It was inevitable that it would happen. It was just a matter of when; they certainly wouldn't continue to try to explain away his behaviour. And as for the public at large, many rarely judged musicians or artists on their work but on what the media said about them. But more importantly, what about Pete's fans?

As long as Pete Doherty keeps writing music and revealing that spark of brilliance, that glimmer of genius that he undeniably possesses, he'll surely keep his fans. They'll be upset at cancelled gigs and they'll endlessly discuss and dissect the tabloid stories, but they'll still be there to support him. No matter how many times Pete comes crashing down again in the future, they'll wish him well. When he's at his lowest ebb they'll help pick him up with words of encouragement. 'Get well soon, Bilo.' And they'll rejoice if he ends up sticking rehab out to the end for once. He clearly has many demons still to battle. But his fans will stand by this imperfect rock star because that's what fans do.

As one fan put it, the tabloid readers had missed The Libertines. 'All they heard were the bitter snarls flung round in their wake. They missed *Up The Bracket*, they missed the gigs-outside-of-gigs and the bringing folks back to the flat to carry on playing 'til the pigs arrived … what they know is Shane MacGowan gets drunk all the time, got f*cked-up teeth, ugly fucker … what they know is Pete Doherty gets high all the time, got f*cked-up teeth, got a supermodel girlfriend.'

For Pete's fans the things that the tabloids focused on were the things that were almost irrelevant to them. It was more complicated than this, but in essence the fans cared about the rock 'n' roll; the tabloids cared about the drugs and the sex.

Bill Wyman of The Rolling Stones once said of being on tour: 'Everyone tried to get us. The papers in every country abused us when we'd get there for being dirty and long-haired. We needed teaching a lesson, they said.'

Whenever Mick and Keith got arrested for anything, it was always 'Stones on Drug Charges', despite the fact that Wyman and Charlie Watts rarely took drugs. 'I don't need half a dozen joints to get a session together,' Wyman told author Robert Greenfield. 'I don't really drink and I don't take pills.'

On their now infamous 1972 tour of the US, Keith was arrested for striking out at a photographer, followed in quick succession by Mick Jagger, who attempted to stop them. Arrests, drug-taking – times haven't changed much. But it's hard to imagine Pete ever conforming and becoming as much a mainstream figure as Jagger has now become.

After emerging from one of his spells in rehab, Pete said his darkest hour had passed. He told fans he had spent hours talking to his probation officer and pouring his heart out to drug workers and that that results had been worthwhile. There was, he said, 'much clearing of rubbish'. Consequently, he appeared much calmer and more peaceful. 'Thank you to all who have shown kindness, undeserved, over these past troubl'd times,' he said. Posting the message on his website he added that he would be playing a gig the following weekend. 'I know many have vowed never to come again, but do come and support me,' he said. 'I will be in good health and promise to play the finest set yet, and it may be my last gig of freedom.'

Some of Pete's fans will look back on this message with sadness, heartbroken that Pete's darkest hour may have passed then, but only for a short while. It wasn't long before the drugs had grappled Pete and pulled him back down again. The truth was that drugs had become bound up Pete's very being; they were a part of who he was.

Pete was genuinely sorry every time he let his fans down; he didn't want to. But the drugs were controlling him, not the other way round, and he knew it. Contrast this to Lou Reed who, while in the very real throes of addiction, simulated shooting up on stage. While his band played 'Heroin', it looked like Reed was injecting himself with a syringe. As author Michael Wrenn points out, 'It's not certain whether it contained heroin or just water.' Either way, it was all part of his act.

Reed was getting pressure to fulfil what he termed 'some kind of role model tag' – something that irritated him and that he felt was being forced on a lot of rock stars of his generation. It's incredible to think this was thirty years before Pete Doherty. 'I was being tutored that I could be an example of this, of that, how someone could move from drugs to spirituality, but I don't want to be an example of anything,' Reed said. 'I think drugs are terrible, for me. I also person-ally feel they're terrible for a lot of other people, but that's for them to go fool around and figure out.'

As long as Pete loved the chaos, as long as he continued in his self-imposed quest to burn out, playing as many gigs as he could, staying blinkered as he shot down that path to self-destruction, drugs would remain part and parcel of that world. It would take a sea-change to distance himself from narcotics. And that wasn't likely to happen – not in the foreseeable future anyway. Pete equated his way of life with free-dom. And by that token, if he gave up drugs he'd have to give up that freedom; and then he would no longer be a libertine. Was life really worth living if he couldn't live as a libertine?

It was that philosophy which led some people to make comparisons with the Cobains, Joplins, Hendrixes of this world: those who had burned brightly before disappearing in a blaze of glory, to be remem-bered forever as artists who helped shape popular music. It was inevitable that comparisons would be drawn. Those who suggested it simply couldn't imagine Pete Doherty straight. It wasn't that he'd be boring without drugs, just that he wouldn't *be* the Pete Doherty they knew. Pete Doherty the myth had become far bigger and burned far brighter than the real Pete Doherty – his legend had overtaken the individual, to the extent that no one, not even Pete himself, could recognise a Pete Doherty who wasn't a libertine.

In their book *Fandemonium*, Fred and Judy Vermorel described punk as the 'positively last gasp of rock 'n' roll romanticism, complete with dead drug heroes and wicked managers'. They obviously didn't see Pete Doherty coming.

Pete has chosen his path and he's stuck to it. He's been given the opportunity to turn back, to take a different route, but his mind's already made up. He embodies the mythology of the iconic musician. He's an outlaw in rock 'n' roll, even incurring the wrath of fellow musicians. But he's not concerned with the views of others, save perhaps for those closest to him. In the beginning Pete wanted nothing more than a regular childhood. Now he's entirely unconfined by society's rules and regulations; the laws do not apply to him. He may still occasionally pine for that normal childhood, may wonder what it'd be like to lead a normal life, but it's not something he could ever have back – not now.

Pete's hero, the comic Tony Hancock, had very forthright views on drugs. His wife, Freddie, said he was 'hysterically against the idea of using them', but apparently not on moral grounds. He just didn't want to know what was inside his mind. 'There's so much there it would destroy me if I knew,' he said. 'It would destroy anyone if they knew what was inside them. It's very wrong.'

If Pete wanted to do the right thing, to give up drugs and stay clean, it was going to be difficult. With a crack habit it's difficult to make that choice, let alone carry it out. As the philosopher Carl Jung said, 'Every form of addiction is bad, no matter whether the narcotic be alcohol, morphine or idealism.' Pete's problem was that he was multiply addicted: he was an idealist and a crack addict. Addicted to his notion of being a rock star, addicted to the stage, to music and to the limelight. But also to class A drugs.

In January 2005 Carl said the end of The Libertines was a poignant moment. He described it as 'laying a tombstone' on what had been before, but at the same time laying the foundations for a future he hoped would be equally bright. 'It's cutting the ribbon into a different realm of freedom. Because The Libertines became constrained,' he said. Pete took that freedom to extremes. If he felt free when he was with The Libertines then he cannot have imagined the freedom he'd taste with Babyshambles. He'd always said The Libertines had gone into decline the minute they'd signed with Rough Trade; he'd foreseen the ending.

The Christmas before, Pete had described 2004 as a 'humdinger of a year'. He had met some 'lovely people' and 'a few scoundrels'. But it is those scoundrels who should now shoulder some of the responsibility for encouraging Pete in his narcotic pursuits.

Carl had no idea how bad it would get for his old friend. And his comments about Pete shortly after he went into rehab back in 2004 have never had more poignancy than they do today. 'You've got to have hope,' he said. 'Without that we'd be stuffed, wouldn't we?'

And so, it's with hope in our hearts that we await the next chapter in the intriguing tale of Pete Doherty – last of the rock romantics. It's a chapter that has not yet been written. And while we're waiting, we could pull that CD out of the rack – the one with the four silhouetted figures on the front; we could skip to track five and reminisce about the time we saw The Libs at the 333, just happy-go-lucky boys in the band, looking like they loved the limelight, loved what they did. Or we could pull out the other album – the one with Carl and Pete on the front showing off their 'Libertines' tattoos; the picture that spoke volumes, taken just after Pete's release from prison. We could listen to the melodies and ask, 'What did happen to the likely lads?' Or maybe we could stick *Albion* on the record player, close our eyes and try to picture Pete's England or remember those clandestine gigs he put on in his East End flat; buying the ticket from the guy in the hat in the photobooth at Whitechapel underground station.

Surely that was the Pete who really mattered: the one who had the vision, who gave so much. Peter Doherty, the doe-eyed boy standing on the stage in the jacket with the epaulettes, pale and wanton, bare-chested and thin; the one who was born to play music. His image had become iconic – it could stand alone and would adorn posters in the future. Pete was a lost rock romantic; one of life's few. He was a wandering minstrel who felt such a closeness to his fans he'd invite them home to hear his music, sift through his records, drink cups of tea, stay up, bleary-eyed, into the early hours to hear his poetry. That was the Pete Doherty the fans loved. And they weren't ever going to give up hope that that Pete was still in there. The gigs may have reached a point where they were uneven, but they were always filled with drama. And occasionally there would be a gem. He'd play a new song and all of a sudden it came flooding back, the reason they were there in the first place: to witness his brilliance, his flashes of genius.

The Vermorels said punk highlighted a tension in showbiz 'whereby when the boy/girl next door turns star, the punter also wants a slice of the action' – the 'anyone can play three chords' mandate that has so often been cited as punk's mantra. Carl said to his fans after The Libertines had disbanded – 'It's over to you now.' The Libertines had taken punk's mantle and carried it for so long. It was time for the next generation of fans to take over. He wanted them to form rock 'n' roll bands, take to the stage, become libertines.

There were already Libertines copyists on the scene, wearing the clothes, walking the walk and, more specifically, taking the drugs. But there was something missing. A Pete Doherty figure. Bands come and go. Some shine brightly before fading into obscurity. Others live on for years, perpetuating their sound or reinventing themselves. But rarely, very rarely do you find some like Pete. The Libertines imploded. Babyshambles may do the same – who knows. But Pete Doherty will remain the one constant. Pete Doherty will live on – regardless of what happens in the soap opera of his life.

The weeping child could not be heard,
The weeping parents wept in vain;
They stripp'd him to his little shirt,
And bound him in an iron chain;
And burn'd him in a holy place,
Where many had been burn'd before:
The weeping parents wept in vain.
Are such things done on Albion's shore?

FROM 'A LITTLE BOY LOST' BY WILLIAM BLAKE

EPILOGUE

EPILOGUE

The hardback edition of this book came out in February 2006 and a lot has happened since. Most notably though, as I write this, Pete and Babyshambles seem to be heading in the right direction. There is new material, a new record deal, gigs that have attracted great reviews, and Pete also, finally, seems to be getting clean. An appearance on the Jonathan Ross show won him a new legion of admirers, silenced some – if not all – of his detractors, and gained him the sympathy vote in some quarters.

Could it be that 2007 will see Pete Doherty do what his fans have always known he is capable of – surpassing the genius of The Libertines?

In the past year I have become close to Pete's mother, Jackie, who has published her own story, *My Prodigal Son*, about coming to terms with her son's fame and addictions. I helped to find her an agent and assisted her when she came to put pen to paper – at times witnessing both tears and laughter in equal measure – even visiting her 'crying place' in Dorset. Back in March, she invited me down to the West Country where she lives on an army base with her husband, Big Pete.

I slept in the downstairs bedroom – a small room in a modest army house. At the foot of my bed was Pete's vintage Gibson six-string acoustic guitar.

The house was warm; the Dohertys were warm. There were no obvious recent photos of Pete on the walls – just one picture of Amy-Jo sporting her mortar board on graduation day. But Jackie's closet, next to the kitchen, was a shrine to her prodigal son – posters, letters, photos, and various other ephemera were almost spilling out.

Major Doherty – Pete's dad – arrived home decked out in full khaki gear after a 'day at the office'. He was incredibly attentive and friendly, passionate about the military, but said he'd become institutionalised. He showed me the thousands of records he kept in his garage. It was cold and he was worried about the damp getting to his collection. He told me that accumulating this vintage vinyl had become a compulsion – he couldn't stop buying 1960s and 1970s rock 'n' roll records, some of them rare and worth a small fortune. He had just sold one of his doubles to an American woman who said it was a gift for her husband, who had been in the backing band for the artist and had played on the record.

Big Pete said he'd only started the collection for his son, who loved music like nothing else. He didn't know if or when he'd ever hand the records over.

Jackie played me a video of a twelve-year-old Pete doing mock interviews with his big sister, at home on an army base. He was an intelligent, inquisitive boy; one revealing episode saw him tell the camera repeatedly: 'I'm a celebrity,' whilst another showed him on stage with a band at school, aged seventeen. He had long, floppy curtains and was singing a Beatles' number, together with the only public rendition of 'Billy The Hamster' – the first song he ever penned. Big Pete was filming the gig and was so proud.

At the end of June I was asked to interview Pete for the cover of *The Big Issue* magazine. By this time I had spent eleven months writing about him. I'd interviewed scores of people who knew him or had worked with him, and probably knew more about him than he did. But I'd never formally met him – and it was a peculiar prospect.

Pete had been clean for over two weeks but he'd had a relapse a couple of days before the interview and was in a bit of a state. Despite this, he was a commanding presence as he wandered into the small recording studio in the basement of the club where Babyshambles were demoing some new material.

Adam Ficek and I chatted for about an hour before Pete's arrival, and he was positive about the future. Despite all the setbacks, the missed shows, the relentless media coverage, and even this recent relapse, he was confident things were finally getting better.

Pete shook my hand and asked if he could speak to me outside the room. 'I'll be totally honest with you,' he said. 'I succumbed again. I flew out to Portugal to get an implant, but customs cut open the implant packets at the airport and they became tainted. I had been clean for sixteen days but as soon as I got back to London … it was a setback and I feel like I let down the boys, but it's the first time in sixteen days.' He assured me he hadn't got his habit back yet.

I had arrived at 5pm and wouldn't leave the studio until well after midnight. During that time Pete would play the new songs the band had recorded and talk lucidly about his plans for the future. This wasn't a man on the brink of self-destruction – not now, anyway. This was a polite, coherent, sensitive person who loved music and loved life.

The interview went something like this:

'We have plenty of new songs. Keep your ears open and you'll see – slowly but surely all your questions will be answered as to where he is, where he was, and more importantly, with whom. The conglomerate that is Babyshambles has expanded and shrunk, and expanded again. Patrick [Walden] has had time aplenty to come back into the fold but he has chosen not to. I really started the band with him, while I was still in The Libertines. And then, as if by magic, I met this other incredible singer/songwriter called Mr Whitnall. And we began writing this rambling, shambling album together called *Whitnall and I*, which I thought was quite clever at the time. [Mick Whitnall has now replaced Patrick on guitar in Babyshambles.] Along with thirteen or fourteen pure Doherty gems, there's some Doherty/Whitnall numbers; there's no shortage of ammunition. It's just a little bit difficult working out who's in the secret police and who's not. If you read the press, then check the weather, check the horoscopes, maybe have a look at the sport, but please, please don't read anything with my name in it and expect it to be even half true.

'I'm sort of at the equivalent of being at the stage in my life where I'm looking for somewhere to live. For the first time, Mick has his own gaff. Adam's settling down nicely. And Drew's at that younger, slightly more romantic time. Me, I live in a supermodel's hat box, and, in between crashing with superfans in Homerton, Babyshambles continues apace.

'Even now, people are telling me to get my own gaff; that I've got to settle down, but I still don't believe in the private ownership of property. It's quite strange, given that I've been crashing at country mansions here and there, and luxury hotels, so it's quite confusing for a young lad. In the end, I'm going to end up with my own gaff and it's not going to be a Peabody cottage.

'This chance to record our music has come like a miracle out of nowhere, so hopefully we can make this opportunity work for us; it really is that simple. If we don't take this opportunity I don't know what we're going to do, because I can't see anyone else giving us the time and the chance. We've still got so much to do.

'It's been difficult with all the shite that people have been slinging at us. The only way to carry on is not to fight fire with fire, but to fight their shite with our lyrical might. That's our power.

'I'm publishing my private diaries – my Books of Albion, books of dabibble, books of derangement, really. They're just a young man's journey over the last six or seven years – in and out of consciousness, in and out of Pentonville, in and out of several hearts, homes and hostels. At times I'm proud. I was always a candid sort of fellow when it came to putting ink onto paper. There's a lot of honesty in there and some horrific stories which I can't wait to tell. If I was a great footballer, I'd have a couple of beers and say "that wasn't a bad goal". Today I've had a beer and a half, and I'll say I'm proud of my writing and I feel that I'm a very open young man – not too young, maybe. And if my dad's still too ashamed to face me and look me in the eye after what's happened, maybe there's a few surprises for him as well; because there's a few gems of the old Irish philosophy in there. There's definitely a lot of sadness in there – a few attempts at thinly disguised fiction. Definitely an attempt at reconciliation.'

At this point Pete began singing and strumming his guitar. 'Three bags full of sorrow/weren't you the one …

'Oh, this is a song I wrote with Dot Allison,' he said. 'That was me trying to woo Dot.'

'I hope she was suitably wooed,' I said.

'She was very *wude*,' Adam said, before they all cracked up laughing.

'You are so *wude*,' added Drew, before playing the opening bars to 'Up The Morning'.

'That song meant so much to me I had it tattooed on my arm,' Pete told me afterwards.

Drew explained: 'We were on tour, playing Sheffield, and Peter and

Patrick spent four hours in the dressing room, writing and practising this song. Peter had it on his Dictaphone, but three hours down the motorway we stopped at a service station and he realised he had lost it. Peter went inside to buy some things, but gave me his guitar and said, "Try to remember it." I tried and tried, but couldn't.

'When I went inside, Peter was walking around the shop in floods of tears. It was the song – it had made him cry like a baby. That's how much music means to him.'

Luckily, a friend of theirs was filming. 'Like some miracle, "Up The Morning" survived,' Pete said.

I asked how the band had met their tour manager, Sally [also the girlfriend of Specials' singer Terry Hall].

'Do you remember *Select* magazine?' Pete said. 'When I was sixteen I put an advert in.' He then began singing: 'I was a troubled teen/who put an advert in a magazine/to the annoyance of my imaginary lover … This is what she said to me: she said "Oh, you're green. You don't know what love means; maybe I could tell you."

'I've never told anyone this before. I was a lonely young man who was the only kid his age living behind barbed wire on a Coventry army base. Sally and I didn't meet for three years, by which time I became a bit too proud to admit to anyone that I'd met this beautiful girl through pen-palism. And she fobbed me right off – and, listen to this – ended up getting off with this new-found friend of mine called Carlos Barât, who was a mate of my sister's. And things went downhill between me and him from there really – long before we got signed to Rough Trade, mate.

'I was just never her type but then later, as soon as I found out she was going out with Terry Hall, I decided I was going to be her best friend. But she's seen me through it all from day one. The first real song I ever wrote was called "Albion", and I remember playing it to her and her laughing at me. She said, "Do you really think you're going to make something of yourself? You can't sing, you can't write." Then I played her "Music When The Lights Go Out" and "You're My Waterloo", and she wrote me a letter saying, "The word stalker would not be inappropriate". Then there was a four-year gap. And now she's like my sister. And Kate took Sally in as a mate. It's a rare thing.

'Fucking hell, I can't believe I told you all that.'

Pete had also been frank and forthcoming about drugs and his dealings with the media. 'I've had a pipe with an off-duty police officer before,' he told me. 'I've had a spliff with a fireman. I'd never grass on anyone, but I will point out that there are people working for tabloid newspapers – scum – who are very hypocritical. They'll take the tax disc off your car and photograph it and say, "Look, Pete Doherty's got no tax." Or they'll find a gig where you've been sober for the entire show, just waiting for that one snap where you look remotely out of it. It's heartbreaking.'

He may have a point. During my research for this book I came across the name of a person linked to Pete who was quite possibly supplying his drugs. There were even rumours he had supplied heroin to a pop star in the 1980s. A police contact confirmed he was known to the police, had form, and ran a suspected crack den. But I wondered why the papers – so desperate for anything Pete Doherty-related – hadn't already exposed him. Surely they could lay off Pete for one minute and go for someone who should shoulder some of the blame for his drug addictions? I sent an email to a contact at a newspaper that I thought would be interested. This was the reply:

'Thanks for the tip. Fortunately, it just sounds like [you're] chasing stuff we know. I've known xxxx for about three years – and have been round to the so-called crack den. We thought about doing an exposé on him last year – on how the same man who corrupted yyyy had turned PD on to heroin. We also went to xxxx about it to see if he'd talk, but we decided to shelve any plans to go for him at the moment. We'd be shooting ourselves in the foot. He's worth more as a contact than for one weak exposé. Undeniably interesting to the right audience. So just treading a careful path rather than we've missed anything. Cheers.'

Cheers indeed. 'Addicted Pete' is clearly better copy than 'Clean Pete'. I credit his fans with more intelligence.

Bibliography

Ackroyd, P, *London The Biography*, Vintage, 2001

Baudelaire, C (translated by Patricia Roseberry), *Artificial Paradise*, Broadwater House, 1860, 1999

Brake, Mike, *The sociology of youth culture and youth subcultures*, Routledge, 1980

Cohn, N, *Awopbopaloobopalopbamboom*, Paladin, 1969

Engell, J, *The Creative Imagination – Enlightenment to Romanticism*, Harvard University Press, 1981

Frith, S & Goodwin, A (Eds), *On Record*, Routledge, 1990

Gillett, C, *The Sound of the City – The Classic History of Rock*, Souvenir Press, 1970

Hall, S & Jefferson, T (Eds), *Resistance Through Rituals – Youth subcultures in post-war Britain*, Routledge, 1976, 1996

Hancock, F & Nathan D, *Hancock*, Ariel Books, 1969

Hebdige, D, *Subculture – The Meaning of Style*, Routledge, 1979

Hodges, C, *The Rock & Roll Years of Chas before Dave*, Lennard Publishing, 1987

Hoskins, B (Ed), *The Sound and the Fury*, Bloomsbury, 2003

Howe, C, *Lovers & Libertines*, Ace Books, 1958

Jordan, F (Ed), *The English Romantic Poets*, Modern Language, 1950

Kerouac, J, *On the Road*, Penguin, 1957

Kumar, Shiv, *British Romantic Poets*, Atlantic, 2002

Kureishi, H & Savage, J (Eds), *The Faber Book of Pop*, Faber & Faber, 1995

Lucas, J, *England and Englishness – Ideas of Nationhood in English Poetry 1688 – 1900*, Hogarth Press, 1990

McNeil, H (Ed), *Emily Dickinson (Everyman's Poetry)*, Everyman, 1999

Pattison, R, *The Triumph of Vulgarity – Rock Music in the Mirror of Romanticism*, Oxford University Press, 1987

Pedrini, L & D, *Serpent Imagery and Symbolism – A study of the Major English Romantic Poets*, College and University Press, 1966

Richards, J, *Films and British National Identity: From Dickens to Dad's Army*, Manchester University Press, 1997

Road, A, *The Facts About a Football Club – featuring Queens Park Rangers*, G. Whizzard Publications, 1976

Savage, J, *England's Dreaming – Sex Pistols and Punk Rock*, Faber & Faber, 1991

Shaar Murray, C, *Shots from the Hip*, Penguin, 1990

Shapiro, H, *Waiting for the Man – The Story of Drugs and Popular Music*, Mandarin, 1988

The Works of Lord Byron, The Wordsworth Poetry Library, 1994

The Works of William Blake, The Wordsworth Poetry Library, 1994

Vermorel, J & F, *Fandemonium!*, Omnibus Press, 1989

Welsh, P, *Kids in the riot: high and low with the Libertines*, Omnibus Press, 2005

Wrenn, M, *Lou Reed – Between the Lines*, Plexus, 1993

Wu, D (Ed), *A Companion to Romanticism*, Blackwell, 1998

Yates, N & Samson, P, *Pete Doherty: On The Edge*, John Blake, 2005

Cloonan, M, *State of the nation: "Englishness," pop, and politics in the mid-1990s*, Popular Music and Society, University of Bowling Green, 1997

Orwell, G, '*In Defence of English Cooking*'; First published: *Evening Standard*, December 15, 1945. Reprinted: The Collected Essays, Journalism and Letters of George Orwell', 1968.

Hancock's Half Hour - Radio Series 6, episode 7; "*Fred's Pie Stall*"; First Broadcast - 10-11-1959

Websites:
http://libertines.twinkling-star.com
www.thelibertines.org.uk
www.libertines.org
www.babyshambles.com
www.babyshambles.net